Smart Leadership – Wise Leadership

There is a strong link between organisational culture and profit; after all, a happy workforce is a productive workforce. Yet a culture of inertia rather than innovation prevails in many organisations. Wise leaders, however, know how to work with the grain of human value and worth, harnessing it, so as to add shared value both for the organisation and for the good of society. So, how can astute leaders set the right conditions for creativity and cultivate non-economic goods, such as time and relationships, that make for a happy, effective workforce? The author proposes the notion of organisational culture as 'environments of value' wherein inner value translated into external value is embedded within the triple bottom line and indeed an awareness of how an organisation is like a force field: it exercises power and leaves a footprint. This construct informs the emerging concept of 'Shared Value' as requiring five literacies about:

- shareholder value and return for risk;
- value for the social environment linked to respect for the natural environment;
- inner value of those in the enterprise, which, when unlocked, releases energies and adds value;
- nurture of non-quantifiable qualities that promote human flourishing;
- understandings of how power relations distort the way organisations operate.

Steed clearly signposts the link between promoting an environment of value within which these literacies flourish and the added value for the organisation arising from such a culture. *Smart Leadership – Wise Leadership* will be a valuable text for industry experts as well as those studying Leadership and Business at degree level.

Christopher Steed is a writer, management consultant, counsellor, educator, and a research fellow at Southampton University, UK. Chris contributes papers to conferences across multi-disciplinary boundaries on subjects he has taught. He holds an MSc in social theory and international relations, a PhD in theology and a doctorate in social sciences. A member of the British Association for Counselling and Psychotherapy, Chris has a private practice in Totton, Southampton, where he works for the Church of England developing a community hub for social innovation, support services and active listening. Chris asks what the leadership and organisations of the future will look like in a digital era. What kind of 'wise leadership', as contrasted with 'smart' (technocratic) leadership, will be needed as business learns to function in a different way?

Forthcoming from the Routledge:

We Count, We Matter
Voice, Choice and the Death of Distance
Christopher Steed
ISBN: 978-1-138-30621-9

Smart Leadership – Wise Leadership

Environments of Value in an Emerging Future

Christopher Steed

Routledge
Taylor & Francis Group

LONDON AND NEW YORK

First published 2017
by Routledge
2 Park Square, Milton Park, Abingdon, Oxon OX14 4RN

and by Routledge
711 Third Avenue, New York, NY 10017

Routledge is an imprint of the Taylor & Francis Group, an informa business

© 2017 Christopher Steed

The right of Christopher Steed to be identified as author of this work has been asserted by him in accordance with sections 77 and 78 of the Copyright, Designs and Patents Act 1988.

British Library Cataloguing-in-Publication Data
A catalogue record for this book is available from the British Library

Library of Congress Cataloging-in-Publication Data
A catalog record for this book has been requested

ISBN: 978-1-4724-8473-4 (hbk)
ISBN: 978-0-415-78891-5 (pbk)
ISBN: 978-1-315-58007-4 (ebk)

Typeset in Bembo
by Taylor & Francis Books

The most exciting breakthrough of the twenty-first century will not occur because of technology but because of an expanding concept of what it means to be human.

John Naisbitt, quoted in F. Laloux (2015), *Reinventing Organisations*

Contents

Foreword

There is an increasing recognition that organisations today are operating in a context that is increasingly volatile, uncertain, complex and ambiguous (widely referred to as a VUCA context). This gives rise to a need for a fundamental rethink about the way in which our organisations operate and are led in times of such transformational change. Indeed, there is a need to question and challenge many 'givens' that have become core to organisational thinking. One significant aspect of such a core review of organisational paradigms is the need to re-consider the nature of value in a VUCA context.

Since the inception of organisational theory a dominant view of value has been embedded in the concept of shareholder value. This view has informed almost all aspects of thinking about organisational life, ranging from strategy through structure and leadership to the role of individuals and related motivation. However, a combination of all too frequent corporate failures and scandals, environmental challenges and the digital revolution have led to a challenge to the primacy of shareholder value and the emergence of a broader concept of stakeholder value. Indeed, we are already seeing a number of organisations adopting the practice of 'triple bottom line' reporting, covering a combination of social, environmental and economic aspects of business value.

Against this background the role of leaders in organisations has been placed under the spotlight. The 2008 financial crisis (and related corporate scandals) has led to a questioning of the role of leaders in organisations and how they are selected, developed and monitored. In trying to understand leadership our armoury of leadership models and theories has been described as being based in a 'top-down' view of the role of leaders within which we seek 'heroic' leaders who are able to deliver organisational performance. This 'heroic leadership' paradigm is being questioned increasingly, leading to the emergence of a range of 'post-heroic' theories, such as authentic leadership, ethical leadership, responsible leadership and shared leadership. A commonality amongst these diverse theories is a core view that leadership is a relational process that requires leaders to work with a complex nexus of relationships with a diverse range of individuals from different stakeholder groups.

Within an organisation a major focus of leadership relationships relates to those with other employees. Alongside all of the other changes facing organisations and leaders the employees are also changing. People come to work with a different set of expectations, beliefs and personal values priorities. Developing engagement of employees with their work, organisation and leaders is seen as being a core challenge facing leaders. The significance of employee engagement to organisations is underlined by a range of research that demonstrates strong relationships between engagement and performance. Therefore, our concept of value in an organisation needs to be extended to include valuing the people who work within it. To achieve this shift in thinking requires a careful examination of the purpose and culture of the organisation, resulting in a need for leaders to contribute to creating a culture that provides an 'environment of value'. It is this proposition that forms a core theme in Chris Steed's argument in *Smart Leadership – Wise Leadership*.

In this book Chris works on a very broad canvas and uses this to explore the changing context and challenges facing today's organisations. In doing this he takes the reader through fundamental rethinking ranging from the nature of an organisation's purpose, through formulation of strategy and creating a culture of value, to the role of leaders and the role of wisdom in leadership. In exploring the role of leadership Chris places his thesis clearly within the frame of 'post-heroic' relational leadership and highlights the core role of value, values and self-awareness. Furthermore, in Chapter 10 he looks to the future, highlighting the need to consider the overall role of education in developing individuals to provide a pool of future leaders fit for the challenges to be faced.

Chris proposes a new construct that probes the association between inner and external value; the inner worth that participants in an organisation may or may not feel and how that is translated into their tasks. For analytical clarity and rooted in client observation, he assembles evidence to show that connection through its contrast prism – what makes staff disengaged or demotivated. The next question is under what circumstances inner worth and value can be channelled positively to create a valuing environment, or 'an environment of value' to use his terminology. If this is valid, it is an important insight. 'Smart leaders' need to know how to work with this grain to maximise their bottom line even if purely self-interested. Wise leaders implicitly understand this is important in itself if the workplace of the present and future is not to damage its greatest asset – people!

Smart Leadership is not 'yet another book on leadership'. The discussion throughout (very usefully illustrated by the use of case studies) explores the complexities of leadership within a fast-changing context and highlights the need for constant reflection and adaptation around a core belief in purpose and the valuing of people.

This is not a 'how to' book with simple rules or formulae for success. Rather, it is a book that causes the reader to think and reflect through challenging much of our 'conventional wisdom'. Most importantly it does all of this in an interesting, refreshing and enjoyable style.

Malcolm Higgs
Professor of Organisation Behaviour and HRM
Southampton Business School University of Southampton
November 2016

Setting the scene

The world stands at the dawn of the Fourth Industrial Revolution. It is a transition to a network economy that has become social; to networked individuals; to a new set of systems, bringing together digital, biological and physical technologies in new and powerful combinations. Much will change fundamentally in the emerging network economy, including organisations and the role of their leaders to nurture enabling environments. The challenges of our time require strategies and solutions that span private, public and civil sector spheres. Digital technologies are unleashing new economic and social dynamics. A country's industrial might no longer determines its future. The prizes will go to highly adaptive leadership; leadership with spirit; leadership with purpose.

> The leadership for this day and age is the leadership of cross-sector experience and collaboration. But where will we find these leaders when our universities still offer siloed professional programmes such as business, engineering, law or medicine? How will such medical schools train the doctors needed to develop user-experience-design for medical technology that will make many doctors obsolete? What business school programme helps students acquire the socio-political business savvy needed to develop legitimate participation for private enterprise in welfare sectors without sacrificing trading quality for profits? What about the socially conscious engineers needed to develop scalable technologies to support social development and catastrophic relief efforts?[1]

Equipping organisations to tackle the future will require a management revolution no less momentous than the one that spawned modern industry. As Gary Hamel described in his 'Moon Shots for Management', most of the fundamental breakthroughs in management occurred decades ago.[2] Work flow design, annual budgeting, return-on-investment analysis, project management, divisionalisation, brand management – these and a host of other indispensable tools were all part of the application of scientific principles to management. Yet management, like the combustion engine, is a mature technology that must now be reinvented for a new age. With this in mind, a group of scholars and business leaders assembled in May 2008 to lay out a road map for reinventing management, charting a new, communitarian approach to capitalism as long as leaders imbue it with a social purpose. In an enormously volatile and unforgiving environment, how in an age of rapid change do you create organisations that are as adaptable and resilient as they are focused and efficient? How, in a creative economy where entrepreneurial genius is the secret to success, do you inspire employees to bring the gifts of initiative, imagination, and passion to work every day? To successfully address these problems, executives and experts must first admit that they have reached the limits of the industrial-age paradigm built atop the principles of standardisation, specialisation, hierarchy, control, and primacy of shareholder interests. Tomorrow's business imperatives lie outside the performance envelope of today's bureaucracy-infused management practices. Chief amongst the tasks of revisiting the philosophical foundations of management is the reality that in tomorrow's interdependent world, highly collaborative systems will out-perform organisations characterised by adversarial win-lose relationships. Looking again at what underpins much management practice is the need to eliminate the pathologies of formal hierarchy which cannot but undermine the self-worth of individuals in an organisation. Leaders of the future will re-define strategy as an emergent process. In the future, top management will not themselves make strategy but create conditions in which new strategies evolve.

This is a definite issue for the turn to 'financialisation' that has been a marked feature of the neo-liberal project. When companies turned from banks to the open market to fund expansion; when, in return, banks turned to consumers as a new source of profit amidst some highly complex loan arrangements with debt re-packaged into financial instruments and traded in the marketplace something new was going on. The systemic dominance of finance over industry had damaging implications for productive activity. Hedge Funds did not care for the industry they were entering or assets they were stripping. Extracting maximum share values was top priority and capital investment now a revenue stream.[3] High-value work was accompanied by a high-octane environment that was often pernicious. Those involved report the restless jockeying for position, the relentless pressure to prove one's worth by following the best bet. The tendencies that can be found everywhere in corporate life – the grasp of position and status, looking over your shoulder to see who is coming up behind you, and personal rivalry – were accentuated in such a pressure cooker.[4] In the process, ethics and responsible business leadership often failed. Too often, as Whyte noted about 'the organisation man', there is conflict between how an individual can flourish and how organisations can succeed.[5]

As a *Harvard Business Review* points out, 'Leaders find it tough to ensure that their people adhere to values and ethics. The prevailing principles in business make employees ask, "What's in it for me?" Missing are those that would make them think, "What's good, right, and just for everyone?"' The notion of 'the wise leader', not just a 'smart leader' is receiving more attention today though hardly mainstream.[6] People behave less ethically when they are part of organisations or groups. Common rationalisations, such as that you are acting in the company's best interest, or justifications, such as that you will never be found out, lead to misconduct.

Those that came of age around the year 2000, the millennials, frustrate managers by being willing to migrate to the next exciting opportunity that calls forth purpose. Yet, as digitally native, entrepreneurial and cosmopolitan world citizens, they are the generation that will have to address unprecedented new challenges and somehow acquire that wisdom. The iconic status attributed to people like Bill Gates and Steve Jobs has encouraged the notion that if a company finds the right leader, everything else will fall into place. The pathway of wisdom, however, points to a different lens; that it is the role of leaders to foster a collaborative sense of common purpose. They can do this through working with the grain of what we will call 'environments of value' that draw out the inner worth of those they work with and translate it into their tasks.

Capitalism and the free market, with their gospel of globalisation and the primacy of growth and GDP as a measure of happiness, are under siege. Against the background of the 2008 global financial crisis and its aftermath, the questions keep coming.

> The impact of the global financial crisis has not only been profound, but enduring. The crisis has not led to any fundamental reappraisal of the nature of capitalism, or how to 'govern' it. For the majority in work conditions have deteriorated, while those without employment have been subject to ever more punitive sanctions. Inequalities are increasing and working lives becoming more precarious.[7]

Perhaps it took the crash and crisis to create the conditions of mass youth unemployment, austerity, poverty and growing inequality that arguably were the precursor to the new business models of digital start-ups and sharing economy platforms. I argue elsewhere that for the future societies to work, we need to get rid of our endemic emphasis on what work and jobs mean to our self-worth.[8] Yet, for all the talk of the meaning and purpose of our jobs being a prime means through which we are validated, most people see work merely as a means to an end. According to a massive global survey by Gallup, only 29 per cent of employees in North America say they are engaged (worldwide, the number is 13 per cent).[9] Perhaps the very nature of work that allowed families to prosper and individuals to build a sense of self is under attack. Work might be losing its value to people.

Ethereum is a software development company founded by a 21-year-old called Vitalik Buterin to help develop decentralised platforms.[10] The first company formed to work with the grain of Ethereum's technology was ConsenSys. 'It became clear to me', said its founder, Joseph Lubin, 'that instead of people wasting their time walking down the street with posters on sticks, we could all work together to just build the new solutions to this broken economy and society.'[11] ConsenSys is attempting to nurture the idea of 'holocracy' rather than bureaucracy. 'Holocracy' is a collaborative rather than hierarchical process for getting things done. It involves dynamic roles rather than traditional job descriptions, distributed not delegated authority, transparent rules rather than office politics and rapid reiterations rather than big reorganisations.

Even in a high tech age, leadership remains vital. As the developing Fourth Industrial Revolution transforms the technological foundations of global enterprise, the phenomenon of firms growing at extremely rapid rates has become unprecedented. What is labelled 'hypergrowth' has moved out of Silicon Valley and gone global; from high tech start-ups to companies both old and new. Challenges facing hypergrowth firms have a huge impact in today's global economy. Yet from talent shortages to regulatory impediments, growth challenges are a consistent management priority. According to *Mastering Hypergrowth*, the World Economic Forum's study of nearly 200 companies around the world, over half (55.6 per cent) of CEOs say that finding, motivating and keeping the best people is one of their most pressing challenges.[12]

As I write these words, issues of culture come inescapably to the fore. Within a few days (in early July 2016), the internal culture of Western intelligence agencies was found to be severely wanting. They had singularly failed to challenge the belief that weapons of mass destruction remained in Iraq at the time of the US- and UK-led invasion of 2003. Confirmation bias had set in.[13] The fall-out from the Libor interest rate-fixing scandal continued to haunt the banking sector. The following day, shootings of black men by the police in America raised angry shouts against institutional racism, quickly succeeded by the shooting of five police officers.[14] A UK Parliamentary Select Committee was preparing to censure a major retailer, Sports Direct, for 'Victorian and inhumane working practices, resembling those of a workhouse', despite the company protesting it was committed to dignity and respect.[15]

Institutions are under strong scrutiny. As we will discuss, the chess game of 'institutional defence' is constantly played out as official bodies rally round themselves in the face of external criticism. A wearying refrain sets in, that certain actions and malpractice are the result of 'a few bad apples'. Lessons must then be learnt. One wonders what this education was, now acquired, that was not known before. There do seem to be systemic structural problems. Public bodies and authorities everywhere are seen as offering remote leadership. The challenge is to do things on a more human scale, as if people come first.[16] De-personalisation is now a major problem in Western societies, both internal and external to an organisation. Part of the distance created by impersonal systems is that government seems over-complicated. It is the combination of distance and complexity that alienates voters. In his book *Simpler: The Future of Government* Cass Sunstein, Barack Obama's regulatory tsar from 2009 to 2012, said he had worked hard at conducting a war against redundant laws and regulations as well as trying to ensure that rules are easier to understand.[17] For the most part, targets, systems, processes and especially bureaucracy are not good words.

How can we ensure that organisations are engaging places – not the kind of toxic environments that are all too frequent?[18] And how can we continue to ensure that organisations are humane places when the future of work is an issue that becomes hugely challenging in the wake of the gathering flood of what may well be the job-killing Fourth Industrial Revolution? What kind of Smart Leadership is needed to cultivate the human dimension in a digital era? What does it mean to cultivate 'leadership with spirit'? Can wise, ethical and responsible leadership that is not off-balance become the default position and not just 'smart leadership'? We will explore the idea that leaders should be wise, lifting organisations to a higher dimension than just technocratic through engendering humane environments that, under certain conditions, best translate the value of people into their collective endeavours.

This book presents a new construct about leadership and how organisations flourish. It is the task of leaders to facilitate a workplace culture where the value of people is best expressed. Our term for this will be an 'environment of value', an organisational 'community of practice' that draws out the inner value of its participants and translates that into external, added value for the enterprise. It acts as a catalyst for the conversion of internal value into the purposes of the organisation. It seeks to build value precisely because it works with the conditions by which a valuing environment can be cultivated. An environment of value therefore digs into motivational drivers because it mobilises the factors that will encourage people to give of their best.

New perspectives on creating positive organisational changes are much needed. As I write, Siemens have just offered a report about the reasons for the productivity puzzle in the UK. Workers seemingly produce for longer hours than their US or European counterparts but their output is up to 20 per cent less. Siemens suggested that 75 per cent of the deficit is due to poor leadership and practices that do not make the most of the potential of their staff.[19]

A generation ago, Peter Drucker, the leading guru of management, argued that we were in the middle of a great social transformation, akin to the Renaissance. The computer was the symbol of this immense change whereby the primary resource was no longer capital, land, or labour but knowledge (hence 'post-capitalist'). Drucker argued that knowledge had become the means of production, creating value by 'productivity' and 'innovation' when applied to work. The new class of post-capitalist society was now made up of knowledge workers and service workers. This presented a major challenge for society. How should we preserve the income and dignity of service workers (who lack the ability to become knowledge workers but constitute the majority of the work force)?[20] Many lament there simply are no quality jobs anymore.

More recently, the financial journalist Paul Mason pondered if we are not on the brink of a change so big, so profound, that this time capitalism itself has reached its limits and is changing into something wholly new. It is the information technology revolution, Mason argued, that has the potential to reshape utterly our familiar notions of work, production and value; and to destroy an economy based on markets and private ownership – in fact, he contended, was already doing so.[21]

As the Fourth Industrial Revolution takes hold, the factors that build value through the human dimension in an enterprise will change. Automation and robotics are threatening to wreak havoc on employment, reshaping the way society works. The march of the machines is giving considerable cause for considerable angst. 'Policymakers need to get going now because, the longer they delay, the greater the burden on the welfare state.'[22] A Universal Basic Income (UBI) is coming to the fore and was voted on at the time of writing in Switzerland. It would be the ultimate benefit. If it had been passed, every adult legally resident in Switzerland would have been paid the same and received an unconditional income of 2,500 Swiss francs (£1,755) a month whether they work or not. Supporters for the Yes vote dressed up as robots to highlight the increased use of technology in factories where retail and finance has replaced human employees with machines. Speaking as hundreds of 'robots' danced on the streets of Zurich, campaigner Che Wagner said: 'The robots are saying "we don't want to grab your work and make you suffer. We want to make you free", that's why they want a basic income for us humans.' In Switzerland over half of all work that is done is unpaid – in the home, care, in the communities – so, that work would be more valued with a basic income.[23] Critics objected that the rich would have to be paid the same as the poor so who would pay for it? The libertarian right to be lazy would undermine society and erode the work ethic so that people will not be industrious. An alienated idleness will break the welfare state.

Nevertheless, the genie of technology has been let out of the bottle. Prospects for a world without work due to a fully automated society co-exist with technological upheaval that is already reshaping the global economy. Automation already holds out the promise of a cyber meadow where we live free from the drudgery of work plus a platform for people to create new jobs. Alternative narratives of a digital future are available. On the one hand is a post-work world where most jobs are low-paid. On the other is the creation of many new platforms on which to build a whole new economy and the worse jobs are done by machines and algorithms.[24]

The plates are shifting, shifting so fast that everywhere on the planet is no further than hours away and no one further than milliseconds on the Internet. Distance has all but died. Everywhere the impact of living in a wired-up, globalised world asserts itself. Everywhere we see the reaction against the impersonal and the imperative towards personalisation. Organisations have to flourish in a very different climate than they did a generation ago before these trends became so accentuated. Leadership and nurturing the human dimension through fostering talent are more important than ever.

Nevertheless, there is a highly significant alignment between jobs being automated out of existence and the new participative paradigm that is emerging. In both the second and third waves of industrialisation, the emphasis was on quantity, on output, on top-down command and control so that ever greater yields could be cranked from given inputs. As the majority of the people on the planet are wired together in a Fourth Industrial Revolution, it is no accident that the Internet being midwife to a new economic infrastructure is taking place at the same time as there is more emphasis on quality. An organisation that stresses industrial scale quantity, not quality, is not thinking deeply enough.

A recent paper (at the time of writing) has suggested that such fears do not take into account the extent to which tasks can be unbundled.[25] Machines can only handle some of these tasks. Bookkeeping, accounting and auditing were susceptible up to a massive 98 per cent risk. However, three-quarters of those jobs involve face-to-face or group tasks. A major shortcoming of the typical arguments about technological non-employment is that there is no clear reason why the effect of new technologies will be different now than in the past when they did not create widespread reductions in employment.[26]

As the age of capitalism yields to the knowledge society and now to the digital economy, the radical effects it will have on society, politics, and business now and in the coming years are far-reaching. Now that since about 1980 far fewer people in the West work in factories – and even China is busy de-industrialising – we have already moved from a society based on capital, land, and labour to a society whose primary source is knowledge and whose key structure is the organisation.

In the digital future, environments of value will be different from the old industrial-era institutions that created public services. It is not solely the case that if an organisation is well managed it is well led. Future organisations will not just be cranking out quantity but quality. Creativity and empathy have not been really needed except for the creative or caring industries. In the future, they will be vital for all enterprises. The leadership needed to foster such environments will be different from the old top-down style where instructions are given. They will be open, transformative processes, where we no longer speak about bosses and workers, processes based on subject–object relations, but about creating space for all involved, if not in equal relation then in creative dialogue. This is surely the workplace of the future, not old hierarchical models but where creativity and empathy fuse to generate all-round shared value. The future of work will still entail successful organisations being those employing worthwhile people doing worthwhile jobs and tasks.

Rooted in the well-rehearsed notion that organisational success or competitive advantage is achieved through its workforce, the proposition for a new construct is this. Human activity in organisations flourishes at its optimum in a valuing environment where the link between inner value and external, added value is optimised. Wherever a human community has a task at its heart and there are jobs to do, this can be expressed as 'significance with belonging'.

Having thought about the smart leadership needed to lead from the emerging digital future, we go on to discuss the ingredients of what constitutes an environment of shared value, the corporate or organisational culture within which the human dimension can be motivated and harnessed. Often one hears statements such as 'culture will take care of itself – leadership doesn't need to support culture'.[27] I argue that it is the role of leaders to build positive cultures within their organisations against the backcloth of empirical factors that generate their opposite. Organisational cultures can become toxic through leaders devaluing their staff. This is not necessarily conscious games of power and control by managers acting as narcissistic individuals. Human experience in the workplace is shaped by valuing environments (or their contrast pole): by micro-cultures that induce systemic behaviour.

Values-driven ethical leadership, not just technocratic competence, is emphasised in leadership literature of recent times. What that needs to be complemented with is the dimension of spirit and soul that translates managerialism from Smart Leadership into wisdom for rushing executives whose own inner world is so often off balance. We will call this 'leadership with spirit'.

What this study now adds to such literature is to configure the experience of participants in the workplace within a construct of what is involved in being a catalyst for turning inner value into external, measurable outcomes. It proposes a typology for such catalytic action. Triggered by my experience in daily work, I was looking for integrated perspectives where theory and practice merge. The client work that illuminates the factors that generate inner worth being drawn out and harnessed (or shut down as the case may be) is reflected in a journey of auto-ethnography. On reflection, this was the most suitable vehicle to allow for gathering and reflecting in a sustained and ethical way about the experiences people have shared over the years and thence to develop some generalisations. This was combined with a relational constructionist approach in which participants construct their own meaning and reality through realising how much they are related.

Crucially, looking at issues of human worth through their contrast polarity – what it means to be devalued – lent greater analytical clarity. It began to emerge what a valuing environment looked and smelt like. Through empirical observation in therapeutic contexts and organisational study of both the popular and academic literature, circumstances that give rise to the experience of feeling devalued can be clustered and summed up as threefold:

- *Not honouring our humanity (inequality)* – the experience of being diminished rather than enlarged, ranging from discriminatory practice to not having one's full humanity included: the politics of insult. Lack of either involvement or inclusion results in a deficit of significance of which these are its ingredients.
- *Lack of purposeful engagement (indifference)* – not being seen, noticed, recognised or listened to.
- *Being invaded (indignity)* – the politics of assault or being set aside, giving rise to feelings of indignation.

When it comes to corporate culture, there will always be problems between managers and employees, even in the most benign situation. Many difficulties are the result of clients' own responses to authority and stress. Some difficulties are the result of company policies. There is, as observed, much good management and leadership out there. Nevertheless, client reports keep coming back to these same factors *again and again*. Moreover, statements in practitioner literature indicate that these can be replicated. There really does seem to be an issue not just with narcissistic managers but with the culture of many organisations. As we will explore, it is the culture and practice on the ground that shapes behaviour and nearly always vitiates 'official' strategy and so often makes it practically irrelevant.

Discerning such negative factors for disvaluing environments leads to turning these back on their head 'to lift the LID' on an organisation, release dynamism and address disengagement through a positive workplace culture:

- Honouring our humanity – **Look**, learn and listen.
- Engage with purpose – **I**nvolve and include so as to elicit significance.
- Set up a non-intrusive environment – **D**ignify.

I sought to develop some theory to propose a new conceptual structure relevant to environments of value and the shape of things to come in a Fourth Industrial Revolution. The grounded theory is:

- There is a strong association between the sense of inner-world value held by staff or workers as they participate in an organisation AND the added, external value they generate that furthers its purpose.
- Smart Leaders understand it is in the interests of the organisation to optimise those factors (proposed here as essentially threefold) that enable a valuing environment to translate inner value into added value.

At first glance, this is a book about how organisations flourish. There is, however, a construct being developed here that potentially provides a lens on the drivers of human action. Getting the best out of people, not just extracting the most, requires attention to the circumstances in which their sense of themselves and their value is translated into their projects.

We ask, what advantages are there to employers, to leadership in non-profit or faith-based organisations in setting up work environments where it is not all about making money and optimum performance? After all, the law does not say leaders must look after their staff and make them feel valued. Yet it is surely a strategy of self-enlightenment to discern what are the ingredients of a high-value environment. About 90 per cent of the overheads of an organisation are still staff salaries.

There is also an emphasis on looking more deeply into what it means to go beyond technocratic leadership into something more akin to wisdom, something rooted in spirit and soul. Technocratic leadership has been fundamental to building the very industrial-era public services that so often de-personalise us. 'Leadership with spirit' takes us beyond the 'smart leadership' that will negotiate the forces that are driving change into wisdom for a digital economy.

Axiomatic in what follows is that human beings are strongly shaped by their social environment, by forces that structure their life and work, not just their own agency. A workplace is a very particular form of social environment. If the circumstances and context are right, people will give of their best. That seems commonplace until it is realised that the experience of so many is that the organisational environment and culture are not conducive. Rather than engendering engagement, they are de-motivating.

Similarly, when a teacher closes the classroom door, he or she is creating a certain culture of what happens and what is acceptable in a learning context. This is a vital ingredient of education generally but it is particularly relevant to the kind of education needed for the digital age that is sweeping all before it. How do we generate the soft skills of creativity and advanced empathy that will be vital tools of collaboration and innovation as the workplace and life generally merge and create new ways of doing things?

Income inequality is already growing because high-skill workers benefit disproportionately when technology complements their jobs. This poses challenges for employers and policymakers: how to help existing workers acquire new skills, and how to prepare future generations for a workplace stuffed full of artificial intelligence (AI). As technology changes the skills needed for each profession, workers will have to adjust. That will mean making education and training flexible enough to teach new skills quickly and efficiently. It will require a greater emphasis on lifelong learning and on-the-job training, and wider use of online learning and video-game-style simulation. AI may itself help, by personalising computer-based learning and by identifying workers' skills gaps and opportunities for retraining.

> Social and character skills will matter more, too. When jobs are perishable, technologies come and go and people's working lives are longer, social skills are a foundation. They can give humans an edge, helping them do work that calls for empathy and human interaction – traits that are beyond machines.[28]

Making human connections becomes all the more important despite an age of individualism. In a digital future, a fixed, static workplace environment changes. For the most part, we no longer work in factories. The impersonal accentuates the importance of the personal. In the global society that is already arriving, technological displacement will radically reshape the workplace within the next 20 years. Creativity and empathy may be given the same status as numeracy and literacy because learning to collaborate and learn (or unlearn) are skills the future will value. These are gifts of the imagination and less easily automated. Alongside human relationships, cultivating empathy will be crucial for making organisations and the workplace more humane places. With the Internet already organising economy and society in a different way, a premium will be placed on factors to do with the human 'touch', such as creativity, empathy and entrepreneurial flair that cannot be replicated by algorithms. There is a vital association between inner value and external, added value that is there to draw out under optimum conditions. Leaders are often unsure how to mobilise the participation and engagement of their people so they are productive and contribute effectively. *That is true anytime, anywhere, but in the Fourth Industrial Revolution even more so if it deprives us of our heart and soul.*

How are we to re-humanise communities of practice to nurture capacity for creative compassion? Computers are already learning pattern recognition. Yet that is only half of creativity. The most important ingredient cannot be replicated technologically, making meaning. Empathy, too, is not going to be replicated by technology soon. It does not depend on electronic connection so much as garnering human capacities for reflection and making connections. Soon, education will need to be redesigned so as to foster skills that nurture the human. Educators will be tillers of the soil, gardeners and guardians of tender shoots so as to nurture connections between learners inside and outside organisations and introduce them to each other – both locally and globally.

In short, if there is definite congruence between inner and outer forms of value, between inputs and outputs, it is surely a wise approach to learn to work differently. Probing the conditions within valuing environments that either function at their optimum or are clearly absent can lead to a conversation about how to set up organisations that best elicit the magic gold of human participation. There is a new trajectory here waiting to happen that has been forming for some time.

If then the proposition is accepted that there is a strong association between internal value and external, added value, it forces reflection on what are the optimum conditions within which that conversion takes place. This then begs a second question. If a valuing environment draws out the potential of people within a given context, why does this dig into human motivation? If we are setting up ripe conditions within which social participants are engaged and motivated, what does this say about how motivational drivers are configured? Can we apply that to voluntary sector and civil society when future workers will have a flexible pattern of employment rather than fixed career structures?

We will therefore ask a deeper question. If certain conditions lead to a culture and practice of being better motivated and having energies and dynamism released, what does that say about the way humans are wired up – the motivational drivers? Proposing a brief account of what it would mean to articulate the motivational drivers in this way, we ask how that might be translated into useful knowledge. Can we apply such insights to the way we motivate paid staff or volunteers in an enterprise? Is this different when it comes to the shape of civil society or the role of faith-based organisations?

And what then do we do with Maslow (or Freud)?

Notes

1 'Fulcrum Capital', http://www.fulcrumcapllc.com/millennials-skills-lead-21st-century/, accessed June 2016.
2 Hamel, G. (2009), 'Moon Shots for Management', *Harvard Business Review*, February 2009, https://www.hbr.org/2009/02/moon-shots-for-management/, accessed June 2016.
3 Fine, B. (2014), *Social Capital versus Social Theory: Political Economy and Social Science at the Turn of the Millennium*. Abingdon: Routledge.
4 Author conversation with those who have worked in the industry.
5 Whyte, W. (1957), *The Organisation Man*. London: Jonathan Cape.
6 Nonaka, I. and Takeuchi, H. (2011), 'The Wise Leader', *Harvard Business Review*, 89 (5), pp. 59–67.
7 BSA Work, Employment and Society 2016 Conference – Call for Papers. Work, Employment and Society Conference 2016, 'Work in Crisis'.
8 Steed, C.D. (2016), *A Question of Worth: Economy, Society and the Quantification of Human Value*. London: I.B.Tauris.
9 Witters, D. and Agrawal, S. (2015), 'Well-Being Enhances Benefits of Employee Engagement', *Gallup Business Journal*, 27 October 2015.
10 https://www.ethereum.org/, accessed June 2016.
11 Quoted in Tapscott, D. and Tapscott, A. (2016), *Blockchain Revolution: How the Technology behind Bitcoin is Changing Money, Business and the World*. London: Portfolio Penguin, p. 88.
12 http://reports.weforum.org/mastering-hypergrowth/, 2016, accessed June 2016.
13 'The Iraq Inquiry', http://www.iraqinquiry.org.uk/, 6 July 2016, accessed July 2016.
14 http://www.bbc.co.uk/news/world-us-canada-36755178/, accessed July 2016.
15 *The Today Programme*, BBC Radio 4, http://www.bbc.co.uk/radio4/thetodayprogramme/, 22 July 2016, accessed July 2016.
16 Hilton, S. (2015), *More Human: Designing a World Where People Come First*. London: Penguin Random House.
17 Sunstein, C. (2013), *Simpler: The Future of Government*. New York: Barnes and Noble.
18 James, O. (2013), *Office Politics*. London: Vermillion.
19 *The World at One*, BBC Radio 4, http://www.bbc.co.uk/radio4/worldatone/, 14 July 2016, accessed July 2016.

20 Drucker, P. (1990), *Managing the Non-profit Organization*. New York: HarperCollins.
21 Mason, P. (2015), *PostCapitalism: A Guide to our Future*. London: Allen Lane.
22 'Artificial intelligence. March of the machines. What history tells us about the future of artificial intelligence – and how society should respond'. *The Economist*, 25 June 2016.
23 'Switzerland votes in historic universal basic income referendum'. *The Independent*, 5 June 2016.
24 Srnicek, N. and Williams, A. (2016), *Inventing the Future: Post-capitalism and a World without Work*. London: Verso.
25 Arntz, M., Gregory, T. and Zierhahn, U. (2016), *The Risk of Automation for Jobs in OECD Countries: A Comparative Analysis*. European Centre for Economic Research. OECD Social, Employment and Migration Working Papers No 189. Paris: OECD Publishing.
26 Karabarbounis, L. and Neiman, B. (2014), 'The Global Decline of the Labor Share', *The Quarterly Journal of Economics*, 129 (1), pp. 61–103.
27 Author's client notes – used with permission and name withheld.
28 *The Economist*, 25 June 2016.

Chapter 1

Smart leadership from the emerging future

'She were accessible, she were a people person; she weren't out for money, she were for us.'
Tribute by neighbours who were stunned by their MP, Jo Cox, being slain
on the streets of her West Yorkshire town, 16 June 2016.[1]

The revolt of unrealistic expectations (leadership in turbulent times)

We are educating children for a society that will be out of date within 15 years. The only technology young people know comes with a twenty-first-century mindset; a frame of reference that has been reshaped and recast in this curious time when technology and nature came together. The social and economic impact of technology is widespread and accelerating. The speed and volume of information have increased exponentially. Experts are predicting that 90 per cent of the entire population will be connected to the Internet within ten years. With the Internet of Things, digital and physical worlds will soon be merged.[2]

The forces that are driving change, that are reshaping the landscape of culture and society, are both rapid and discontinuous. They are rapid because the pace accelerates with each passing year. They are discontinuous because the transformations are disruptive and unpredictable. Discontinuous change creates situations that challenge our assumptions and mandate different ways of working. The new network economy that is emerging is post-capitalist: the utility is provided through abundant information technology that, in a wired-up world, is social on a global scale.

One of the seven sweeping transformations we will note, the Fourth Industrial Revolution courtesy of the new infrastructure of the Internet, is the first-ever truly two-way media. Amidst its Janus-type quality of facing both ways simultaneously towards both human flourishing and destructiveness, the Internet has brought many new voices to the fore. Instead of sitting back and being broadcast at, we are now active participants and contributors. We place a priority on connection, on being part of the conversation, on participation. This offers potential for human flourishing that has never been seen in world history at the very same time as it threatens de-personalisation.

The plates are shifting. The way the world works is changing rapidly. Change is beginning to stir at a deeper level than that of governments calling the tune. Smart leaders in politics know that pulling the old state levers to make things happen is not going to do the job in the same way. Historical forces are reshaping things. A de-personalised world is experiencing blowback. The blowback takes the form of an assertion of (or retreat into?) identities, translated into populist demands 'to bring back control' as Gordon Brown frames it.[3] It is an illusion. There is no going back.

When Philip Bobbitt, American lawyer, historian and government adviser, along with other champions of the liberal global order evoked the 'end of history' after the end of the cold war they imagined a deepening network of international bodies, running on liberal rules, which would cooperate to tackle such all-embracing problems as climate change, pollution and, of course, residual poverty and disease.[4] That was all before the 9/11 attacks and the banking crisis of 2008/9, when the scale and speed of China's recovery to worldwide authority was far from clear. So it has not proved so easy. Globalisation has proved a mixed blessing, with the rise of religious fundamentalist militancy and the mass migration of peoples across the world. The American-led war on terror set out to disrupt and destroy the emerging franchise known as al-Qaeda. But they reckoned without a newly emerging bit of tech known from 2000 as a 'smartphone'. It was the terrorist organiser's dream weapon.

The World Economic Forum's Meta-Council on Emerging Technologies, published in collaboration with *Scientific American*, highlights technological advances its members believe have the power to improve lives, transform industries and safeguard the planet. It also provides an opportunity to debate any human, societal, economic or environmental risks and concerns that the technologies may pose prior to widespread adoption.

> Horizon scanning for emerging technologies is crucial to staying abreast of developments that can radically transform our world, enabling timely expert analysis in preparation for these disruptors. The global community needs to come together and agree on common principles if our society is to reap the benefits and hedge the risks of these technologies.[5]

To give a snapshot of the breathtaking acceleration of the new digital world, the top ten technologies for 2016 were the following.

Nanosensors and the Internet of Nanothings

With the Internet of Things expected to comprise 30 billion connected devices by 2020, one of the most exciting areas of focus today is now on nanosensors capable of circulating in the human body or being embedded in construction materials. Once connected, this Internet of Nanothings could have a huge impact on the future of medicine, architecture, agriculture and drug manufacture.

Next-generation batteries

One of the greatest obstacles holding renewable energy back is matching supply with demand, but recent advances in energy storage using sodium, aluminium and zinc-based batteries makes mini-grids feasible that can provide clean, reliable, round-the-clock energy sources to entire villages.

The blockchain

Much already has been made of the distributed electronic ledger behind the online currency Bitcoin. With related venture investment exceeding $1 billion in 2015 alone, the economic and social impact of a blockchain's potential to fundamentally change the way markets and governments work is only now emerging.

2D materials

Graphene may be the best-known single-atom-layer material, but it is by no means the only one. Plummeting production costs mean that such 2D materials are emerging in a wide range of applications, from air and water filters to new generations of wearables and batteries.

Autonomous vehicles

Self-driving cars may not yet be fully legal in most geographies, but their potential for saving lives, cutting pollution, boosting economies, and improving quality of life for the elderly and other segments of society has led to rapid deployment of key technology forerunners along the way to full autonomy.

Organs-on-chips

Miniature models of human organs – the size of a memory stick – could revolutionise medical research and drug discovery by allowing researchers to see biological mechanism behaviours in ways never before possible.

Perovskite solar cells

This new photovoltaic material offers three improvements over the classic silicon solar cell: it is easier to make, can be used virtually anywhere and, to date, keeps on generating power more efficiently.

Open AI ecosystem

Shared advances in natural language processing and social awareness algorithms, coupled with an unprecedented availability of data, will soon allow smart digital assistants to help with a vast range of tasks, from keeping track of one's finances and health to advising on wardrobe choice.

Optogenetics

The use of light and colour to record the activity of neurons in the brain has been around for some time, but recent developments mean light can now be delivered deeper into brain tissue, something that could lead to better treatment for people with brain disorders.

Systems metabolic engineering

Advances in synthetic biology, systems biology and evolutionary engineering mean that the list of building block chemicals that can be manufactured better and more cheaply by using plants rather than fossil fuels is growing every year.[6]

Automation has also enabled the rise of 'big data' based on deep-learning. Given enough data, computers can imitate the neural networks of the human brain and undertake tasks like powering search engines. Internet-based firms can experiment with big data, the accumulation and collection of vastly more data than before to analyse and improve performance. The 80–20 rule used to be a management adage; that out of the things that could be changed to make for improvement, working on 20 per cent would drive 80 per cent of what needs to improve. With big data, it becomes possible to analyse all the factors and all the detail rather than work on a few tweaks. Big data is transformative because it produces any amount of small improvements.[7]

Citizens have 24/7 access to high-quality information and inspiration, so they no longer need to go to the regular channels for those things. Slowly but surely, global, societal shifts are changing how things are done. More and more communities are finding creative ways to prioritise connection, dialogue, participation and empowerment. There is a new 'participative paradigm'. People expect to work collaboratively. Political and economic turbulence have destabilised communities and dislocated individual lives. Faith in many democratic institutions is undermined. In a global economy and rapidly changing business environments, competition and hierarchy are being replaced by collaboration and shared leadership.

As Giddens notes, 'there are good reasons to believe that we are living through a major period of historical transition. The changes affecting us are not confined to any one area of the globe but stretch almost everywhere.'[8]

First transformation – distance in politics

Across the world, we are entering an era of fragmented politics and multiplicity of party. As witnessed in the 2016 US presidential elections or concurrent debates about the European Union, sentiment against the European project has risen dramatically in recent years. Citizens everywhere seem more fearful of immigration, more distrustful of global actors. This is a pronounced cultural anxiety, widely reported on. The 'return of the public' is fraught with both risk and opportunity.

Though citizens hold on to the belief that in theory the state can pull the levers and make things happen, this goes hand in hand with a marked sense of powerlessness in the face of remote forces. The distrust of institutions in general and politicians in particular is strong. Official policy does not seem to take into account the effect it has on ordinary people. As one voice put it, 'I'm fed up with my representatives doing things that don't come down to me.'[9]

It has become commonplace to observe that there is a marked 'anti-politics' mood across the Western world. What the Tea Party in the US or the Trump candidacy has in common with support at the time of writing with a self-confessed socialist candidate is the same principle as strong grassroots support for a socialist Leader of the Opposition in the UK. Old ways of doing things seem sterile. The stables need drastic cleansing. There is also a broad anti-establishment, anti-politics mood playing out in the European referendum debate in the UK, the 2016 US presidential elections and beyond. People are fed up with politics as usual. Politicians are branded as being too grey, too bland, too unrepresentative of 'people like us'.

Everywhere, the cry is 'power to the people' or 'Wir sind das Volk', as the Saxons proclaimed in 1989; the first East Germans to take to the streets crying freedom for a life without communism. We are in an age of critical citizenry demanding authentic politics and politicians. 'It makes him a whole person, a real person', declares a supporter of Marco Rubio in the 2016 US presidential election.[10]

Post-industrial workers are much less inclined to vote by fixed allegiances. Party managers and activists alike are struggling to grasp why voters are not as excited as they are and how we are to make sense of seemingly contradictory outcomes such as, in the UK, the Labour Party being too 'left wing' for England perhaps but too far to the right for Scotland. These trends tell us something about the politics of distance. Westminster is 'too far away', just as Europe is too far away for many English voters. Indeed, many Highlanders and Islanders feel Edinburgh is a long way. Distance is the new frontier. There is far greater emphasis on the need to reconnect people and politics, born perhaps from distrust of 'the system' run by vested interests and elites. Infantilising the electorate won't work now. Grassroots activism in economic and political life as people exercise agency shows they are less prepared to be passive observers of what is going on. The debate across Europe about Europe arguably is not about the shape of bananas but remoteness. Along with citizens not identifying so much with their traditional base because it has passed them by – witness the white working-class voting Labour in England or older, middle-class men in Germany anxious about social decline and cultural alienation[11] – comes the rise of nationalisms. Just when the post-war generation thought nationalism had lost its potency and fascist overtones, from Greece to Scotland, from UKIP and Tory euro-sceptics to Marine Le Pen, people want a national story. The Scottish National Party stormed to victory in the 2015 British general election because they created a mass movement mobilised at the speed of a smartphone and a text. They drew on the enthusiasm of ordinary voters, on crowd funding and instant donations. Everyone felt part of the project. The decision for Brexit in the EU referendum debate in June 2016 told a similar story.

Beyond doubt, globalisation has, for many people, been a great force for good. Life expectancy has risen by more in the past 50 years than in the previous 1,000. When the Berlin Wall fell, two-fifths of humanity lived in extreme poverty. Yet as Joseph Stiglitz contends, lack of rewards of globalisation being spread evenly is the root cause of the current backlash against globalisation. 'We've never had a democratic globalisation. The lack of transparency and openness has meant that we've wound up with a form of globalisation that works for a few, but not for all of us.' 'Citizens now are beginning to understand that globalisation matters. They are demanding a voice.'[12] In short, the EU referendum outcome in the UK was about more than the EU. It was a vote of no confidence against globalisation.

The importance of Facebook and other social networks to politics will continue to grow. In the 2016 US presidential election, candidates spent a billion dollars on digital advertising, more than 50 times what they spent in 2008.[13] Facebook can now generate targeted advertisements. Politicians can say different things to different groups without anyone noticing.

There is a strong sense that politics is not doing what it should be for people and that politicians are far too remote, not 'people like us'! Politics has passed them by. Many white working-class people feel marginalised. The subjectivity, the mood behind this is 'They want to recover a sense that they matter'. Yearning to feel a sense of being from somewhere, people retreat into assertions of identity. Amidst cultural anxiety that 'this isn't my country anymore', populism is alive and well.

Second transformation – the economy

At the same time as the shift in the mood of Western publics, we are witnessing extraordinary global forces restructuring the world economy.

The impetus to create an intricate web of a global economy had been especially intensified in different periods, such as the nineteenth century. In particular, the spread of trade, capital and people brought an expansion of the world capitalist economy in the period from 1870 to 1914 characterised by railroads spanning many continents, refrigerated rail cars, steamships based on coal and then oil turbines, and global capital (facilitated by currencies pegged to the price of gold). World trade more than doubled in the two decades leading up to the First World War. Edwardian era globalisation was stimulated by a massive free flow of people and emigration.[14]

The period after the First World War witnessed a closing of markets to overseas trade and retrenchment. It was not until post-war reconstruction after 1945 that trade barriers were discredited as having contributed to nationalism and suspicion of other countries. The Bretton Woods conference in 1944 created the foundations for a huge rise in international trade, enabled by new institutions such as the World Bank and the International Monetary Fund (IMF).[15] Increased trade in goods, and greater flow of investment restored prosperity in the 1950s.

After the stagnation of the 1970s, there was a new phase of capitalist world development with the accession of Margaret Thatcher and Ronald Reagan. There had been growing dissatisfaction with the role of government in the economy alongside the welfare capitalism associated with social democracy. The turn to the market led to a freeing up of regulation and reduction of trade tariffs (the Uruguay Round). Communist regimes began to totter and then collapsed spectacularly. They had been very good at producing iron and steel but not the items people wanted, such as their own car. The year 1989 represented the revolt of the frustrated consumer. Capitalism had finally won over communism as a way of organising society and the economy. Backed by container ships and continuing growth of communications (such as satellite technology), globalisation had become a new reality. Global movements of capital, trade and transport annihilated distance and brought intensified compression of the world combined with an increasing awareness of it.[16] The days had passed when a widget was made in one country and exported to another. Products were now built from parts from all over the world manufactured by the same multinational firm according to where it made economic sense to locate. Built on manufacturing, low labour costs and large factories took advantage of the same economies of scale that had powered the first phase of the industrial revolution in the West.

Global flows of finance, goods and services rose from $2 trillion in 1980 to $28 trillion in 2014. McKinsey argues that this figure could rise to $84 trillion by 2025.[17] Globalisation – the linking together of national economies into a global market economy – is a strongly contested phenomenon. To its critics, it continues to stand accused of undermining sovereignty, weakening democracy, widening inequality and foisting exploitative multinational corporations onto consumers.[18] There is another narrative, that difficulties in connection with globalisation are to do with politicians and policies, trade deals and so on rather than markets. The inter-dependence of nations is here to stay. People are able to communicate with each other instantaneously in a way that leaps across borders. Cultural globalisation means we buy clothing and food or listen to music from anywhere. It goes hand in hand with a globalised world where economic transformations continue to be far-reaching. With high labour and high energy costs, the rich world cannot compete with producers worldwide of low-value, bulk steel. Entire steel industries and communities dependent on them are declining fast.[19]

We are witnessing reaction against the central planning and statism of a former generation towards an agenda acknowledging the need to release free enterprise and personal responsibility (strong themes in the new democratic economy that is emerging following the economic crash of 2008). A centrally planned economy is a failed model – as China's economic explosion attests. Doing economics as if people matter is a growing emphasis, witness the rise of social enterprise amidst a recurrent emphasis on consumer rights as businesses fuss about that most precious of all commodities, the consumer. Small businesses can enter market space and, under the right conditions, thrive. The lifetime of a FTSE 100 company is falling fast due to churning. Though insurgent companies have a hard time against big concentrated power that controls a market, we could be seeing the eclipse of the capitalist model of organising society. Either that or the democratisation of productive forces by consumers is its latest evolution. The old corporate top-down machine model is passé. Old state monopolies have been broken up. Traditional lines between producers and consumers have blurred. The communications Internet, energy Internet and logistics Internet are converging to create a neural network at a global level that connects everything.[20] From bitcoins creating a dispersed public ledger to nimble enterprises seizing opportunities, virtually everywhere we are seeing new forms of economic organisation. Customers are just as likely to stay in an Airbnb as in a hotel or take an Uber taxi as a state-licensed one. The notion of renting a car, rationalising resources is enabled by new platforms. Traditional businesses are being unbundled. The digital economy poses changes and challenges that are vast in scope and urgent in timescale.

It is growing exponentially. In Egypt, for example, 90 per cent of the young adult population do not have bank accounts. 'Going digital' and 'mobile-first' strategies are fundamental to how maximising customer experience maps on to vast new opportunities for growth and investments. Robotics and artificial intelligence (AI) are now prevalent in wealth management. Completely new vistas of interaction and customer service have become possible.

Many voices urge that under no circumstances should official bodies print money. With the Internet of information we have trust. Banks, governments, and even social media companies like Facebook work to establish our identity and ownership of assets. They help us transfer value and settle transactions; powerful intermediaries need powerful intermediaries. They use centralised servers, which can be hacked. They take a fee for their services – say 10 per cent to send money internationally. They capture our data, not just preventing us from monetising it, but often undermining our privacy. They are sometimes unreliable and often slow. They exclude two billion people who don't have enough money to justify a bank account. In sum, they capture a lopsided share of the benefits of the digital economy.

Enter the blockchain, the first native digital medium for peer-to-peer value exchange. Its protocol establishes the rules – in the form of globally distributed computations and heavy-duty encryption – that ensure the integrity of the data traded amongst billions of devices without going through a trusted third party. Trust is hard-coded into the platform. The Trust Protocol acts as a ledger of accounts, a database, a notary, a sentry, and clearing house, all by consensus. Every business, institution, government, and individual can benefit in profound ways.[21] Blockchain offers the potential for:

- including billions of people in the global economy;
- protecting rights through immutable records like land titles;
- creating a true sharing economy by replacing service aggregators as Uber are doing, with distributed applications;
- ending the remittance rip-off, helping diasporas return funds to their ancestral lands;
- enabling citizens to own and monetise their data (and protect privacy) through owning their personal identities rather than identities being owned by big social media companies or governments;
- unleashing a new halcyon age of entrepreneurship by enabling small companies to have all the capabilities of large companies;
- helping build accountable government through transparency, smart contracts and revitalised models of democracy.

The growth of technology is both exponential and digital. As middle-class jobs disappear in the wake of computers learning to think, the gap is set to widen considerably between those whose skill set is enhanced by technology and those who have to compete for the chance to wait at tables and other low-grade work. Tasks involving brain power are susceptible to rapid technological displacement. How we can educate accordingly? The task is urgent. How can we embed skills and approaches that will be at a premium in the new world unfolding before our eyes, a world where the extraordinary is the new ordinary?

A few companies in the sharing economy are performing particularly well, overtaking established competitors in traditional industries. Yet there are commentators who counter that these commercially successful companies are not really part of the sharing economy. Others question whether the sharing economy is actually a new phenomenon or, for example, if it is simply renting by another name. The sharing economy has become confusing in recent years as technology has enabled diverse business models to emerge under the system. Many find the growth of new online platforms to be disorienting. The movement began with locally based, grassroots-funded initiatives such as tool libraries and timebanks, but now seems to be led by global, venture-backed corporations and new forms of corporate power. Uber is now the world's largest taxi company (owning no taxis), Facebook, the world's largest media owner (creating no content), Alibaba, the world's most valuable retailer (with no inventory) and Airbnb, the world's largest accommodation provider (owning no property).[22]

While the sharing economy is exceeding most expectations of its business potential, it is disappointing those who were more excited by its social promise. As online platforms have scaled, they have found it increasingly difficult to sustain their initial social impact. Nevertheless, the sharing economy reflects a dramatic shift in labour relations that could offer a dynamic new marketplace for workers and employers alike, or leaves workers to compete for meagre rewards while platform owners reap fees from every transaction.

Third transformation – the death of the father

One of the increasingly strong themes in this new global culture is that people are less willing to put up with big institutions. They want relationships with real people. Governments are perceived as professional elites, patronising and paternalistic.

Social theorists can ponder the rise of feminism concurrent with the decline of paternalism. But there is no doubt we are seeing a paradigm shift. The attitude of 'we know what you need' is on the way out, especially if politicians don't actually meet real people (apart from situations of grievance) let alone ask them! Whether it is perceived long-term dependency of benefit recipients on state welfare or developing countries on foreign aid – an attitude of 'we know best' is not the way the world works anymore. An empowered citizenry is realising its own agency. Local communities assert the need to wrest power back and re-build voluntary association. A strong feature of the twentieth century was for governments to do more based on the power of the state to get things done. Doing things for and to people is not as effective as unleashing the power of ordinary people coming together and doing things for themselves. Such trends are closely aligned with more relational ways of working and constructing knowledge communally than using top-down evidence-based knowledge to do something 'to you ... about you ... for you'. Distant, disconnected leadership is rejected everywhere.

The same mood is working, too, against international development aid. A stance of throwing money at a project but not coming alongside and respecting the people is less likely to succeed. As the finance minister of Rwanda remarked, endeavouring to lure international economic investment and reduce the aid that accounted for more than 40 per cent of the budget, 'no country can depend on development aid forever. Such dependency de-humanises us and robs us of our dignity.'[23] There has been greater emphasis in recent years on a multi-dimensional approach to poverty that sees develop- ment not just in terms of what you have but what you can do and be – the capabilities and functionings approach emphasised by the Nobel prize economist Amartya Sen. This is a shift from the achievement of project objectives to a broader sense of impact on people's lives and fostering well-being.[24] Witness Asset-Based Community Development, a large and growing movement that considers local assets as the primary building blocks of sus- tainable community development. Building on the skills of local residents, the power of local associations, and the supportive functions of local institutions, asset-based community development draws upon existing community strengths to build stronger, more sustainable communities for the future. Finding leadership at local level is vital.

Fourth transformation – the rise of accountability

In many parts of the world, the digital revolution is fuelling demands for a more sophisticated, efficient and less corrupt state. In Latin America, for instance, this is com- bined with a parallel trend, the growth of the middle class. There is a strong imperative of mistrust against the impersonal, impatience with a plodding bureaucracy and demand for accountability and transparency. The mood in the global zeitgeist is that states as well as institutions should be held up to scrutiny. Although the practice of this and the exercise of a free press is patchy, the Internet has enabled a great leap forward in public and international scrutiny. Across the Western world, the Internet era fuels constant scrutiny. There is a right to know that is felt with increasing strength. Clandestine, undemocratic conduct is much less tolerated. Holding elites to account, not letting criminal state actors get away with it is a feature of our age. Recent events to do with FIFA and world athletics are relevant here. Due to pervasive scepticism about institutions, increasingly, whistle- blowing is seen as an honourable response to needful exposure of injustice rather than a disgraceful breach of gagging orders.

It is not just about what happens in demanding Western style electorates; witness the way that in, for example, the authoritarian state of Vietnam, ordinary people are remarkably outspoken about social issues such as sub-standard hospitals. China is seeing the rise of civil society. Though the government tries to block access to online information it considers sensitive, social media plays a growing role in China's public life. Yet, as with all these transformations, there is a problematic aspect. In China, accountability is also associated with confessing one's crimes on TV in a public confessional. Academic opinion is divided over whether this is an expression of the shame culture common to East Asia or an expression of submission to an over-mighty state. We read of young Vietnamese outraged by Chinese claims to islands in the South China Sea. Those born since the country ditched its planned economy in the 1980s are growing more assertive on social media. Or social media pokes fun at leaders in Tanzania. In Kenya, anti-corruption campaigners begin organising on Twitter. If they are arrested, soon the whole world knows of it. In countries where age is revered, new media allow younger people to make their voice heard.[25] For many, social media is not just a way of connecting with friends, it is an important source of news and interrogating power.

Fifth transformation – health care

The rising sense of 'we count, we matter' in the human subject is played out in another trend where the second half of the twentieth century has seen a steady reaction against the conversion of human agents into non-subjects. The shift towards adoption of the consumer voice as having great authority is related to a growing mistrust of institutions and bureaucracy and political elites. Institutions – formal and informal – remain the contexts of our freedom, the secure foundation for the diversity and innovation that modern life offers us. With public service, voice and choice are shaped in no small measure by the emphasis on driving up standards and offering free of charge the allure of choice to parents and other customers that the better off have always been able to afford. It is connected with the way social groups feel entitlement to an equalising of voice and levelling of power as old deference breaks down.

All over the world, the health sector is predicted to be the largest source of job creation for the next decade as economies the world over are undergoing a transition from youthful to ageing societies. Its growth is being driven by increasing numbers of older people and by the expansion of the global middle class. As these two groups grow, the higher levels of health care they demand will cause seismic shifts in the amount of money being spent in the health sector, driving employment. This is not just a European story, where the World Bank expects more than a third of people to be aged over 60 in four decades. In Asia, China has revised its one-child policy. Japan and South Korea already experience population decline. Demand for welfare provision will grow in these countries, just as its burden already affects developed economies. Even without these trends, the world would need millions more health workers. But even though more health workers are being trained than ever before, population growth is currently outstripping increases in training. Ageing societies make it difficult to generate economic growth. They consume more and produce less. If older people remain in or re-enter the workforce (90 per cent of new employment in the UK in 2008–14 was accounted for by those over 50), their presence can depress wage growth. Increasing longevity also makes pensions, health care and other social services costlier.

The extent to which society in the West is characterised by 'Voice and Choice' is seen with transformations in health provision; for example, one-to-one patient care, affirming the dignity needs of the elderly or those with dementia or applying consumerism to health care. Personalised care is increasingly seen as vital in the treatment of cancer. There is growing impatience with bureaucratic focus on hierarchies and procedures; a greater demand for excellent service and outcomes. Sweeping changes are needed as states try to work out how to pay for the needs of an elderly population. People used to see a GP as someone who tells them what to do. In such groups as the UK Patients' Forum, language is important: 'we are part of a team' – rather than GPs being the expert out there. 'We're working on this together.' There seems to be more understanding of the pressures GPs are under. A doctor is not just 'a doctor' but a person with skills. The question that health care leaders ask more is: 'What would the clients or patients want to see?' Often the answer to this is a less macho style of 'the expert'. It is such 'factory' issues that prevent humanisation of health care. Being person-centred is more accepted as the right way of delivering care. As a sign in a care home stated,[26] being person-centred means: 'Listen to me. Think about me as a whole, I am an individual. See my essence. Involve me. Keep my identity. Remember I'm a person not a resident. Look after the whole person that is me. Include me!'

Sixth transformation – education

Despite the march of technology, there is little sign that industrial-era education and welfare systems are yet being modernised and made flexible. As Addison observes, the 1988 Education Reform Act imposed on schools a bureaucratic system of targets, monitoring and controls of all kinds which the Atlee government had attempted without much success to apply to industrial production.[27] Yet 'Voice and Choice' is also a growing mindset when it comes to education. Amidst sweeping reforms to re-tool education systems, there is huge concern about standards and standardisation. Should student learning be the subject of market forces where there is no incentive to improve? As Weber saw it, the very essence of industrial society and the regime of rule-governed activity accompanying it lay in it being impersonal.[28] Education has become formidably pressurising; students must achieve at all costs. Inspection regimes raise the stakes hugely; the blame culture can be oppressive. Teachers are leaving the profession in droves and there is very real concern about retention.[29] The UK has seen the spectacular growth of Free Schools, a purpose-driven exercise of allowing parents, charities and churches to start a school providing they meet the conditions.

Education has an important role in helping us to achieve our potential, but the processes by which we assess ability were designed for an industrial age. Though performativity reigns, there is considerable agitation about how we nurture the whole person and restore joy both to teaching and learning. For example, Ken Robinson is one of the world's most influential voices in education. His talk, 'How Schools Kill Creativity', is the most viewed in the history of TED talks and has been seen by millions of people all over the world. In *Creative Schools* he sets out his practical vision for how education can be transformed to enable all young people to flourish and succeed in the twenty-first century. Robinson argues for an end to the outmoded, industrial systems of mass schooling and proposes a highly personalised, organic approach that draws on today's unprecedented technological and professional resources to engage all students to develop individual abilities and love of learning. Already, people and projects are revolutionising education by innovative approaches to teaching, learning and school culture.[30]

So much is changing. The advent of Massive Open Online Courses is challenging expensive university and college providers. Free higher education is no longer in the gift of governments struggling to pay the bills. In the Fourth Industrial Revolution that is already arriving, empathy and creativity will be goals of education as the rise of artificial intelligence and the pervasive algorithm allow machines to supplant people. Technological displacement is unlikely to replace the human dimensions that robots cannot replicate anytime soon. The advocates of expanding pupil data through digital means believe the tools are available now to produce hyper-personalised profiles of performance. Parents will be able to see whether their children are on track to win admission to a given university course. At present, the problem is a way of combining accessing and data easily. 'It is like we have invented the car but haven't yet built the roads.'[31] The infrastructure is about to come.

Seventh transformation – changes in organisational style

Struggling to grapple with huge societal shifts, organisations are changing. We are seeing the need to respond to the needs of the customer or the imperatives away from top-down hierarchies towards smaller teams where collaboration is vital; new ways of leading around awareness of what makes organisations productive, reactions against workplace bullying, etc. A people-orien-ted, relationship-building process is 'in'; team working is widely hailed as the way to get things done. Modern industrial relations are built on respect. 'Top-down' styles are going out of fashion.

One term that has captured some of this is 'post-Fordism'. Up until about 1980 when many in Western societies worked in factories, 'Fordism' was the car manu-facturer's mechanical production line; the dominant form of making things happen. People were just components in a machine. They knew their place, did what they were told and enjoyed secure if not exciting and fulfilling lives. The same model worked in every form of administration – whether in the public or private sector. The big top-down bureaucracies needed to operate public services ruled through elite command and control. Production and politics were both driven by hierarchies that say, in effect, 'there is a way that the world really is ... and I know what it is'. It was the cult of the rational manager needed to regulate large-scale systems to address mass urban society.

Against a bewildering and highly complex backcloth as the twenty-first century has unfolded, new ways of thinking about economics and new patterns for organisations are in the air. The Internet is already organising economy and society in a different way. This changing climate in the direction of networks rather than hierarchies presents a challenge to organisational leadership. The problem is that would-be transfor-mative leaders often do not know how to operate when the modus vivendi is NOT top-down command control. They are unsure how to mobilise the participation and engagement of their people so they are productive and contribute effectively. It is beginning to go out of fashion to be too dominant. Nevertheless, because of the imperative to solve problems or operate protocols, the prevailing mindset remains 'this is what is wrong, let's fix it'. The way power is constructed means we get back to modes of control through such strategies as enforcing company 'vision', acquiring the skills of negotiation to persuade others to shift position or laying down what is or what is not 'scientific' or market-tested 'official' knowledge.

With completely new possibilities offered by the Internet economy, what happens to the corporation, the pillar of modern capitalism? With this global peer-to-peer platform for identity, reputation, and transactions, we will be able to re-engineer deep structures of the firm for innovation and shared value creation. So what does the organisation of an automated future look like that is intent on motivating its people to produce quality and not just quantity, to generate dynamism and innovation, to address growing social problems and challenges within a wider dimension of shared value?[32] An example of the new thinking coming through is from the Nordic region during the past few years where we have seen smaller companies becoming involved with banking. We have seen a more vibrant financial technology community and start-ups, enabled by an accelerator programme.[33]

In this new organisational climate, motivation becomes more important as a way of evoking quality and not just industrial-scale quantity. *How to nurture more humane work environments that maximise the well-being of employees is a top priority for leaders concerned with organisational health.*[34] In the days when management by objective was in vogue, the guru Peter Drucker argued in a similar vein that staff setting their own goals is vital to modern business.[35] People need to feel part of the decision-making process. Respect is vital for modern industrial relations. In the Fourth Industrial Revolution, new forms of operating platforms that are emerging force companies to move much faster and respond with flexibility.

Amidst the systems that both represent and shape social life, these are significant trends. This new global zeitgeist based on authentic autonomy has at its heart a participative mindset, people creating their own reality combined with an imperative towards asserting the value and worth of social participants. It is fundamentally to do with citizens realising their own agency; a mood that asserts, 'we count, we matter' against the de-personalisation of existential distance. Geographical and spatial awareness has shrunk dramatically in the communications and transport revolutions. But the sense of needing to assert ourselves against the power of remote forces shaping our lives is a strong force also: the revolt perhaps of the disconnected as well as the devalued and de-personalised.

Watch out then for the growing assertion of the value of the human, as ever, competing against the forces of entrenched power that, as the sociologist Michel Foucault observed, is everywhere. Is this a rediscovery of the value of the human, a gasp for individualism or a sign of better educated, middle class.

In short, we see the interplay between two megashifts in our world. One is the shift towards the global, towards an increasingly wired-up world in which no one is more than 20 hours from anyone else on the planet or barely a second on the Internet. The other is to a strong degree a reaction against the runaway train of globalisation and impersonal forces that highlights our sense of powerlessness. In the new participative paradigm, everything is more dispersed, dynamic, distributed. Organisational leaders and political parties alike must work with these trends. Old certainties that shaped our thinking are no longer valid; assumptions that shaped very different circumstances are of dubious relevance. New models, new ideas are needed to make things work on a specific, human level so that people do not feel locked out of the system.

One methodology that helps in the journey of working backwards is a Theory of Change approach to try to capture the transformative change in a given project. It aims at a clear, concise and convincing explanation of what you do, what impact you aim to have and how you believe you will have it is a vital foundation of any programme, and a prerequisite for effective evaluation. Theory of change methodology is a diagram that explains how a programme has an impact on its beneficiaries. It outlines all the things that a programme does for of its beneficiaries, the ultimate impact that it aims to have on them, and all the separate outcomes that lead or contribute to that impact. In short, it helps chart the course to answer 'how did we get there?'[36]

The social theory to try to explain all this must wait for another volume. Is it the rise of an educated middle class that fuels public dissatisfaction and distrust of politicians and business leaders? China's middle class, for instance, has gone from about 5m households in 2000 to 225m today. They are not clamouring for the vote, but they are unhappy – financially insecure, and victims of pollution and official corruption. One way or another, the Communist Party will have to meet their demands.[37]

Or is it the rise of the networked individual increasingly in combination perhaps with a subjectivity that reacts against the de-personalisation that is the sign of our times?

Notes

1   *News at Ten*, BBC 1, http://www.bbc.co.uk/programmes/b007mplc, 16 June 2016.
2   Park, Y., Chair, Infollution ZERO Foundation, World Economic Forum. https://www. weforum.org/agenda/2016/06/8-digital-skills-we-must-teach-our-children/, 13 June 2016, accessed June 2016.
3   Brown, G. (2016), *Britain Leading, not Leaving*. Selkirk: Deerpark Press, p. 146.
4   Bobbitt, P. (2002), *The Shield of Achilles: War, Peace and the Course of History*. London and New York: Penguin.
5   Dr Bernard Meyerson, Chief Innovation Officer of IBM and Chair of the Meta-Council on Emerging Technologies, World Economic Forum. Newsletter, June 2016.
6   Dr Bernard Meyerson, Newsletter, June 2016.
7   Mayer-Schönberger, V. and Cukier, K. (2013), *Big Data*. London: John Murray.
8   Giddens, A. (1999), *Runaway World*. London: Profile Books, p. 1.
9   Author's client notes – used with permission and name withheld.
10 'Marco Rubio: The Moral of his Story'. *The Economist*, 27 February 2016.
11 Vorländer, H. (2016), 'The State of the American Manager: Analytics and Advice for Leaders'. *PEGIDA – Entwicklung, Zusammensetzung und Deutung einer Empörungsbewegung*. Wiesbaden (i.E. 2016) (zusammen mit Maik Herold und Steven Schäller). http://www.dresden.de/die_ tu_dresden/fakultaeten/philosophische_fakultaet/ifpw/poltheo/mitarbeiter/kurzvorstellung_ vorlaender_englisch/, accessed February 2016.
12 Stiglitz, J., Global Policy Forum. https://www.globalpolicy.org/social-and-economic-policy/ the-three-sisters-and-other-institutions/internal-critics-of-the-world-bank-and-the-imf/, accessed June 2016.
13 'Censors and sensibility'. *The Economist*, 21 May 2016.
14 Hobsbawm, E. (1982), *The Age of Empire 1875–1914*. London: Abacus.
15 Skiddelsky, R. (2004), *John Maynard Keynes 1883–1946*. London: Pan Books.
16 Roberston, R. (1992), *Globalisation*. London and Newbury Park, CA: Sage.
17 McKinsey (2014), *Global Flows in a Digital Age*. New York: McKinsey.
18 Stiglitz, J. (2002), *Globalisation and its Discontents*. London: Allen Lane.
19 Wolf, M. (2004), *Why Globalisation Works*. London: Yale.
20 Rifkind, J. (2014), *The Zero Marginal Cost Society*. New York: Palgrave MacMillan.
21 Tapscott, D. and Tapscott, A. (2016), *Blockchain Revolution: How the Technology behind Bitcoin is Changing Money, Business and the World*. London: Portfolio Penguin.
22 Goodwin, T. (2015), 'The battle is for the customer interface'. *TechCrunch*, 3 March 2015. https:// www.techcrunch.com/2015/03/03/in-an-age-of-disintermediation-the-battle-is-all-for-the-customer-interface.
23 *The New Economy*, Summer 2009. http://www.theneweconomy.com/.

24 White, S. and Abeyasekera, A. (eds) (2014), *Wellbeing and Quality of Life Assessment: A Practical Guide*. Rugby: Practical Action.
25 *The Economist*, 16 January 2016.
26 Author's client notes – used with permission and name withheld.
27 Addison, P. (2010), *No Turning Back: The Peacetime Revolutions of Post-War Britain*. Oxford: Oxford University Press.
28 Weber, M. (1978), *Economy and Society: An Outline of Interpretive Sociology*. Berkeley: University of California Press.
29 OECD (2013), *Education at a Glance 2013: OECD Indicators*. Paris: OECD Publishing. DOI. http://www.dx.doi.org/10.1787/eag-2013-en/, accessed May 2016.
30 Robinson, K. (2015), *Creative Schools*. London: Penguin.
31 'Heads in the clouds'. *The Economist*, 21 May 2016.
32 Tapscott and Tapscott (2016).
33 http://www.computerweekly.com/news/4500250273/Nordea-Bank-launches-startup-accel erator-to-boost-fintech-innovation/, accessed June 2016.
34 Fowler, S. (2014), *Why Motivating People Doesn't Work and What Does: The New Science of Leading, Energising and Engaging*. San Francisco: Berrett-Koehler.
35 Drucker, P. (1964), *Managing for Results*. New York: Harper and Row.
36 Guidance for Developing a Theory of Change for Your Programme http://www.nesta.org. uk/sites/default/files/theory_of_change_guidance_for_applicants_.pdf
37 'China's middle class'. *The Economist*, 8 July 2016.

Chapter 2

Re-conceiving strategy

> Creativity, as has been said, consists largely of rearranging what we know in order to find out what we do not know. Hence, to think creatively, we must be able to look afresh at what we normally take for granted.
>
> George Kneller[1]

It is an oft-repeated observation that the best laid military plans rarely survive first contact with the enemy.

The future is a network of possible pathways that is constantly evolving, constantly expanding. Artificial Intelligence will change the nature of many tasks and jobs. Developments in neuroscience and genetic engineering have the potential to change how we think about diseases and their consequences. Virtual reality will transform healthcare and travel. Climate change, food production, and water scarcity know no national boundaries. As if this were not enough, consider the changing nature of relationships (how we make friends, keep friends and stay in touch with friends), religious strife and challenging economic conditions. 'At best, the future represents a veritable petri dish of uncertainty affecting every aspect of life.'[2]

The seven transformations we have referred to are about the emerging future. They raise intriguing questions about what happens to the human subject in this consumer-oriented, Internet society. Does the digital human replete with 'Voice and Choice' pose a new form of subjectivity in Western, if not global, culture? This is vital for how we process our world, for sociology as well as for organisational leadership and the political arena where it plays out.

If, as Warren Bennis argues, the organisation is now 'the primary social, economic and political form',[3] organisations must deal with sweeping and profound shifts. Given the dominance of business and public service provision in contemporary society, workplace culture and leadership in particular represent a key focal point of such societal changes. How to create the workplace that is a more humane environment and releases people, their value and worth, is a crucial question today.

It will become even more prominent in the new platforms created in an Internet economy as the Fourth Industrial Revolution takes hold. How and where can we ensure that spaces are cultivated for our humanity, for the digital human? Leadership that nurtures the human dimension is the theme of this book.

When faced with complexity and constant change at work, what do the best leaders and teams do? They invent. The spotlight these days is on maturing the competency for innovation with organisations so they keep up with a rapidly changing environment.

The problem is that the way we manage organisations seems increasingly out of date. But then the culture is shifting; shifting so rapidly that everything is out of date before it has settled in. Disruption is here to stay. In a condition of rapid and discontinuous change, smart leadership takes on board the turbulent times we are passing through and accepts that fast-paced uncertainty is the new normal. As the social theorist Walter Benjamin remarked, disjuncture and disruption (i.e. revolution) is the normal state of affairs.[4]

So how do leaders reckon with the emerging future? Is there a way they can actively lead from it rather than try to plan towards it? That would utilise creativity as well as technical management skills. It would be 'wise leadership' and not just 'smart leadership'. Although technology will soon make the old jobs obsolete, the skills needed for a new era will have to be those that allow for human imagination and innovation to flourish, the driving forces behind economies led by talent. It will remain governments that create the environment that allows innovation to thrive in order to make the most of the transformations reshaping the world. Innovation is highly prized across the piece, but an innovation that is rooted in a 'think differently' mindset, an entrepreneurial mindset or even 'intrapreneurial' within the company.

Creativity is vital. *How Google Works* is a management and leadership book that seeks to explain the astonishing success of Google, the search engine that became a verb. Eric Schmidt and Jonathan Rosenberg write evocatively about the principles they learnt as they built the company into the world-leading platform and way of life. Technology, they argue, has shifted the balance inexorably from companies to consumers. The only way to succeed in an environment that is restlessly shifting, in an age of dizzying speed, is to create superior products and with them, to recruit a new breed of 'smart creatives' and 'give them an environment where they can thrive at scale'.[5]

It seems to be a call that is nigh-on universal. Leadership is needed that releases potential; leadership that uncorks the dynamism needed in a commercial environment, that responds to the cultural mood that resists the 'I know what's good for you', top-down styles of yesteryear; leadership that delivers public services in an era where the old state planning apparatus and mindset have been dismantled.

In a similar vein, three-time Nobel Peace Prize nominee Dr Scilla Elworthy, a realist with 40 years' experience at the sharp end of politics and conflict, presents a bold but realistic vision for the future in *Pioneering the Possible*.[6] Human beings worldwide are anxious, afraid for their children's futures, dissatisfied by their lives, but unsure what to do. Our global ecosystems and supply chains are under threat and our leaders appear to have failed us. *Pioneering the Possible* addresses these anxieties head-on by envisioning a future that could work for everyone, rich and poor, demonstrating with real-life examples how that future is already emerging. *Pioneering the Possible* tackles the deeply embedded twentieth-century values that get in the way of addressing global problems, and shows how these destructive values can be – and are being – reversed. We know the world is in crisis: we are spoiling our planet at such a rate that soon it may be unable to sustain human life. This crisis is in fact a vast opportunity, because a secure and satisfying future for all of humanity is perfectly possible if we make the right choices. But building such a future will require the leap in consciousness that Einstein indicated when he said that no problem can be solved from the consciousness that created it. To envision the kind of future that is possible – a lift-off into 'life as it could be' – Elworthy calls on some experienced specialists to look through their telescopes into the future, then brings in the pragmatists who know what to do in their fields, because they've done it, tested it, and made it work.

Emergence and the unpredictable

As a concept applied to management and leadership, 'strategy' rarely appeared before the 1960s. Before that, strategy was the preserve of military leaders. The nineteenth-century Prussian military theorist Clausewitz observed that strategy is the employment of battles to gain the ends of war.[7]

Strategic management is the oxygen that organisations breathe. Boardrooms and meetings of senior management talk incessantly of 'managing' change, 're-engineering', 'TQM' (Total Quality Management), 'vision and values' and the myriad of change initiatives that require executives to go on staff away days to work out a pathway to the future. The leader had the supreme picture of the organisation – the vision – and his or her task was to convince others of the worth of that vision.

Michael Porter's five-forces model describes strategy as taking actions that create defendable positions in an industry.

- In general, the strategy can be offensive or defensive with respect to competitive forces.
- Defensive strategies take the structure of the industry as given, and position the company to match its strengths and weaknesses to it.
- In contrast, offensive strategies are designed to do more than simply cope with each of the competitive forces; they are meant to alter the underlying cause of such forces, thereby altering the competitive environment itself.[8]

According to the management writer Bruce Henderson, strategy 'depends on the ability to foresee future consequences of present initiatives'.[9] What is needed, he suggested, is extensive knowledge of the environment and an ability to assess that knowledge in a dynamic environment. It is an act of seeing, of vision, of logic fused with imagination. Strategic management is deemed to be fundamental to an organisation; how it will position itself now and in the future and how it will therefore thrive. Literacy in reading the runes of the times is vital to the arts of leadership. Yet strategy is so often a joyless, tedious process devoid of spirit that fails to capture because it does not paint an inspiring frame of what the future looks like. But strategy as an approach often fails to draw on the dreams and visions participants have and gets sabotaged. Are there approaches to strategy that will inspire and command greater 'buy-in'?

The task of strategic management is to assess options and opportunities. In a commercial environment, this involves examining the scope for market leadership, increasing market share, creating niche markets and withdrawing from unprofitable activities. Leadership is required for assessing trends or likely developments in the economic environment, technological advances, political changes, social change and consumer behaviour. The positioning of the existing business needs to be clearly understood in ten key areas that undergird financial performance objectives:

- the cost of the head office and desirability of de-centralising
- the costs of producing its outputs in various locations and its organisation structure
- how and where it sells what it does
- customer service
- design issues

- distribution networks
- innovation and research
- marketing and Internet strategy
- how the organisation manages assets
- scope for chasing unnecessary costs out of the company.

A much-used tool in contemporary organisations is SWOT analysis. An organisation will understand how to position itself and in what direction to drive change by assessing:

- **Strengths** – what gifts and talents run through the organisation, where the energy is to take it forward.
- **Weaknesses** – the things that the organisation is not very good at, areas where it can fail or that will hold it back.
- **Opportunities** – the possibilities to expand, develop and go forward in the same or even another direction.
- **Threats** – scanning the field will indicate the potential problems an organisation will face that to a greater or lesser extent could derail it completely.

That is what has come to be the usual way of doing business. Or, as expressed by Mintzberg, strategy involves five 'P's:[10] Plan – Pattern – Position – Ploy – Perspective (all to achieve a directed course of action).

Post-industrial leadership models assume that people will follow a person who inspires them, and support the tenet that a person with vision and passion can achieve great things. Transformational leadership starts with the development of a vision, a view of the future that will excite and convert potential followers. The narrative used to be told that once the vision is crafted by a leader (in collaboration with a senior team) the next step is to constantly sell the vision. But is that so?

The problem with usual approaches to strategy is that they assume practitioners and leaders are outside a problem, in this case global futures and where the organisation will soon be positioned, before they make intelligent extrapolations of where we will be and how we get there. This has similarity to experts or researchers assuming they are outside the issue they are addressing in order to solve it before stepping out again. There is little sense in strategists being active players who help shape the future they are mapping. Neither is there a sense of co-emergence, that the future develops from numerous open 'micro' systems that together form the emerging but continually shifting landscapes of what is to come. Organisations are seen as machines. Some push, some energy needs to be injected. 'The words that are used are telling: managers talk of "forcing" "driving through" "bringing about" change: many of the metaphors are ones of violence and force.'[11] Invariably, the assumption is that people are naturally conservative and need external force to stir the pot. If participants just let change happen, leaders will not get the results they seek. Hence the need for clear direction and 'telling people what the vision is'. As a CEO put it, 'self-generated strategic change requires the stamina, the endurance and the resilience to just keep coming back to that strategy'.[12] Effective visions are needed to inspire so that fellow participants have a vision of the future and can see where the organisation is going. It rests upon an assumption that change can be known, planned and predicted. Yet an organisation is not a machine but a dynamic flux of interactive people.

There is a close association that needs exploring between an emerging future and the concept of 'emergence'. 'Emergence' is the process whereby larger entities arise through interaction of moving parts at a lower level. The 'higher order' is not reducible to those initial properties.[13] At each level of complexity entirely new properties appear. The whole becomes not merely more, but very different from the sum of its parts. Something new has come about that itself is on the way to becoming something else. The whole system of moving parts is creating something new.

Emergence is an essential component of complexity theory. Much scientific endeavour has been about seeking to reduce complex phenomena to simpler ideas and smaller units of analysis – witness the move in twentieth-century biology from organisms and cells down to genes.[14] Complexity theory takes us beyond the traditional categories of 'macro' and 'micro' levels of analysis or, in sociological terms, 'agency' or 'structure'. It provides a new way of theorising the connection between the individual and society, between individual agents as the prime lens through which we see the world. Applied to the realm of economics, Goldstein suggested this definition of emergence:

> the common characteristics are: (1) radical novelty (features not previously observed in systems); (2) coherence or correlation (meaning integrated wholes that maintain themselves over some period of time); (3) a global or macro 'level' (i.e. there is some property of 'wholeness'); (4) it is the product of a dynamical process (it evolves); and (5) it is 'ostensive' (it can be perceived).[15]

Emergence is built on a number of different possibilities rather than being dictated by strategising that closes down. It also arises from many contributors and multiple voices co-constructing their future rather than one leader laying it down. The whole market economy is one enormous field of constantly moving parts, a dynamic system that is self-organising. There is no one in charge. The stock market regulates the price of securities and shares across the world without a leader; in fact, the ability of governments to pull the levers is strictly limited. Any investor has knowledge of only a limited number of companies within a portfolio. Similarly, the Internet is an example of an emergent, dynamic system. It is a de-centralised system, having no central organisation rationing the number of websites or links.[16] Almost any pair of pages can be connected to each other through a relatively short chain of links.[17]

The fact is that there are no facts. Social systems are far more complex than is often thought. There will be always be missing information, elements that escape a simplified picture. 'We were gripped by the illusion that we were the drivers of the world, the ones truly in control.'[18]

With the Internet being the major highway of the economy and culture in our times, global systems are becoming steadily harder to control. The point about emergent behaviour is that it is hard to predict since the number of interactions between components of a system increases exponentially with the number of components. Many new patterns can emerge. Rapid changes are taking place everywhere.

This is the backcloth to the global economy and transformations reshaping the landscapes of our times. The world is becoming vastly more complex.[19] Yet the human factor remains a major dynamic that, still less than the moving parts of economic and social systems, does not follow the rules. Humans bring an unpredictability to any system or organisation. Organisations are adaptive living things with an inbuilt potential to grow and change like the individuals of which they are composed. Peter Corning observes:

> the game of chess illustrates … why any laws or rules of emergence and evolution are insufficient. Even in a chess game, you cannot use the rules to predict 'history' – i.e. the course of any given game. Indeed, you cannot even reliably predict the next move in a chess game. Why? Because the 'system' involves more than the rules of the game. It also includes the players and their unfolding, moment-by-moment decisions among a very large number of available options at each choice point.[20]

Warren Bennis said that 'people, unlike solids, fluids and gases, are anything but uniform, anything but predictable'.[21] These ideas point towards a de-centralised, relational model of change, rooted in a way of looking at the world that goes beyond strategists as master chess players controlling everyone else's moves. An organisation is a living system with unpredictable people at its heart.

The participative paradigm is a feature of a more collaborative age. It reflects a different lens and possibly a cultural shift away from 'monologic' thinking characteristic of modernity. Since the time of Descartes in the seventeenth century, this was about:

- The rational agent – the person is a contained individual, a separate knower with his or her own mind.
- 'Give us the facts' – data and evidence base is produced through empirical observation and investigation. We combine information about the world that comes to us with what goes on in our heads and do something with it.
- A certain attitude to the way words and language shape our thinking – conceptual thinking and language represents what goes on in the world. Realism in art, for instance, implies 'it looks like what it's supposed to be'!
- The assumption of progress and improvement – knowledge is cumulative. Workers may be irrational but the 'rational manager'[22] should be able to ensure that proper analysis of what is going on results in progress for all.
- Each individual self is a contained, separate existence – there is a continual struggle for who will be the 'subject' (the 'I') and who will be the 'object' (you!). The object is passive, waiting to be known. This is where you get reactions as if to say 'I don't want to be object to your subject'. In an organisation, for instance, there are separate but linked interactions between autonomous beings with their own boundaries.

The assumptions here are widely viewed with suspicion today as giving license to power and exploitation. It was scientific rationalism that, it is often said, led to both Auschwitz and Hiroshima. The Polish sociologist Bauman argued that the Holocaust was the ultimate expression of modernity.[23] 'The Club of Rome published *Limits to Growth*, a now famous report that warned of environmental catastrophe unless leaders radically cut the use of resources,'[24] noted Sebastian Buckup. This was the era when the green movement started to form. It marked the crisis of modernity. Average productivity growth since the global economic crisis is down to just over 1 per cent.

> Our dreams have taken a darker turn. We believe in innovation, but have given up on progress, and the possibility of moral and social improvement. The defining

feature of our days is that we feel like we live in an era of incredible innovation, mostly thanks to staggering breakthroughs in science and technology; but, at the same time, we feel like there are insurmountable limits in the form of economic, political and environmental risks.[25]

The alternative to this assumption of an independently existing world is to think that we are formed through interaction. The 'person' emerges through relational processes rather than being pre-formed. Rather than killing something through definition, ideas and understandings, insights and actions emerge naturally. This lies at the heart of the Relational Constructivist Approach to research and social change.[26]

It is a very different approach. Instead of the rational manager saying 'this is where we are; this is where you need to be', instead of saying to leaders 'it's your task to make things happen', this is a truly collaborative approach to people and plans. New leaders will be encouraged to put their stamp on an organisation and come up with new vision statements or to put in a task force. What would it mean, however, for the organisation of today and tomorrow to be co-constructed, not seeing the company or charity as 'out there and we are somehow separate from it'? It would enable new understandings of power as a range of voices are listened to. It would mean a different approach to change management. And it would mean a different lens on strategy.

Whether strategy as usually conceived is the right approach to chart that future for an enterprise begs vital questions. Can leaders pull the levers and hope that something will happen that corresponds to what they have determined is the correct outcome? Who is to say what that correct outcome should be? How was that conclusion arrived at?

Strategy, as usually conceived, is a plan that is put together at a given point in time in order to 'freeze the frame' now to enable a future point to be mapped. That time-fixity is illusory. Strategy is a process which will always have an element of the unplanned which enters the field disruptively, requiring that we work with it. Yet it is also instructive to see strategy as a process of 'engaged unfolding' in which collaborative practice comes to the fore.

Another way

All these concepts of strategy are future-oriented from a present perspective. They are goal-directed, mobilising the resources of the organisation towards a course of action. Directives in wartime, school mission statements, company vision or the plans of a faith-based voluntary entity have this in common. They look down the road and see what is coming up and where action should best be directed to achieve outcomes.

It is the WHY that shapes the WHAT. The practical steps by which strategy is translated into action are shaped by purpose. WHAT we are aiming to do is determined by WHY we are doing it. Strategic management is, however, usually concerned with those practical, carefully elaborated steps rather than the imperatives that compel a particular mission (be it commercial or social). This is where dreams and imagination come in – not the usual stock of tools available in the inventory of managers. As Laloux observes, 'we can expect that purpose, more than profitability, growth, or market share will be the guiding principle of organisational decision-making'.[27]

Strategy is vital because it is about purpose; what the organisation exists to do and why it is there. It goes to the heart of what leadership is – to focus on the things that are especially important to get things done and to do this through leading people (rather than managing them).

This kind of approach depends on logical and carefully sequenced steps. That is its strength but it is also its weakness. It fails to inspire. It fails to ignite. Especially in public service provision, its machine-like tendency renders the reader as a dry and often passive observer of those buzz words that are designed to demonstrate credibility. If so few get excited about a strategy document, is that an inevitable corollary of 'governing in prose'? A failure in the style of management-speak or is it a failure to connect purpose and goals in wide-screen format?

Another field of vision is possible. This is to conceive of strategy as an orientation not towards the future but to the present-past. It draws on the imagination rather than a purely rational assessment of prospects which are then elaborated step by step using the terminology of key performance indicators. Imagination has given us science fiction which has inspired many dreams and breakthroughs.

Instead of adopting an approach of 'thinking forward' from where we think we are (even if we could fix a precise location), what about turning it on its head? Rather than thinking ahead, could 'thinking back' help in aligning strategy and culture? In other words, move immediately to an intended goal that seems desirable and realistic within an evolving time frame, and ask a question. 'How did we get here?' 'What was our journey by which we came to this imagined future that is still open and evolving?' Such a stance could combine some dreams with a realistic perception of the obstacles we faced and the change that had to be undertaken. It helps put the battles of today and tomorrow with a future orientation.

This is important. Strategy involves a direction of travel from 'here' to 'there'. However, where is here? And where is 'there'? And are they fixed points in time? Is where we are now a point or a circle; that is, a limited and determined point in time or a small circle as a feedback loop? It is a question of how and from where we get information. Do leaders discern information from a multiplicity of voices rather than look in one direction only?

Any organisation needs to know what the point is in time from which it is moving. That may be difficult to encapsulate, as invariably there is no fixed point of reference to aim at. A fixed point in time may be more realistic as 'the present' is likely to be a dynamic picture in flux with many moving parts. Nevertheless, some kind of snapshot is vital to know the place along the journey that best describes where we are now. It is more realistically part of a moving video.

'The present' is not only a place in time with its own frame of reference. It is a state of mind. Moreover, it is a sign. What is wrong with where we are? Why would we need to change? What are the reasons why we cannot stay 'here' in this particular state of flux? It will be a dynamic factor. I propose an approach entitled 'leaning back' that repositions strategy as a reverse journey, to utilise imagination and 'spirit' in constructing a future that we then help to create. It is rooted in the concept of 'emergence' that matches an emerging future where it is virtually impossible to describe the system. It is shaped by purpose.

For organisations, purpose is a powerful thing. It tells your story, it builds your teams and it defines your culture. As David Hieatt argues, the most important brands in the world make us feel something. They do that because they have something they want to change. Customers want to be part of that change. These companies connect with us because they have a reason to exist over and above making a profit: they have a purpose.[28] Consumers love the product they make. But the thing they love most about them is the change they are making. Hieatt offers insights on how to create, build and sustain a purpose-driven company. They do not just make something, but change something as well:[29]

The approach might work in this way:

> Leaders carve out a quality space of time in which dreams and imagination project us forward in time to an evolving horizon at least several years hence. 'Let's dream some dreams.'
>
> They ask, why do we want to go there? What possibility might penetrate the present? What does that horizon just over the present look like? What is realistic? What is desirable?
>
> Leaders look back from that desired point. How did we get here? What were the steps by which we evolved here?

The benefit of working in this way, approaching the present from the perspective of the future, is that it engages a different part of leaders and change managers than is usually the case. It is right-brain rather than just left-brain, to use late-twentieth-century terminology. It does not just draw on conceptual thinking and logical steps but on the (ordered) imagination. It draws on the kind of thought experiments that began the scientific breakthroughs Einstein offered to the world.

This approach could be termed 'leaning back'. It is future-oriented, purpose-driven rather than adopting the present (messy, complex and difficult to determine) as the starting point. There is, however, no firm fixed point. And that is just the problem. How do you 'lean back' from a future that, by definition, is open and evolving? Flexible imagination is clearly called for; an imagination that can envisage several open-ended possibilities.

Part of that transformation implicit in the perspective of the future will be thinking through the way the organisation had to shift, not only in its positioning but in its culture. Strategy from the future back might also help impart perspective to weary leaders who are immersed in the trials of today.

There is similarity, though not convergence, between this approach and what has been called 'Theory U'. Drawing on earlier work in the Netherlands by Glasl and Lemson, C. Otto Scharmer and colleagues developed a change-management process intended to transform unproductive situations. The main concept was that the current self meets with the future self. Presencing from the future enables new possibilities to be born that are waiting to emerge.

> Why do our attempts to deal with the challenges of our time so often fail? Why are we stuck in so many quagmires today? The cause of our collective failure is that we are blind to the deeper dimension of leadership and transformational change. This 'blind spot' exists not only in our collective leadership but also in our everyday social interactions. We are blind to the source dimension from which effective leadership and social action come into being. We know a great deal about what leaders do and how they do it. But we know very little about the inner place, the source from which they operate. And it is this source that 'Theory U' attempts to explore.[30]

What is being proposed here is not a focus on the internal horizon of the leader but from the collective messiness of the organisation as a whole. How does a future that seems visionary, desirable but also realistic impact the past? How does the perspective of an imagined horizon beyond this one shape the world of today? What would it mean to say 'yes' to the mess?[31] The task of leadership surely is to set up the conditions within which the natural tendency towards change and flux can grow naturally, counterbalanced by the need for stability rather than keep issuing edicts and new directions so as to 'drive change'. 'It is to release the potential for change, leading and encouraging it in the directions that will help the organisation and its people to flourish.'[32]

Not-for-profit organisations often work in this space. They deal not just with the world as it is but with the world as it should be. The 'ought' calls to them. Invariably there is an ethical imperative behind this. What is wrong with the world, or at least this corner of it? How can it be fixed? Where would we like to be with this situation? For schools, the call for students and places of learning alike to be 'the best they can be' can sometimes provide a driving force. Faith communities and charities will usually endeavour to position themselves based on moral and spiritual imperatives that call for a certain course of action. Invariably, they too are let down by their micro-culture.

It is not just dependent on a journey of consultation. Whether a CEO, chair of a charity, bishop or leader of a faith community or an operating officer of any institution, asking and listening may range anywhere between being a fig leaf or a genuine and lengthy exercise. It matters not. Pulling levers, issuing an instruction or policy directive stands or falls on whether the culture of the organisation supports those aims, whether it will help or hinder.

The problem is that invariably culture wins over strategy. What happens on the ground is so potent, so strong and pervasive that it has the power to rout both strategy and structure. Imagination would need to address this as well rather than espouse the invincibility of formalised strategy. The role of imagination, dreaming dreams and positing the future is vital. What does that future 'look like'? It is an act of seeing. Such an approach is a corrective to the carefully planned sequence of 'where we go from here' that translates into target-driven apparatuses and ubiquitous key performance indicators.

It is worth noting that, in his marketing of the personal computing revolution, Steve Jobs told a story of what people wanted to be, suggesting the kind of person who owns Apple products. It was strategy that was infused with vision that could be encapsulated in narrative.[33] The culture of an organisation is expressed in story, in narratives of 'this is who we are' or 'this is what we do round here'. The challenge is to understand the creative processes that undergird the discernment of purpose. Leadership is surely about telling those stories of what is possible, discerning what the narratives are that either create energy for change or that block it, and then putting new stories into the dynamic flux, stories from the future.

This does not assume that when leaders look back, and plan back to where we are in the present, they will necessarily make a sudden change in course. When the journey is plotted back to the present from where an organisation would like to be x years hence, there is also room to map the path forward to the same time point from where they are now, see how great a divergence there is, and then perhaps manage a controlled change in direction where possible so as not to lose the momentum of the current progression.

The future is not a destination or goal. It is somewhere that we help to create. There is, however, a problem with strategy, however devised. It is that of being eaten alive for breakfast!

Notes

1 http://www.izquotes.com/quote/346035/, accessed May 2016.
2 May Lee, R., Dean, School of Entrepreneurship and Management, Shanghai Tech University. 'How can we teach innovation? A view from China'. World Economic Forum, June 2016.
3 Bennis, W. (1989), *On Becoming a Leader*. New York: Addison-Wesley, p. 177.
4 Roberts, J. (1982), *Walter Benjamin*. London: Macmillan. See Benjamin's 'Theses on the Philosophy of History'.
5 Schmidt, E., Rosenberg, J. and Eagle, A. (2015), *How Google Works: The Rules for Success in the Internet Century*. Google Play.
6 Elworthy, S. (2014), *Pioneering the Possible*. Berkeley, CA: North Atlantic Books.
7 Wilson, A. (2012), *Masters of War: History's Great Strategic Thinkers*. Chantilly, VA: The Teaching Company.
8 http://faculty.bcitbusiness.ca/kevinw/4800/Bobs_porter_notes.pdf/, accessed June 2016.
9 Henderson, B. (1981), *The Concept of Strategy*. Boston: Boston Consulting Group.
10 Mintzberg, F. *et al.* (1998), *Strategy Safari: A Guide through the Wilds of Strategy Management*. New York: The Free Press.
11 Biney, G. and Williams, C. (1995), *Leaning into the Future*. London: Nicholas Brealey, p. 41.
12 Eccles, T. (1994), *Succeeding with Change*. Maidenhead: McGraw-Hill.
13 Bunge, M.A. (2003), *Emergence and Convergence: Qualitative Novelty and the Unity of Knowledge*. Toronto: University of Toronto Press.
14 Rose, N. (1997), *Lifelines*. London: Allen Lane.
15 Goldstein, J. (1999), 'Emergence as a Construct: History and Issues'. *Emergence: Complexity and Organization*, 1 (1), pp. 49–72.
16 Smith, R. D. (2008), 'The Dynamics of Internet Traffic: Self-Similarity, Self-Organization, and Complex Phenomena'. *Advances in Complex Systems*, 14, (6), pp. 905–949.
17 Johnson, S.B. (2001), *Emergence: The Connected Lives of Ants, Brains, Cities, and Software*. New York: Scribner's.
18 Peat, F.D. (2008), *Gentle Action*. Grosseto, Italy: Pari Publishing, p. 29.
19 Morowitz, H.J. (2002), *The Emergence of Everything: How the World Became Complex*. Oxford: Oxford University Press.
20 Corning, P.A. (2002), 'The Re-Emergence of "Emergence": A Venerable Concept in Search of a Theory'. *Complexity*, 7 (6), pp. 18–30.
21 Bennis, W. (1988), *On Becoming a Leader*. New York: Addison-Wesley, p. 1.
22 Kepner, C.H. and Tregoe, B.B. (1965), *The Rational Manager: A Systematic Approach to Problem Solving and Decision Making*, 1st edn. New York: McGraw-Hill.
23 Bauman, Z. (1991), *Modernity and the Holocaust*. Cambridge: Polity.
24 Meadows, D.H., Meadows, D.L. and Randers, J. (1972), *Limits to Growth*. Rome: Universe Books.
25 Buckup, S., Head of Programming, World Economic Forum. https://www.weforum.org/agenda/2016/06/the-poetry-of-progress/, 13 June 2016, accessed June 2016.
26 McNamee, S. and Hosking, D.M. (2012), *Research and Social Change: A Relational Constructivist Approach*. New York: Routledge.
27 Laloux, F. (2015), *Reinventing Organisations*. Brussels: Nelson Parker, p. 50.
28 Hieatt, D. (2014), *Do Purpose*. London: The Do Book Company.
29 Hieatt, D. (2014), *Do Purpose: Why Brands with a Purpose Do Better and Matter More*. London: The Do Book Company.
30 Scharmer, C. Otto. (2007), *Theory U: Leading from the Future as it Emerges*. Cambridge, MA: Society for Organisational Learning, Sol.

31 Barrett, F. (2012), *Yes to the Mess*. Boston, MA: Harvard Business Review Press.
32 Biney and Williams, p. 32.
33 Isaacson, W. (2011), *Steve Jobs*. London and New York: Abacus.

Chapter 3

Eating strategy for breakfast

We will look to you to drive a culture of high performance ... you will create a know-ledge driven workforce, whilst promoting human resource policies that recognise a per-formance driven corporate culture, rewarding creativity and talent. You will seek to attract a world class workforce into the Bank.[1]

It is clear to us, therefore, particularly as a conduct regulator, that the cultural characteristics of a firm are a key driver of potentially poor behaviour.[2]

Culture cannot be fixed by simply fixing mistakes. Culture is what creates the mistakes and it will always remain no matter the organisational chart or the structure chart. One of the main reasons why senior managers pursue restructures is that they believe that structure determines culture.[3]

The totality is not, as it were, a mere heap, but the whole is something besides the parts.[4]

Culture wars

Susan Long describes a shift in society from a culture of narcissism to one of perversion. Perversion reigns where instrumental relations flourish: people are used as means to an end, commodities and tools. Long argues that these kinds of relationships dominate the culture of modern organisations.[5]

Clearly, being culture-driven in a positive sense is a huge asset. Employees are more engaged and passionate about what they are doing; they feel they are more important than process and structures. Culture is the black box that offers a reliable guide to what exactly is going on. It is the mediating element between corporate expectations and expectations of those on the ground charged with delivery. The climate within an organisation is crucial to whether it succeeds in its endeavours. Company directives, mission statements, vision planning, aims and objectives are all dependent on whether the internal culture allows them to be realised. Corporate history or the sagas of not-for-profit organisations, charities or faith communities are bedevilled by a gap between edicts and outcomes.

The reason why that defeats strategy most days of the week is no doubt because of the much cited 'resistance to change'. Yet it is worth pondering why there is often such resistance that manifests itself as rearguard actions fought through fiefdoms or, more passively, organisational yawns. Directive-fatigue sets in. Workers and staff have heard it all before. They suspect it is about cost-cutting, laying-off, downsizing; changing the familiar into ways of working that are a source of apprehension. Organisations may not be comfortable places but they become familiar. New workers and even bosses quickly 'go native'. Emotional cognition – perceptions that are emotionally laden and not just rational – is the norm.

Organisations know how important it is to have motivated, engaged employees, but most fail to hold managers accountable for making it happen. When they do not, the bottom line suffers. Research from the University of California found that motivated employees were 31 per cent more productive, had 37 per cent higher sales, and were three times more creative than demotivated employees. They were also 87 per cent less likely to quit, according to a Corporate Leadership Council study on over 50,000 people. Combine that with Gallup research showing that 70 per cent of an employee's motivation is influenced by his or her manager and the observation arises that employees do not leave jobs; they leave managers.[6]

Issues to do with workplace environments are very much in the news at any given time. During 2015, the troubles surrounding VW for being caught out cheating in their diesel emission tests were clearly not, as was claimed to begin with, a question of a handful of rogue engineers. It was widely considered to be an issue of the culture within the company, pressurising employees towards ultra-high performance for profit. 'A few bad apples' is the standard apologia everywhere a company or an institution is found to have been failing or even being criminally negligent. Learning lessons becomes the wearying mantra.

Bloomberg reported in April 2016 that a number of banks were having difficulties hiring managers for senior roles as new rules, such as the Senior Managers Regime, came into force. These new rules mean that bankers in job functions with senior level responsibility face potential personal liability for wrongdoings and conduct failures under their watch. They are in effect liable for the mistakes of others.[7]

As Steven Goldstein, the executive coach working with banks and financial market businesses to help them transform their risk culture, observes:

> Behavioural change and cultural change in banks' trading and investment banking businesses require the breaking of deeply ingrained habitual responses, entrenched organisational attitudes, and long held processes and practices. The path to success in these businesses is a well-trodden path which gets passed down from managers to traders and salespeople who become the next set of managers. This creates [a] series of self-reinforcing loops which becomes the system and defines the culture. It is this which creates the 'bad apples'.[8]

As I write these words, it has just been announced (31 December 2015) that the UK Financial Conduct Authority (FCA) is suspending its review into the culture of UK banks. This came as a surprise to many commentators. As the Director of Supervision at the FCA, Clive Adamson, observed in a speech when it came into being in April 2013, underpinning concerns about financial regulation or malpractice was the issue of culture:

> In many cases, where things have gone wrong, whether it is mis-selling of PPI or in attempting to manipulate LIBOR, a cultural issue is at the heart of the problem. It is fair to say that to many in the outside world, the cultural approach of doing the right thing has been lost for financial services.[9]

Now the FCA said it would be dropping its review and announced it will instead 'engage individually with firms to encourage their delivery of cultural change ... a focus on the culture in financial services firms remains a priority.'[10] Whether this was because leading banks were threatening to re-locate headquarters away from the City of London unless the 'banker bashing' came to an end will be a matter for the economic historians. What is clear, however, is the importance of culture in these discussions and its power to trip up the best laid plans.

As the Financial Conduct Authority had earlier observed:

> Culture is like DNA. It shapes judgements, ethics and behaviours displayed at those key moments, big or small, that matter to the performance and reputation of firms and the service that it provides to customers and clients. For us, we view culture through the lens of what matters to us as a conduct regulator ... The challenge for many firms is that culture is hard to change and requires dedicated and persistent focus over a number of years in order to embed different approaches and ways of behaving. As the Salz Review recently concluded, if culture is left to its own devices, it shapes itself, with the inherent risk that behaviours will not be those desired.[11]

The review referred to by corporate lawyer-turned-investment banker Anthony Salz was commissioned by Barclays into the circumstances behind the Libor-rigging scandal in 2012. In the judgement of Salz, the culprit was 'cultural shortcomings'. The bank needed a 'transformational change' to restore its reputation amongst the public. Barclays had become too focused on profit and bonuses rather than the interests of customers. The result of fast-paced growth was that Barclays became complex to manage, tending to develop silos with different values and cultures:

> We believe that the business practices for which Barclays has rightly been criticised were shaped predominantly by its cultures, which rested on uncertain foundations. There was no sense of common purpose in a group that had grown and diversified significantly in less than two decades.[12]

Economic crisis highlighted the pressures of the workplace and the sheer cost of negative cultures. A 2013 Report by the UK Chief Medical Officer put mental health issues in the workplace firmly on the agenda. Mental health-related absence in the workplace was rising, with the number of days lost to stress, depression and anxiety up by 24 per cent since 2009. The estimated price tag was a £100 billion a year in working days. Urgent measures were necessary.[13]

Dysfunctional organisations are partly to blame for this – the psycho-social environment where stress at work is a pressing issue will very likely have a detrimental effect on the identity and self-worth of employees. Yet that organisation may be embarking on such practices as making hospital ward managers, for example, apply for their own jobs. The result of such re-engineering will often be to move staff to different wards and specialisms, thereby breaking up well-functioning teams. The systematic denigration of attachment seems to be a feature of contemporary organisational life.[14]

Teachers in schools have been feeling the effects of the overwhelming demands being increasingly placed on them. Schools are being called upon to find the remedies for many of society's ills. They are often blamed for what goes wrong even if they do not have complete control over the matter. They are constantly called upon to incorporate new content and approaches into the curriculum; to develop new educational programmes and pedagogical practices. Computing and information technology bring their own set of challenges. All these demands often have to be met in the face of cuts to education budgets and staffing schedules and calls for economies of every kind on all levels of school life.[15]

Case study

Teacher stress – A personal view[16]

Over recent decades teachers in state schools have been faced with an ever-increasing workload that has little to do with the actual task of teaching children. Successive governments have demanded more and more paperwork – planning, assessing, recording and reporting the progress of their pupils. Whitehall bureaucrats and politicians claim that this is all about improving standards and improving outcomes for the nation's children, but the sheer volume of work wears teachers out and detracts from the quality of their interaction with their pupils.

After retiring from teaching at the age of 54 – and I was told to take early retirement due to stress – I did not enter a school for around 17 years. I then joined a team which goes into schools to present assemblies. I was immediately struck by how young the teaching staff seemed to be. It is clear that more and more teachers get out of education after only a few years because of work-loads and stress.

There is another aspect, though, that is rarely talked about – denigration. For over 30 years there has been a widespread tendency for governments to be constantly denigrating the work of teachers and questioning their commitment. This began in the 1980s with legislation that was passed to 'ensure that teachers worked a minimum of 35 hours per week'. Most teachers were already working over 50 hours per week – including marking and preparation time, much of it done at home late into the night.

The introduction of the National Curriculum should have helped level the playing field of education content across the country, but the demands to keep records to prove what every child was achieving made the whole process a bureaucracy overload. The subsequent push to introduce regular testing to 'prove' that children were reaching standards of attainment (the dreaded 'SATS') and then the introduction of league tables became more sticks to beat teachers with. OFSTED (Office for Standards in Education, Children's Services and Skills) inspections further added to the pressure – inspectors were required at every inspection to find a minimum of three items which the school was failing in. Politicians and bureaucrats focused almost all of their attention on these 'failings' rather than all the glowing reports of success highlighted in the majority of reports.

So the whole ethos of state education has become one of denigrating the teaching profession as a failing profession and many teachers have become dispirited. When someone is repeatedly told that they are falling short of imposed standards, is repeatedly under a cloud of fear of what the next OFSTED inspector will find fault with, it is little wonder that there is so much unrest in the profession and that so many teachers are giving up. Increasingly over recent years the real quality of a good education – the relationship between tutor and taught – has been sacrificed to the opportunity for politicians to batter the profession in a constant demand for higher and higher standards, and the opportunity for capitalists to make profit from education – in much the same way that the quality of the NHS has been sacrificed on the same altar.

I referred above to my retirement at the age of 54 due to stress. At about that time a friend – vice-principal of a large secondary school in Derbyshire – was asked by his professional association to undertake some research. The thrust of the research was to learn about the needs of teachers approaching retirement to enable them to make the most of their years *in* retirement. The intention was that the association would then offer advice and training to prepare people better for retirement. The research threw up some unexpected information.

The researcher discovered that teachers who worked right up to retirement age of 65 had an average life expectancy in retirement of 2–3 years. Teachers who retired at age 60 had a life expectancy in retirement of 10–15 years. Teachers who retired at 55 had a life expectancy afterwards of over 25 years.

Given a normal career start age of around 22–23, this meant that many teachers were achieving 30–40 years of service. That research – in the 1990s – showed the increasingly detrimental impact of the stress of teaching as individuals aged. Twenty years later, research shows that the average length of service in teaching is now only seven years. After three to four years of training to achieve a degree and enter the profession many teachers find the working conditions and stress unsustainable. Their talents are lost to schools and the cost of their training largely wasted.

It is certainly the case that Health and Safety Executive research has found teaching to be the most stressful profession in the UK, with 41.5 per cent of teachers reporting themselves as 'highly stressed'. For comparison, the incidence of any kind of stress across the working population was then around 20 per cent.[17] A survey on occupational stress published in the *Journal of Managerial Psychology* in 2005 ranked teaching as the second most stressful job out of 26 occupations analysed. The study found that only ambulance drivers experienced higher levels of stress than teachers. A 2008 survey of local authorities found that stress-related absence amongst teachers in Britain led to the loss of around 500,000 teacher days.[18] Since that time, the situation has, if anything, got worse. The culture is exacerbated by successive administrations telling teachers, 'You are the problem! This is what you will do and this is how you will do it'.[19] It is a prime example of how the external environment impinges upon the internal environment. In many primary schools, numeracy and literacy are tested daily and the results must be entered by a busy teacher on the software used to track relentless progress.

In today's typical workplace, stress is seen as becoming increasingly common. People appear to be working longer hours, taking on higher levels of responsibility and exerting themselves ever more strenuously to meet rising expectations about job performance. Competition is sharp. There is always someone else ready to 'step into one's shoes' should one be found wanting.

The culprit so often is the culture of the organisation, what goes on on the ground. There is a generational shift towards organisational culture, defined by Deal and Kennedy as 'the way things get done around here'.[20] The concept has been much critiqued. Do organisations have a common culture as distinct communities of their own with distinct rules and values? How are we to understand the idea of culture when applied to firms, companies and public institutions?

Nevertheless, the notion of organisational culture has received general acceptance as a way to study human systems in the workplace. It is now widely recognised that an organisation's culture will influence human behaviour and human performance at work and is crucial to its success. It is formed by values and visions, working practices and, crucially, management style. 'Culture change must mean changing the corporate ethos, the images and values that inform action and this new way of understanding organisational life must be brought into the management process.'[21] Deal and Kennedy argued that culture is the single most important factor accounting for success or failure in organisations. They identified four key dimensions of culture:

1   Values – the beliefs that lie at the heart of the corporate culture.
2   Heroes – the people who embody values.
3   Rites and rituals – routines of interaction that have strong symbolic qualities.
4   The culture network – the informal communication system or hidden hierarchy of power.[22]

Peters and Waterman suggest a psychological theory of that link based around reward systems. This was reflected in one of the best-selling business books ever – *In Search of Excellence* – rooted in putting people first.[23] Charles Handy also proposed a fourfold typology rooted in contrasts between power cultures, role cultures and task culture. His account of organisational culture stressed the role of motivation in the workplace to ensure people thrive.[24]

The focus in the contemporary scene is less now on 'what the man in charge actually does'. It is not so much on the leader as leadership. In the leadership literature, there is much greater acceptance than there was in the heady days of 'scientific management' that the prime task of a leader is to create cultures: micro-cultures that allow the right objectives to be realised under the right conditions. Leadership and management are not just a set of professional competencies but the translation of the guiding values of an organisation into practice in a way that connects with the values of the workforce.

As we will explore, the obvious ways this perspective shows up is with respect to the ethical stance of a leader, the management of people and change management. Arguably, there are no competencies that are not shaped in their application by values. Few actions, policies or interventions in an organisation are neutral with respect to values. This entails a close connection between the leader and the leadership he or she exercises. If leadership is about creating positive values in the micro-culture of their organisation, this begs a deeper question about what those values are? Put another way, what are the ingredients of success?

Perspectives on leadership have been extensively analysed according to:

● results[25]
● traits,[26] especially Myers Briggs[27]
● relationality[28]
● stewardship and being guardian of resources[29]
● situation and appropriate power[30]
● charisma[31]
● values[32]

- creativity;[33] see also Amabile;[34]
- servanthood.[35]

Recent emphases in leadership development have been on emotional intelligence[36] or the concept of 'flow'.[37] Knowing the varied ways organisational cultures work makes us wary of big generalisations.[38] Metaphors and models in an organisation must reflect being an environment of value.

Throughout the literature, there is widespread consensus, however, that, beyond managing systems, the role of the CEO is to create cultures in which staff and workers contribute effectively to the purpose of the organisation.[39] The leader needs to find a balance between purpose and people,[40] to utilise the human resources available towards effective ends.[41] Central to this is learning to relate, to attend to the interaction and emotional dynamics of personnel and professionals and to harness this towards aims and objectives.[42]

Transformative leaders realise, usually painfully, that to change an organisation, you need to change its culture, how it works, its traditions. For how an organisation works does not just emerge from lines on paper that tell an accountability or hierarchical story. Those lines do not actually exist. They are representations of exchanges, of the flow of power within an organisation, who goes to whom. Organisational identity, 'who we are', is more rea-listically told through stories and narratives about 'this is how we do things around here'. People learn the rules of the game and operate a kind of collective agreement.

Organisational culture has been much studied in the leadership literature of the past 50 years. Many if not most academics and practitioners alike would concur that it is a prime task of leaders to create and sustain micro-cultures and often to challenge and change them. A recent roundtable of CEOs involved with mergers and takeovers agreed that re-shaping an industrial enterprise was only 5 per cent manufacturing and producing; 95 per cent was of the issues concerned with the human factor, the emotions and reactions of people on the ground.[43]

The essence of organisational culture is 'what goes on on the ground'. Yet building the right kind of culture is a vital ingredient of success. A positive climate adds to the bottom line. A successful school is characterised by strong leadership that relishes the challenge of putting in place school improvement factors to do with a culture of high expectations and learning as well as teacher recruitment and retention. Put another way, we are here exploring what it means to construct valuing environments. 'Environments of Value' are those that facilitate the crucial link between a felt sense of inner value and worth and the added value for an organisation as that value is mobilised. Rooted in client observation, post-doctoral work and practitioner experience of a variety of workplace environments, this book probes the factors that promote or hinder that link.

Culture is messy. It is to do with identity. The culture of an organisation is more than a list of values, despite a list of values often pointed to as representing that culture. Culture is made up of the myths, stories, and accepted practices that infuse an organisation and explain what happens on the ground. If leaders want to have a handle on the culture of their organisation, they must listen to the narratives, the stories told on the ground floor that encapsulate attitudes and beliefs. These can be changed gradually. They are malleable. 'A new normal' can be achieved.

The literature around the role of leadership in organisational culture is vast and extensive. The way that CEOs create an environment in which value at all levels informs the culture of the organisation is integral to the leadership style. This is highly problematic when it comes to how institutions operate.

The institutional defence game (and its opponents)

'The families were not listened to for twenty-three years.' – 'You expect to be treated with respect, with dignity and with justice but instead the opposite happens.'[44]

The police failed them, the emergency services failed them. The police even doctored the evidence so as to pin the blame for the Hillsborough football disaster in 1989 on Liverpool fans being unruly rather than failure in crowd control. Those were the staggering findings of the independent report on the Hillsborough disaster. A slur on a whole city could be lifted at last. The distrust of discredited institutions was high. It was a complete breakdown of the services people were supposed to trust.[45]

When agencies of the state let people down, a culture of institutional defence is involved. This presents a united front against which whistleblowers and campaigners require dogged persistence. The degree to which the public services were capable of cover-up was not just a story of a few rogue operators: the usual narrative. A complete absence of people coming forward represented systemic failure. This added up to a massive failure of public administration. The public clearly felt as separate from the institutions of the state as those institutions often appeared to do towards them. All too often, the innocent suffer and the guilty are protected.

Contrast this reprehensible episode with a report on the state of Britain's hospitals published the same day. 'Hospitals on the Edge' reported that over-65s accounted for seven in ten hospital beds but 'the system continues to treat older patients as a surprise at best or unwelcome at worst'.[46] The system! These are words that send shivers down contemporary spines, possibly because people have come to expect more from public services. Being disregarded is one of the prime inputs into erosion of personal value and worth we are tracking in this book. The themes of indifference, indignity and diminishing crop up constantly in episodes of institutional failure, witness reactions to the Hillsborough cover-up.

This feature of public service response was all the more ironic for it clustering around police action, for police forces have felt considerable disrespect from successive governments that clearly felt they were unreconstructed, despite the waves of reforms that broke over the public sector as a whole.

The game of institutional defence is about covering your back, agreeing with the boss rather than the people and ticking the box – all so as to preserve the institution which now has a life of its own and rallies round itself.

The emphasis in the UK has been on targets, delivering outcomes based on spreadsheets from a Whitehall desk. Assessed against mission statements and stated aims of public organisations, everything can seem on track and acceptable. The boxes have been ticked. If the emphasis is instead on lived experience, however, the conditions on the ground, as it were, of human interaction with the state and its various associated institutions, a different picture emerges. There, experience is neither rich nor rewarding. It is often a report of not being heard, being disregarded, so that your life situation does not count in contrast with the overall picture that is being measured. Concern in health provision has been about meeting targets at the expense of patients; targets set in the name of raising standards. The human factor, the lived experience of those on the ground is often at odds.

It was health care where the protest against the impersonal most strongly came to the fore amongst the agendas of our times. A wave of reports expressed concern about the quality of health care provision in the UK. In October 2011, the Care Quality Commission found that many patients, especially amongst the elderly and more vulnerable, were being neglected. Then the National Health Service Future Forum outlined a series of concerns about the lack of focus on compassion and caring. Nutrition, mental well-being and even spirituality should be on the agenda. Health care was too important to leave to the professionals. In December 2012, the Chief Nursing Officer in the UK said that a new culture would need to be built to re-develop compassion. It was clear that very highly qualified nurses were needed to take on the increasingly complex nature of nursing but had skills been emphasised at the expense of compassion? Care seemed in short supply.

Anecdotally, those involved with health care systems care about patients but the constant number-crunching and auditing makes a job joyless. Nurses were encouraged to place dignity at the heart of their work but practitioners still appear to be struggling against a system that 'wants' the opposite. 'Patients seem to be becoming numbers not people. I am having to fight against what the system wants in order to provide dignified care to my patients.'[47] The Secretary of the Royal College of Nursing commented that, 'Dignity should not be an afterthought or an optional extra. Each and every patient – whether they are in a hospital, a GP's surgery, in the community or in a care home – deserves to be treated with dignity and respect.'[48] So often health care professionals are developing a standardised package to people for whom it doesn't seem appropriate. They are burnt out by the time they get to 60. Professionals work at a frenetic pace in contemporary society. Huge burdens of paperwork and administrative overload cause great stress. 'You have to keep proving that you are a worthy person,' complains a health care professional. 'It's important to gain funding.'[49] Social worth and value for money are clearly intertwined in narratives such as these. Yet what such regimes do to those that have to deliver the service should also be factored in. It erodes their personal worth, feeling the stress of never doing the best job, always playing catch.

Far too many areas of one of the largest employers in Europe, the UK National Health Service, are squeezed and chaotic. Counsellors working with staff report that far too many employees are demoralised and burnt out. Although absenteeism is a perennial concern of a human resources department, stressed managers are often more concerned about 'presenteeism' – those who continue to work when they should be off sick, grateful to get to the end of a shift.[50]

The report on serious failings at the Mid Staffordshire NHS Foundation Trust between January 2005 and March 2009 that resulted in the appalling suffering of many patients highlighted the negative organisational culture that was endemic to the systemic failings. As the Chief Officer of the NHS Confederation observed, 'staff give of their best when they feel valued, not inspected'. There seems to be a strong and intrinsic connection between a culture of value and the value that is generated from that environment; in that case, the value of the human being served. Value is the key ingredient.

Analysis of the Trust's board meetings from 2005 to 2009 found that discussions were dominated by finance, targets and achieving foundation trust status. Yet between 400 and 1,200 more people died than would have been expected at Mid Staffordshire NHS Foundation Trust over three years, the Healthcare Commission report said.

> On behalf of the Government and the NHS I would like to apologise to the
> patients and families of patients who have suffered because of the poor standards of

care at Stafford Hospital ... There was a complete failure of management to address serious problems and monitor performance ... This led to a totally unacceptable failure to treat emergency patients safely and with dignity.[51]

Three years on, observers said the same culture was prevalent.

Institutional behaviour through discrimination has been much studied as a major means by which groups create and maintain dominance over other groups.[52] Institutions obtain a fit between the organisation's members and the predominant ideologies, values, and agenda of the organisation, or a person–environment fit, through several processes.[53]

There are many concerns about the limits of corporate or neo-liberal globalisation; 'to the extent that the state has been instrumentalised by a combination of global market forces and a general antipathy towards bureaucracies and regulation, the sphere of governmental autonomy with respect to promoting the well-being of the territorial citizenry is diminished.'[54] Nevertheless, reaction against objectification by targets and standardised solutions in favour of the local and the personal has become part of a growing political discourse. Indignation against indignity has been a key input into these debates. There has been a growing call for greater accountability and transparency, the effect of which is to shore up the value and worth of those who would otherwise have been trashed.

Personalisation was the police you knew, the local officer with a face and a name. There was a strong reaction against police who seemed to greet a complaint or problem with a yawn. It was reported that the London police themselves were frustrated by the way they performed their tasks. 'There's been a detachment from the people we're here to serve', said the Chairman of the Police Federation. It seems the public too felt estranged. In 1981, 43 per cent of the public had contacted the police usually just to ask directions. By 2006, it had fallen to 27 per cent, of whom most had reported a crime.[55] There is an irony here. It was partly to avoid ethnic bias that a culture of obsessive recording had developed. It is that loss of face and presence that compounds a sense of distance.

In an Internet age, the angry swarm of the Twitter sphere is a massive step-change towards promoting accountability and transparency. It does also promote gossip that is intentionally malicious. Yet politicians, CEOs and leaders of organisations alike now live in glass houses. They are increasingly vulnerable to genuine whistleblowers and those with a grudge seeking revenge. The boss of BP, Tony Hayward, never got over the storm that broke following some unwise comments at the time of the oil spill in the Gulf of Mexico. When 200 million gallons of crude oil flowed from Deep Water Horizon in April 2010, an exasperated CEO said, 'I want my life back!' For a while, before resigning, Tony Hayward was the most hated man in America, vilified for these comments and the BP oil spill they referred to.[56]

This applies to the church and faith communities as much as it does to other institutions. The game of 'institutional defence', with its trademark response of 'yes and that's why we've done x', shows it is about protecting the system rather than people. For too long, the story was that of a fortress within which tea and sympathy could be offered to some individuals who were obviously upset but nothing systemic was offered by way of explanation. 'A few bad apples' had become synonymous with hiding them away.[57]

Where the line is drawn between intrusion and valid public comment is a question as old as a free press. There is no doubt though that the digital revolution has returned power to critics of organisations, public and private alike. The whistleblowers or spies of yesteryear, anxiously copying documents after hours, are creatures from the past. Now, anything that looks incriminating can go global in seconds. Transparency and account-ability are given new technology twists.[58] The risk of reputational damage has bosses running scared. Even adding corporate social responsibility to business interests seems to be no defence against company critics, indeed can seem to be hypocrisy.

The overwhelming majority of those who work in public service institutions are well-intentioned people seeking to operate in a benign way (and combine some idealism with pragmatism) even though the system may be dysfunctional. For the most part too, targets, systems, processes and especially bureaucracy are not good words. A feature of our times is response to institutions and public service provision as being sites of imper-sonal forces. It may well be that what drives visceral attitudes towards the European project is its remoteness as well as perceived lack of democratic accountability. Then there is the way that public institutions find it woefully painful to admit mistakes. This emerges especially with the call for 'lessons to be learnt' that has become a depressing litany of our times. What is this education that has been generated supposedly by insight, previously absent and now taken on board? What was learnt that had been hidden knowledge beforehand?

Yet the notion of a post-bureaucratic age is illusory. Rational and effective action is the hallmark of modern society. The choice is not between bureaucracy and no bureaucracy but good bureaucracy and bad bureaucracy. Delivering fair provision for the benefit of all characterised the state-run bureaucracies set up after the Second World War. As Weber pointed out:

> precision, speed, unambiguity, knowledge of the files, continuity, discretion, unity, strict subordination, reduction of friction and of material and personal costs – these are raised to the optimum point in strictly bureaucratic administration … The 'objective' discharge of business primarily means a discharge of business according to calculable rules and 'without regard for persons'.[59]

It is commonplace that public services as much as anywhere are characterised by the game of institutional defence, of covering your back. Moves to protect whistleblowers are at least a recognition that such a culture is harmful to health. Institutional defence is a paranoia that seems to be intrinsic to how contemporary organisations operate – especially those in the public sector but by no means exclusively. The system closes ranks to pro-tect itself. It churns out the weary mantra of needing to learn the lessons. What kind of education is it that such learning was not in place before an incident?

Cultures of working excessive hours invariably lead to ill health, poor morale and a negative rather than positive environment.[60] Critics of the BBC institutional culture identified as being detrimental to its functioning spoke of internecine warfare as a prime culprit.[61] Here you had highly talented people pursuing levels of rivalry and striving for esteem that descended into bitterness. It was to feature prominently in the release of documents highlighting how a culture was vitriolic and not just competitive.

Boeing had spent several years struggling to get ahead in the global economy. Amidst high-level negotiations between management and union leaders, management had a new headache – a union contract that was about to expire. The company wanted the public to think workers were too self-interested, too unaware of the realities of global competition. Yet, as the *Seattle Times* remarked:

If Boeing workers strike next week, it's not just over the contract. It's the feeling of human devaluation they say permeates plants from Everett and Renton to Wichita.[62]

Across the board, people voice a recurrent protest about contemporary organisations. It applies to public services and private companies, to commercial and non-profit-making sectors alike. It is the complaint of not being heard. It seems to arise because of the coincidence of two factors – the fragmentation and sense of reaction against de-personalisation combined with higher expectations under media scrutiny as to what people want and demand from the institutions that affect them. In Russia for example, anti-government feeling has not resulted in mass protest due perhaps to a resigned tolerance and adaptability.[63] Western societies, however, face a crisis of systems drowning the human voices, a crisis of not being heard. This shows up as a crisis of institutions, part of the post-modern configuration of life in which the personal reacts against the impersonal and big government is suspect.

Organisational cultures differ according to the way human devaluation operates through their regimes. There is nothing new about such insights. Back in the 1930s Elton Mayo was an Australian Professor of Industrial Research at Harvard University Graduate School of Business Administration. He was the founding father of the 'Human Relations Movement'. Workers and managers must first be understood as human beings. Central to the Hawthorne Experiment he directed was the fuller realisation of the 'human factor' in work situations.[64] For generations, organisations have been designed and managed along the same lines. They are machines. In the second and third wave of industrialism, staff and workers are cogs. To achieve quantity and output, management was about balancing the books and fulfilling certain policies. To effect change, we go into the entity in order to tinker and change from outside. This notion is associated with that of Action Research, propounded by Kurt Lewin at the end of the 1940s.

Managers and workers create a workplace culture through symbols, beliefs, management style, corporate philosophy and conditions of work.[65] A positive example is reported to be uncommon practice at Harley-Davidson with an 'open, non-status culture.'[66] How we think about these things can bring clarity or confusion. New approaches challenge well-trodden paths built around command and control, paradigms aligned with the purpose for which the organisation exists. This is to see companies as functioning within a web of stakeholders, of groups or individuals motivated by human interests, and compare it to a kind of biological entity – an organism and not just an organisation formed and re-formed. At the heart of organisational culture is a continuing and almost endless circular set of conversations and memories that express what is important to us and why. Understanding this dynamic is important to creating power through people.

That applies to a dysfunctional culture as much as one conducive to human. Mental health issues in the City seem to be on the increase. In his book *Fear and Self-Loathing in the City*, Michael Sinclair, a chartered psychologist who practised there, described a range of issues presented by clients. Anxiety, depression, eating disorders, drug and alcohol abuse were the main culprits, but behind them, Sinclair argued, lay a generalised fear of failure and a strong self-loathing. The need to be a perfectionist and always in control bumps up against failure when City workers do not measure up to such exacting standards.[67] These individual pathologies are, however, sharply accentuated by an organisational culture that is so often downright toxic. A long-hours culture is driven by the fear of new people coming up who may outrun you. Many companies exhibit these tendencies. In such environments, people are not judged by their merits so much as ability to play the political game. There are all too many narcissistic individuals and indeed psychopaths motivated by power.

It is important to say too that organisations do not exist in a vacuum. Consideration of organisational culture can hardly be separated from social contexts and the embeddedness of participants within wider society. Because of the presence in the self of wider culture, management practices that shape what happens in a particular organisation are culturally constructed. If a firm is the mediating structure between the value generated in that particular site and the value produced overall in the economy (the micro and the macro), the culture of an organisation is vital. It is a mediating dynamic between the purpose of that organisation and the outcomes it seeks at any one moment in time. What takes place on the ground is crucial for determining whether or not the organisation succeeds in the tasks it sets itself.

As I write these words, the UK Care and Quality Commission (CQC) has just published the first comprehensive report on Britain's hospitals and care facilities under a new inspection regime. The results were not encouraging.[68] 'From the evidence we've analysed, we don't believe that more money is the answer to delivering higher quality care.' What counted for more were engaged leaders building a shared ownership of quality and safety. Amongst the critical aspects of good leadership were said to be:

- effective engagement and communication with staff and people using services;
- the skills, experience and visibility of management.

The Austrian philosopher Martin Buber describes 'I–Thou' relationships we can have with another, opened via the door of empathy.[69] This contrasts with 'I–It' relationships, which stay on the surface. The emotional indifference of an 'I-It' relationship has a very different feel than the connection made with an 'I–Thou' mode. The boundary between them though is fluid. Even in close relationships, we slip into the 'I–It' mode when we are busy. The 'Thou' can become an 'It' to me. That is surely the significance of how we have come to relate to public service provision in contemporary society. We want more, we demand more and the recovery of the personal thus becomes a major challenge for institutional provision everywhere. Humanise the landscape! Certainly, in reforming the public sector, empowered citizenry is becoming a major theme.

Having a culture that draws out human potential is a vital issue. Pfeffer asks why – despite long-standing evidence that a committed work force is essential for success – firms continue to attach little importance to their workers. The answer, he argues, resides in a complex web of factors based on perception, history, legislation, and practice that continues to dominate management thought and action. Yet, some organisations have been able to overcome these obstacles. In fact, the five common stocks with the highest returns between 1972 and 1992 – Southwest Airlines, Wal-Mart, Tyson Foods, Circuit City, and Plenum Publishing – were in industries that shared virtually none of the characteristics traditionally associated with strategic success. What each of these firms did share is the ability to produce sustainable competitive advantage. They achieved it through managing people.[70]

The culture of the workplace runs through its DNA. It is also highly subversive. It devours not just breakfast but also lunch and tea. Senior managers believe that restructuring will solve problems but culture stands in the way, mocking all efforts at reform. If the structure is wrong, it is changed because the culture is working. The changed structure will not bring a new culture. As they realise the importance of culture within the team, and the wider culture of the organisation, successful managers reject the belief that minor adjustments within a team or teams can be scaled up to the whole organisation to achieve the result seen within the team. They have forgotten culture.[71]

A major UK retailer is facing strong condemnation on the grounds of audit and financial regulation (or its lack). Eye-watering sums have been fudged in the accounts. 'Things are always unnoticed, until they're noticed,' Tesco Chairman Richard Broadbent said when asked how Britain's biggest retailer had failed to spot a £250m-sized hole in its first-half profits for 2014.[72] An insider tells of the culture that drives employees to falsify or at least exaggerate the profits.[73] It can be summed up in one word – 'fear'. It is the fear of not keeping up profit margins, fear of falling sales, fear of falling behind, fear of pressure from above, fear of pressure from outside: fear is the driver in this culture.

Yet there is a wide difference between being culture-driven and being driven by culture. A client working in the City returns every night profoundly depressed to the point of hating his job. He has continually to crack down on employees, to 'put the screws on them'. The need to get the most out of the staff drives the workplace but it comes at a price. The result is not a happy, productive environment but a restless place, joyless and sullen.[74] A driven culture is part of how things are done. A female senior executive in a major US investment bank has a baby. Not wanting to give any signals that she could not manage a top job, within TWO HOURS OF HAVING A BABY, she is back on the phone doing her job.[75] In South Korea, the punishing work culture is gradually being relaxed in the country's family-owned conglomerates – the chaebol. Within Hyundai's new office culture, junior staff are allowed to speak freely with bosses and there is a cut in bonuses for managers whose staff do not take enough leave. In 2003, Eric Surdej, a French sales expert with experience working at Sony and Toshiba, decided to join, seeking out new challenges in his career. He knew about Koreans' reputation of being extremely difficult to work with, but didn't care too much. He was determined to see for himself the inner workings of the enigmatic Korean company he believed would soon pose a major challenge to more established brands from the US, Europe and Japan. This company would be unstoppable once it got on a roll, his instinct was telling him. Surdej was half right and half wrong, he writes in his memoir *Koreans are Crazy!*[76]

Yet, the extreme ways the Koreans worked, or the Korean company worked, were well beyond his expectations. It was more than a cultural difference he had thought he could overcome with ambition, passion and professionalism. 'The 10 years at LG was the most bizarre experience of my life, much more than just a professional challenge in (my) career,' Surdej recalled. Long, gruelling hours, rigid, militaristic hierarchy, after-work parties that felt like cult gatherings, overly controlling bosses and the unyielding obsession with numeric growth – none of these were easy for Surdej to adjust to, but he somehow managed to immerse himself in the environment so that he earned the nickname, 'LG addict'. 'I couldn't understand how a company on solid footing to grow can cause such a high level of stress on its employees … The company looks strong, products are attractive and innovative. Growth seems assured. Then why are they so insecure?' Surdej writes, recalling his first day at LG. Slowly, he begins to understand that every element of the Korean office exists for one reason – to perform. In a top-down, command hierarchy like an army unit, LG moves in perfect unison, principle and efficiency. Everyone competes on one's own respective field and level to beat competitors or self. 'Inhumane? Absolutely. But ruthlessly effective,' Surdej says. LG's market position in the French electronics market moved from fifteenth to third place between 2003 and 2010. Revenues rose sevenfold.[77]

Two stories in the UK media at the moment of writing conclude these concerns. The service company G4S were embarrassed to discover that a BBC *Panorama* report had investigated maltreatment at a Kent young offenders centre. Seven members of staff were suspended after filmed evidence of abuse was presented by the BBC. The allegations involved unnecessary force, foul language and cover-up.[78] This despite the website for the company proudly proclaiming: 'Securing our people. Why it matters as a service provider, our customers rely on us to have a motivated and healthy workforce.'[79]

The second story concerned the British Army. Unofficial practice of punishments, known as 'beastings', had led to the death a young soldier. Some argued that beasting is a necessary part of training, designed to toughen up soldiers and push them to their limit. Others claimed it fast becomes bullying, with damaging physical and psychological effects. Though the practice seemed endemic in its culture, the Army boasted of serving 'with heart, with soul'; where everyone is treated equally.[80] It was the same British Army that surprised its American counterparts during the Second World War by stopping to shave in the morning or pausing to brew regular cups of tea.[81] This was a micro-culture in operation; 'how we do things round here'.

Between rhetoric and reality, a great gulf is fixed.

Notes

1 https://www.afdb.org/, accessed November 2015.
2 Adamson, C. (2013) 'The Importance of Culture in Driving Behaviours of Firms and How the FCA will Assess This'. http://www.fca.org.uk/news/regulation-professionalism/.
3 Serewicz, L. (2013), 'Culture Eats your Structure for Lunch'. https://www.thoughtmanagem ent.org/2013/07/10/culture-eats-your-structure-for-lunch/, accessed December 2015.
4 Aristotle (1998), *Metaphysics*, Book H 1045a, 8–10. London: Penguin.
5 Long, S. (2008), *The Perverse Organisation and its Deadly Sins*. London: Karnac.
6 Travis Bradberry, President, TalentSmart, World Economic Forum, 4 November 2016.
7 http://www.bloomberg.com/news/articles/2016-04-06/u-k-banks-struggle-to-lure-talent-for-top-jobs-as-rules-bite/, 6 April 2016.
8 Goldstein, S., http://www.traderbehaviour.blogspot.co.uk/2016/04/investment-bank-cul ture-few-bad-apples/, April 2016.
9 Adamson, (April 2013).
10 *The World at One*, BBC Radio 4, http://www.bbc.co.uk/radio4/worldatone/, 31 December 2015.
11 Adamson (April 2013).
12 http://www.bbc.co.uk/news/business-22012261/, April 2013.
13 *Annual Report of the Chief Medical Office 2013*. London: Department of Health.
14 Campling, P. (2016), 'A Crisis of Containment', *Therapy Today*, 27 (8), pp. 34–46.
15 http://www.ieu.asn.au/resources/workplace-health-safety/stress-burnout-amongst-teachers/, accessed June 2016.
16 Author's client notes – used with permission and name withheld.
17 Health and Safety Executive (2000), *The Scale of Occupational Stress*. The Bristol Health at Work Study. http://www.hse.gov.uk/research/crr_pdf/2000/crr00265.pdf/.
18 Hackitt, Judith, Speech to NASUWT conference, Chair of HSE, March 2008.

19 Author's client notes – used with permission and name withheld.
20 Deal, T.E. and Kennedy, A.A. (1982, 2000), *Corporate Cultures: The Rites and Rituals of Corporate Life*. Harmondsworth: Penguin Books, 1982; reissued Perseus Books, 2000.
21 http://www.oup.co.uk/pdf/bt/fincham/Chapter15.pdf/.
22 Deal and Kennedy (1982, 2000).
23 Peters, T. and Waterman, R. H. Jr. (2004), *In Search of Excellence*. London: Profile Books.
24 Handy, C. (1999), *Understanding Organisations*. London: Penguin.
25 Ulrich, D., Zenger, J. and Smallwood N. (1999), *Results Based Leadership*. Boston, MA: Harvard Business School Press.
26 Lord, R.G., De Vader, C.L. and Alliger, G.M. (1986), 'A Meta-analysis of the Relation between Personality Traits and Leader Perceptions: An Application of Validity Generalization Procedures', *Journal of Applied Psychology*, 71, pp. 402–410.
27 Myers, I.B., McCaulley, M.H., Quenk, N.L. and Hammer, A.L. (1989), *MBTI Manual: A Guide to the Development and Use of the Myers Briggs Type Indicator*, 3rd edn. Palo Alto, CA: Consulting Psychologists Press.
28 Uhl-Bien, M. (2006), 'Relational Leadership Theory: Exploring the Social Processes of Leadership and Organizing', *Leadership Quarterly*, 17 (6), pp. 654–676.
29 Davis, J.H, Schoorman F.D. and Donaldson, L. (1997), 'Toward a Stewardship Theory of Management', *Academy of Management Review*, 22 (1), pp. 20–47.
30 Ktter, J.P. (1985), *Power and Influence beyond Formal Authority*. New York: Free Press.
31 Conger, J.A. and Kanungo, R.N. (1987), 'Toward a Behavioral Theory of Charismatic Leadership in Organizational Settings', *Academy of Management. The Academy of Management Review*, 12 (4), pp. 637–647.
32 De Ciantis, C., and Hyatt, K., 'Values Perspectives'. http://www.kairios.com/, accessed 2014.
33 Kirton, M. (1989), *Adaptors and Innovators*. London: Taylor & Francis.
34 Amabile, T.M. (1996), *Creativity in Context*. Boulder, CO: Westview Press.
35 Greenleaf, R.K. (1991), *Servant Leadership*. Mahwah, NJ: Paulist Press.
36 Goleman, D. (1996), *Emotional Intelligence*. London: Bloomsbury.
37 Csikszentmihalyi, M. (1991), *Flow: The Psychology of Optimal Experience*. New York: Harper & Row.
38 Schein, E. (1985), *Organisational Culture and Leadership*. San Francisco: Jossey-Bass.
39 Bass, E.M. (2008), *The Bass Handbook of Leadership Theory, Research, and Managerial Applications*, 4th edn. New York: Free Press. See also Zaleznik, A., 'Managers and Leaders: Is There a Difference?', *Harvard Business Review*, Best of HBR, 1977, pp. 1–11; Hurst, D., 'Of Boxes, Bubbles and Effective Management', *Harvard Business Review*, May–June, 1984, pp. 78–88; Kotter, J.P., 'What Leaders Really Do', *Harvard Business Review*, Best of HBR, December 2001, pp. 85–96; also RBR Reprint no. r0111f.
40 Fiedler, F.E. (1967), *A Theory of Leadership Effectiveness*. New York: McGraw-Hill.
41 Hersey, P. and Blanchard, K.H. (1977), *Management of Organizational Behavior: Utilizing Human Resources*, 3rd edn. Englewood Cliffs, NJ: Prentice Hall.
42 Baxter, L. and Montgomery, B.M. (1996), *Relating: Dialogues and Dialectics*. New York: Guilford Press.
43 *The Bottom Line*, BBC Radio 4, http://www.bbc.co.uk/radio4/, 2 November 2013.
44 Lord Falconer and a representative of Liverpool families affected. *The Today Programme*, http://www.bbc.co.uk/radio4/, 15 September 2012.
45 hillsborough.independent.gov.uk/repository/report/HIP_report.pdf HC 581, 12 September 2012.
46 Royal College of Physicians Report, http://www.rcplondon.ac.uk/, 15 September 2012.
47 'Nurses Need to Consider Residents' Dignity in Personal Care', *Nursing Times*, 6 June 2008.
48 http://www.rcn.org.uk/, accessed June 2008.
49 Author's client notes – used with permission and name withheld.
50 Campling, P. and Ballat, J. (2011), *Intelligent Kindness: Reforming the Culture of Healthcare*. London: RCPsych Publications.
51 http://www.healthcarecommission.org.uk/, 17 March 2009.
52 Haley, H. and Sidanius, J. (2005), 'Person–Organization Congruence and the Maintenance of Group-based Social Hierarchy: A Social Dominance Perspective', *Group Processes and Intergroup Relations*, 8, pp. 187–203.

53 Sidanius, J. and Pratto, F. (1999), *Social Dominance: An Intergroup Theory of Social Hierarchy and Oppression*. New York: Cambridge University Press.
54 Falk, R. (2002), 'An Emergent Matrix of Citizenship: Complex, Uneven, and Fluid', in *Global Citizenship: A Critical Reader*, ed. N. Dower and J. Williams. Edinburgh: Edinburgh University Press, p. 16.
55 'A New Beat', *The Economist*, 24 January 2009.
56 'Tony Hayward, Genel Energy CEO: now he has his life back'. http://www.ft.com/, 14 September 2014.
57 'Ministers and Clergy Sexual Abuse Survivors', http://www.macsas.org.uk/, accessed April 2015.
58 Dezenhall, E. (2014), *Glass Jaw: A Manifesto for Defending Fragile Reputations in an Age of Instant Scandal*. http://www.dezenhall.com/, accessed October 2014.
59 Gerth, H.H. and Wright Mills, C. (1970), *From Max Weber*. London: Routledge & Kegan Paul, pp. 214–215.
60 TUC, 'About Time: A New Agenda for Shaping Working Hours'. http://www.tuc.org.uk/publications/, 2010.
61 *The World at One*, BBC Radio 4: http://www.bbc.co.uk/radio4/worldatone/, 12 December 2012 and 24 June 2013.
62 'No wonder the workers are so mad'. *Seattle Times*, 26 August 1999.
63 'Protests against Putin sweep Russia as factories go broke'. *The Guardian*, 7 June 2009.
64 Mayo, E. (1933), *The Human Problems of an Industrial Civilisation*. New York: Macmillan.
65 Gherardi, S. (1995), *Gender, Symbolism & Organisational Cultures*. London: Sage, p. 67.
66 Milligan, A. and Smith, S. (eds) (2002), *Uncommon Practice*. London: Pearson Education, p. 47.
67 Sinclair, M. (2010), *Fear and Self-Loathing in the City: A Guide to Keeping Sane in the Square Mile*. London: Karnac.
68 'State of Care 2014/15 Summary', http://www.cqc.org.uk/, 15 October 2015.
69 Buber, M. (1937), *I and Thou*, trans. Walter Kaufman. New York: Simon & Schuster.
70 Pfeffer, J. (1996), *Competitive Advantage through People*. Cambridge, MA: Harvard Business School Press.
71 Serewicz, L. (2011), 'Culture Eats your Structure for Lunch'. https://www.thoughtmanagement.org/, accessed December 2015.
72 'Tesco's 250-million-pound black hole: Who was minding the shop?'. *Reuters Business*, 2 October 2014.
73 Author's client notes – used with permission and name withheld.
74 Author's client notes – used with permission and name withheld.
75 Author's client notes – used with permission and name withheld.
76 Surdej, E. (2015), *Ils sont fous ces coréens!: Dix ans chez les forcenés de l'efficacité* (Documents, Actualités, Société), French edn. Paris: Calmann-Lévy.
77 http://www.koreaherald.com/index.php 8 June 2015, accessed January 2016.
78 http://www.bbc.co.uk/news/uk-england-kent-35260927/, accessed January 2016.
79 http://www.g4s.com/, accessed January 2016.
80 http://www.army.mod.uk/join/, accessed January 2016.
81 Barr, N. (2015), *Eisenhower's Armies: The American-British Alliance during World War II*. London: Pegasus.

Chapter 4

The Fourth Industrial Revolution and the human dimension

'I don't see why I should carry the can when I'm treated as rubbish.'

Author client notes

If environments of value are those that mobilise the worth of participants, it begs the question: 'What are the inner ingredients of that sense of value and worth that can be aroused and recruited?' Yet the context of valuing environments is about to undergo (and is already experiencing) rapid transformation.

Kevin Kelly argued for the existence of an emerging new economic order in a wired-up world. 'It is global. It favours intangible things – ideas, information and relationships. And it is intensely interlinked. These three attributes produce a new type of marketplace and society.'[1] The system of fluid networks, he suggested, will replace traditional linear models of business interrelationships. Kelly argued that as the marginal cost of producing data and physical products becomes cheaper due to information technology, paradoxically a company's goods become more valuable as their price moves closer 'to free'.

In this chapter, we will discuss the huge concern that the coming wave of industrialisation will sweep away millions of jobs and the implications this has for how organisations of the future will be able to nurture the human dimension. Rapid progress has also led to concerns about safety and job losses. For decades, computers have substituted for a number of jobs, including the functions of bookkeepers, cashiers and telephone operators. The Fourth Industrial Revolution will generate huge social challenges as well as radically reshaping the future of work. What space there is to safeguard and indeed cultivate our humanity will be a vital question for organisational leaders of the future. It matters fundamentally to the creation and conversion of 'value' and where we see 'value' coming from – whether from human labour or, increasingly, from capital and technological investment. Such concerns are not new.

As the Great Depression of the 1930s was taking hold, John Maynard Keynes warned that mass unemployment would be a feature of modern societies. This, he argued, was 'due to our discovery of means of economising the use of labour outrunning the pace at which we can find new uses for labour'.[2]

Britain in the mid nineteenth century went through enormous changes in the transition from land to town and city and from agriculture to manufacturing. Expansion of population and urbanisation from about 1780 onwards brought about social metamorphosis.[3] In 1790, country labourers were twice as numerous as town labourers. By 1841, the reverse was true.

It was economic change on a scale that the world had never seen. Across the country, new machines could be heard clanking night and day, heralding powered manufacturing that transformed the world far more than any class-war revolutionaries with fire in their minds.[4]

Industrial production and services were becoming more important as the way the economy and society are organised. In tandem there was a consumer and also a financial revolution. The concept of limited liability brought in by such measures as the Joint Stock Companies Act of 1856 in the UK allowed capital to be raised from a wider swathe of the population. You were only liable for what you put in – no more, no less.

In Western economic landscapes, productive forces have de-personalised us by making us objects of relentless production. The classic analysis of this was that of Marx in the nineteenth century:

> the alienation of the worker means not only that his labour becomes an object, an external existence, but that it exists outside him, independently of him and alien to him, and begins to confront him as an autonomous power; that the life which he has bestowed on the object confronts him as hostile and alien.[5]

According to that analysis, the factory system left us little say over the conditions in which we work, how that work is organised, and how it affects us physically and mentally. We are, in addition, alienated from our fellow human beings and from those who control the things we produce. To cap it all, there is our alienation from being human, our ability to consciously shape the world around us. Work bears no relationship to our personal inclinations or our collective interests. Those who create the wealth are deprived of its benefits. Marx's descriptions of this process in his *Manuscripts* were powerful indictments of the industrial revolution. 'It replaces labour by machines, but it casts some of the workers back into barbarous forms of labour and turns others into machines.'[6]

The human obsolescence of the workforce means that half of the workforce in the UK and the US may eventually lose their jobs to robots, as technological automation trends spread across all industries and service sectors, the Bank of England's chief economist advised the Trades Union Congress. Unveiling the Bank's new statistics, based on the historic trends in the market economy, Haldane warned that half of UK workers might find themselves unemployed in the coming decades.

'Taking the probabilities of automation, and multiplying them by the numbers employed, gives a broad brush estimate of the number of jobs potentially automatable,' Haldane said, stressing that 15 million people might be affected on the island nation that currently has a workforce of 31.21 million. The same trend, the chief economist argued, will also be witnessed in the US, where the current labour force of roughly 160 million Americans will see half of its jobs go to automation.

'For the UK, that would suggest up to 15 million jobs could be at risk of automation. In the US, the corresponding figure would be 80 million jobs,' Haldane said. The economist noted that previous predictions concerning the impact of modernisation on the workforce had been proven wrong since the beginning of the industrial revolution. However, citing fears over the growth of artificial intelligence, Haldane said that if the Bank's predictions are correct, the labour market patterns of the past three centuries would 'shift to warp speed'.[7]

Panics about 'technological unemployment' featured in the 1960s with the advent of computers and the 1980s and 1990s when PCs became part of office life and checkout or automatic facilities in car parks, etc., became common. Widespread automation of skilled workers' jobs was about to take place. Western democracies have become used to seeing some jobs outsourced to overseas economies that can offer lower labour costs. However, automation was a different sort of transfer: outsourcing to robots. How wide and deep will this technology transfer go? To try to answer this question, Frey and Osborne conducted a research exercise for the US that assigned probabilities of jobs being automated away. They examined how susceptible jobs are to computerisation by implementing a novel methodology to estimate the probability of computerisation for 702 detailed occupations. They examined the number of jobs at risk and the relationship between an occupation's probability of computerisation, wages and educational attainment. According to their estimates, about 47 per cent of total US employment is at risk.[8] That amounts to about 80 million jobs over the next few decades.

It is not only manual labour jobs that could be affected. Computers are taking over many cognitive tasks due to the impact of big data and algorithms. In the first wave of computerisation, computers are substituted for people in such areas as logistics, transportation, administrative and office support. The impact of the second affects jobs depending on how well engineers crack computing problems associated with human perception, creative and social intelligence. Extending this work to the UK in 2015, the business advisory services firm Deloitte analysed Office for National Statistics labour force data between 2001 and 2015. Matching changes in employment against occupations predicted to be at high, medium and low risk of being automated in the next 20 years, Deloitte's research found that, in the last 15 years across the UK, those occupations with the lowest risk of automation have created 3.5 million jobs while those occupations with the highest risk have lost 800,000 jobs.[9] On balance, that sounds a good news story. However, what kind of jobs are being created? Occupations that created the largest boost to employment across the UK since 2001 were:

- care home workers and home carers – 275,000 new jobs, growth of 55 per cent;
- teaching assistants – 250,000 new jobs, growth of 202 per cent;
- business and financial project managers – 170,000 new jobs, growth of 842 per cent.

Occupations with the largest fall in employment were:

- personal assistants – 210,000 jobs lost, down 50 per cent;
- typists – 110,000 jobs lost, down 75 per cent;
- bank and post office clerks – 100,000 jobs lost, down 44 per cent.

The Bank of England's more recent study showed that approximately one-third of jobs in the UK were at high risk of technological displacement (above a 66 per cent probability of being automated away), one-third were at medium risk (between 33 and 66 per cent vulnerability to automation) and one-third in the low-risk category (less than 33 per cent vulnerable). They took the probabilities of automation and multiplied them by the numbers employed. The conclusion was that as many as 15 million jobs in the UK might be susceptible to being automated away.[10]

Clearly there is a big divide between the kind of work that will be swept away and that which is generated. If machines are increasingly capable of taking over professional work, where does it stop? Accountants face a 95 per cent chance of being despatched to the dole queue. Vocational extinction is unlikely to be faced by hairdressers or care workers where empathy and caring are important. Yet the reality is that machines now perform tasks that even ten years ago we thought could never be done except by a human being.

It seems likely that technology forces a distinction between routine tasks that burden every job professional people do AND the empathy needed to handle real human beings. Automation may enable a practice nurse to encourage patients to self-diagnose and that could replace some aspects of what doctors do. Yet there is no real substitute for a caring, informed and personalised service that doctors are supposed to exercise. Customers at supermarket checkouts routinely look for staff assistance even with automated facilities. Robots have not taken over yet. They can, however, streamline professional work.

So where does value added come from if a digital future is either replacing skilled human labour at best or sitting alongside it and streamlining the routine?

The labour theory of value revisited

Economics is about value, how it is generated through work and profits and how prices are determined that reflect what something is worth at any one time. I am arguing that there is a different form of value − 'value-in-oneself' − the drive for which is fundamental to social processes. So it is worth recalling that there is a value theory relating to goods and services to explain how their price is determined through the wage and salary system. The idea is that the value of any commodity is determined by the average amount of labour time needed to produce it.

Marx re-wrote it but did not originate the idea of a labour theory of value. It was given classic form by Adam Smith, the prophet of capitalism, as he sought to explain how the price of goods and services is determined:

> The real price of everything, what everything really costs to the man who wants to acquire it, is the toil and trouble of acquiring it. What everything is really worth to the man who has acquired it, and who wants to dispose of it or exchange it for something else, is the toil and trouble which it can save to himself, and which it can impose upon other people.[11]

Behind the value of a good, Adam Smith argued, is the human labour in producing it:

> The value of any commodity ... to the person who possesses it, and who means not to use or consume it himself, but to exchange it for other commodities, is equal to the quantity of labour which it enables him to purchase or command. Labour, therefore, is the real measure of the exchangeable value of all commodities.[12]

It was David Ricardo who formulated the classic statement of the link between economic value and the value of the labour involved:

> The value of a commodity, or the quantity of any other commodity for which it will exchange, depends on the relative quantity of labour which is necessary for its production, and not as the greater or less compensation which is paid for that labour.[13]

These classical economists saw prices and value as reflecting primarily the costs of production. 'The scientific development of economic theory began as an attempt to solve the value problem.'[14] Marx defined the value of the commodity somewhat differently. Agreeing that products are exchanged in the marketplace roughly in line with the labour costs of producing them, he argued that value is the 'socially necessary abstract labour' embodied in a commodity. The usual outline of factors of production – capital, land and labour – were subsumed into labour. Profit is created within the workplace, not initially the marketplace. It is human capital alone that creates all the value and therefore the source of profit incentives. Human value is without qualification, an intrinsic worth independent of how much you are worth on the market.[15] It is socially unacceptable for the rich to derive income from the ownership of property. It is equally undesirable for factory owners to cream off the 'surplus value' produced by the workers above and beyond the wages they receive. Surplus value is the amount that the factory owners pocketed. In the Marxist view of the world, this was a route that leads to the exploitation and impoverishment of the working classes. Communism played on the desire for justice as well as a desire for revenge.[16]

Yet there is another Marx, the author of a much lesser-known work than *Das Kapital*. It is the Marx of what is known as the *Grundrisse: Foundations of the Critique of Political Economy*.

> Once adopted into the production process of capital, the means of labour passes through different metamorphoses, whose culmination is the machine, or rather, an automatic system of machinery (system of machinery: the automatic one is merely its most complete, most adequate form and alone transforms machinery into a system).[17]

The main role of workers in a future economy, Marx suggested, was to supervise the machines. Knowledge – the 'general intellect' as Marx termed it – would become a productive force in its own right, going far beyond the human labour that went into making the machine in the first place. In that scenario, he predicted, what is locked up in the machine is shared, social knowledge.

This was remarkably prescient, highly relevant to a future based on the sort of information technology we know today. Two statements can be made.

First, productive labour is about value added.

The very nature of work takes what has been or can be produced and adds value to it. Humans take their labour and their skills to add to the raw material all around them. What they are doing is to add value, the value they have accrued within themselves. This is human capital and it builds up as any other capital. It is relative value, value in proportion to the value others can bring in the market place. But in any enterprise, we are adding value to what we have in front of us and becoming creators – bringing something new into being. In the Western world, governments came to tax the added value as an important source of revenue, a tax that recognised the human element in the extra piece of work that has been undertaken at every stage.

There is a case to be made that globalisation and the new technology are doing for white collar workers what the industrial revolution did for trades. Menial, repetitive tasks that are generated involve the separation of thinking from doing. In our time, craftwork has become devalued. Yet it rests on the notion that making is thinking. There are modes of thought characteristic of skilled labour based on human interaction.[18]

Craftsmanship may become more important in these conditions. It shows us not only how twenty-first-century society values its work but arguably teaches us how to value ourselves.[19]

As Paul Mason observes, the amount of labour always adds value to the product yet productivity is shaped not just by trained workers but by machinery that drives down the average unit cost per labour hour and hence price. As other firms copy innovation and automation, profits will inevitably fall leading to crises within capitalism. That will be subject to mutation as new sectors will be created that ensure there are workers rich enough to generate demand.[20]

We don't need to go all the way with a labour theory of value to agree that human action is the prime instrument by which the raw materials of goods and services are shaped and extended. This applies to the production of metals, ladders and wheat. But a teacher turning out a lesson plan and delivering it, an office worker checking planning applications or a journalist constructing an article is doing this no less; generating output that, if sold on the open market, will be taxed by governments. Value Added Tax was widely adopted as a source of revenue in the second half of the twentieth century. But, in a non-monetary sphere, value added measurements began to be adopted in many schools also as a way of looking at the progress that pupils were making, not just their GCSE output. Education is argued to have an economic, measurable value.[21] There is resonance between value added in education and intrinsic human worth.[22] Any work is taking something (or someone) and extending it in a way that is deemed to be higher in value.

Second, the human dimension lies at the heart of an enterprise.

Wealth creation and economic dynamism or what is sometimes referred to as 'driving companies up the value chain' comes through releasing the value and talents of the people working for them. In any enterprise, the concept of human capital is being taken as vital. Coined in the 1960s by the economist Theodore Schultz,[23] the idea was that human capital was like any other type of capital: it could be invested in through education and training. Benefits will arise that will lead to an improvement in performance. Broadly speaking, it is about training, not natural ability, developing the human element in economic activity as a form of investment.

The notion of human capital is problematic. Have we fallen prey to the illusions of capitalism that all can be quantified? Is it time to ditch the very notion of 'social capital'? Social capital epitomises all this criticism; assuming this capital is social but other forms are not. The basic problem is treating social relations as physical in all but form; the imperative to accumulate capital. It displays a reductionism that recognises nothing but material interest and the maximisation of profit, regarding non-economic forms of capital as equivalent to the economic.

That aside, the concept of a labour theory of value has its roots in Adam Smith. Yet Karl Marx argued that training of the labour element in an organisation helped to explain wage differentials. The idea was developed more recently by economists such as Gary Becker of the University of Chicago.[24] A Nobel Prize winner, Becker has estimated that in a modern industrialised economy, 75–80 per cent of economic output comes from human capital as against land or machinery. Acquiring a skill with a specific application helps to generate production and therefore wealth. Wealth creation depends on human capital. According to Soumitra Dutta, Professor of Innovation at the INSEAD Business School, Fontainebleu, innovation has become a broader, horizontal concept.

We can talk of social innovation and market innovation. The need to invest in human capital has become much more apparent. Investment in human capital is not just the investment required in universities but in people as they go through their careers. 'You can only compete on the human mind and on the capacity of the human mind to create ideas and take them to market.'[25]

At first blush, it seems apparent that things are worth what they cost to make them. Yet, though superficially attractive (including to the president of South Africa at the time of writing),[26] the labour theory of value is problematic. It is by no means the case that all the effort of our labours results in something that can be traded. Also, as Adam Smith observed, there are many natural objects that have not had labour expended on them. Gemstones and berries have an economic value in their natural, unworked state. Marx failed to take into account that consumer demand changes over time and within time – wine that ferments over years is more valuable than wine that is newly made. The labour theory of value fails the need often for reforms in the labour market that are necessary. It also fails the test of what economists call 'time preference'. Consumer demand is usually for items that are readily purchasable here and now rather than waiting. If an item is sold on later, a worker cannot usually be expected to wait until he or she gets paid. A labour theory of value may have been valid for the first industrial revolution when machines began to do the work. The second wave of industrialisation early in the twentieth century when assembly lines took over meant that industries began to be less labour-intensive. But in the third wave, wage costs are growing less and less important because labour represents a small part of making and selling things. In 2012, a $499 first-generation i-Pad included only about $33 of labour costs.[27] Few items now reflect the cost of components and the labour that goes into their manufacture, rather the price that consumers are prepared to pay.

Productivity is more than investing in capital in the form of new machines or managing to boost the performance of the workforce. It seems that machinery and labour accounted for only 14 per cent of growth in the industrial era.[28] The value from human labour per se was limited. The missing 86 per cent was accounted for by energy efficiency: the extent to which energy and raw materials can be converted into work and output.[29] In the first industrial age it was unleashing the revolutionary power of the steam engine based on coal. The combination of coal and rail provided a platform that powered unprecedented growth and change. For example, by harnessing the power of the steam engine in the British textile industry, production of cotton soared exponentially from 22 million pounds in 1787 to 366 million pounds in 1840.[30] It was the first industrial economy. As Hobsbawm noted, 'it harnessed the power of a million horses in its steam engines, turned out two million yards of cloth in over seventeen million mechanical spindles, dug almost fifty million tons of coal'.[31]

As manufacturing goes digital, it will change how goods are made and therefore the human element. When jobs are automated away, the human element decreases. This is increasingly true of manufacturing and financial services. It is also increasingly true of the knowledge industry as witnessed, for example, by the growth of Massive Open Online Courses (MOOCs). An automated system is neutral with respect to human concerns; mechanical functions are not dependent on the emotions of the workforce. Nevertheless, even in an age of robotics the human dimension is still alive and present.

Replacing some bank workers with ATMs, for example, has made it cheaper to open new branches, creating many more new jobs in sales and customer service. E-commerce has increased overall employment in retailing. Replacement of jobs is likely to be more than offset by the creation of new jobs in the long term. In a wired-up world, production takes place anywhere. Supply chains leap continents. Global value chains are forged. This makes it increasingly hard for tax authorities to tax added value. The interplay of different forms of value changes in the Fourth Industrial Revolution, or 'Industry 4.0' as it was termed at the Hannover Fair in 2011. In an interconnected world replete with 'smart factories', virtual and physical systems of global production are flexible in the way they work together. Emerging technologies such as nanotechnology and quantum computing fuse with physical, biological and digital landscapes that are then diffused quickly. It took less than a decade for the Internet to go global. The infrastructure it created will enable very rapid transfer of technologies that harmonise biology, architecture or computing in completely new mutations.

In such an automated future, the human dimension is squeezed. As represented by units of wealth, value is created with far fewer workers than at the dawn of the third millennium. Value generated more and more by technology reflects huge capital investment but less labour. In 1990, the three largest companies in Detroit, that were then the centre of gravity of economic activity and worth $36 billion, employed about 1.2 million employees. In 2014, the three main companies in the new industrial hub of Silicon Valley were worth 30 times more but had ten times fewer employees.[32] The great majority of developed and growing economies have experienced a decline in the share of labour as a proportion of GDP. Returns to the factors of production are less to labour than to the investors and innovators who provide the capital. Increasingly, the robotics being used across all industrial sectors represents a substitution of capital for the human dimension. Information as the basis for economic goods can be transported and replicated at close to zero marginal costs. It is a vastly different world than that populated by labour-intensive industries.

As the on-demand economy grows, the relationship between employers and employees will shift fundamentally. As more employers use the human cloud to get things done, discrete units of work are parcelled out to anyone on the planet who can do the job. Employees are converted into independent workers. Aspiring workers are essentially self-employed; free of the regulations, pensions, national insurance and workers' rights that we have been used to. It will be a trade-off. A world of unregulated zero-hours contracts or enormous flexibility for people with Wi-Fi who can work anywhere they choose and accept that life is now a series of transactions with work opportunities anywhere. New forms of employment contracts will have to emerge that protect against exploitation where the model of work that has been a relatively stable relationship between employers and employees undergoes serious transition.[33]

Gender discrimination will be central to these concerns. At the going rate, economic parity will not be achieved round the world for over a hundred years.[34] Without it, organisations and societies in general will simply not be drawing on the talent available to them.

Will the automation avalanche adversely affect the role of women in society and in the workforce? It seems clear that significant job displacement will affect both female and male dominated professions. Cuts in jobs currently performed by working men – such as manufacturing and construction – will be savage. This has serious political consequences. But so too will jobs done by young female workers in developing markets such as call centres or admin work that provide livelihoods in more developed economies. The future for new jobs and opportunities remains to be written. At present, men still dominate in IT and engineering so increased demand in these areas will favour male workers as things stand. On the other hand, skills that automation and robots cannot replicate will be at a premium – such as providers of health care, coaches, therapists and psychologists. Traits and capabilities that have been associated with female professions will continue to be needed.

Disruption on a massive scale is on the way. It is a question of 'when?' not 'if'. As a result of disruptive innovations, the global economy is seeing an emergence of new industries, business models and behaviours. 3-D printing means manufacture can be customised. The way people are working is changing – technology, big data analysis, social media and ways of communicating are evolving. These developments will have a fundamental impact on how global business will attract, retain and motivate a skilled workforce. Organisational leaders of all kinds will have to ask radical questions about how this will affect them and what kind of value is generated that makes the digital economy a place of opportunity.

There are many voices in this growing introspection that is essentially about what it will mean to be a digital human. The commodification of the human dimension is exacerbated by the hugely ambiguous Internet: the infrastructure of the emerging 'third wave' of industrial technology. At the same time that democratisation of open access means anyone with a lap-top and smart phone is wired-up and connected 24/7, the big corporations have moved in. Most consumers do not realise the Faustian bargain struck as the Internet took off. When they visit websites, advertisers bid to sell. Following Facebook and Twitter contains a double-bind. You are being followed! Pressing the 'Like' or 'Tweet' buttons carries a code that means other websites can track users. On most popular websites, on any given day, around 1,300 companies are watching, observing and waiting.[35] By giving information about yourself, you have become a commodity. You are worth something to somebody.

Yet the new network economy based on information as an economic resource portends another reality – the rise of the 'networked individual'. These are able to draw freely on global knowledge that is an open source, able to operate in a network way across culture, consumption and relationships.[36] The move to networked individualism has expanded personal relationships beyond households and neighbourhoods; transformed work into less hierarchical, more team-driven enterprises; encouraged individuals to create and share content; and changed the way people obtain information.

When it comes to the future of work, at least two narratives are available. One is that robotics and automation squeeze the human dimension severely. The rise of the robots pushes humans to the wall as they take over tasks and drudgery but also learn to think. Accountants will have to look for employment elsewhere. The 'mission-creep' of algorithms has been a threat already; a threat that is on the rise. The human voices are becoming silent as we no longer talk to each other. Women's jobs will be even more at risk than those of men.

A second narrative is available. The Internet of Things (IOT) offers a relationship between things and people; between products, services and places that are enabled by the new platforms and connected technologies. Workers with skills are in great demand. It will remain the case that the human touch is what combines art and science to create something new. The effect of technological substitution will indeed be considerable; destroying many jobs. But many others will be created. Just as the numbers working in farming went down dramatically in the twentieth century and domestic service all but evaporated, there were many new employment possibilities created. Major social change was accomplished with minor disruption.

The possibilities lie between automation being a threat or technology enhancing the human dimension. That, however, is to polarise the debate. A theoretical lens is also available, the lens of object relations that mean the subject–object dichotomy blends, if not dissolves. As originally conceived by the psychoanalyst Karl Abrahams, 'object relations' offer a theory of relationships between people, in particular within a family and especially between the mother and her child. The key idea is that we are driven to form relationships with others. Failure to form successful early relationships leads to later problems. Yet the notion of object relations is also concerned with the relation between the subject and their internalised objects, as well as with external objects. Can this idea help dissolve the dichotomy between humans and robotics if we see humans as no longer playing subject to an object of technology but working with, being enhanced by it?

It is not either/or. The Fourth Industrial Revolution will have a major impact on the workplace and indeed global labour markets. Yet technology will have many positive elements that give cause for optimism. Witness the following.

It is the human dimension that has superintended and is interactive with robotic technology.

The possibility already exists of connecting human brains to the Internet. That truly opens the door to a potential future in which cyborgs, half-machine, half-human, are with us. That is, however, dystopian. The future need not be nearly so bleak.

The way we build social networks and use apps can amplify and accentuate the existing inequalities on the global scene. That does not have to be the last word, however. Optimism is both called for and highly appropriate.

Helper robots are now available that live with us, get us through the day, and yes, become trusted friends. User-friendliness is achieved through natural speech and affective computing which allows the AI to 'get to know you' by recognising the cycles of people's emotional states over time, inferring it from tone of voice and body language. The big names in the tech world, such as Google, Microsoft, Facebook and Apple are putting much effort into software that can understand language, known as chatbots, seeing them as the next big thing. According to Microsoft CEO Satya Nadella at the 2016 Build conference in San Francisco in March, chatbots, or 'conversations as a platform', are the next big thing in computing, as important as the shift to graphical user interfaces, the web browser and touchscreens.[37]

All these are important steps forward in the way humans interact with the digital era. 'As the internet revolution unfolds, we are seeing not merely an extension of mind but a unity of mind and machine, two networks coming together as one.'[38] Witness researchers within the University of South Wales' Genomics and Computational Biology research group who are making use of HPC Wales' supercomputing technology and services to help them revolutionise the way in which cancer is treated. As the project lead commented:

> One of the problems with cancer treatment is that drugs are not made specifically for individual patients: medicine should take into account a person's genotype, not just age and gender, and should be tailored to their needs. Computational biology

has the potential to do this. It is a tool used to rigorously and mathematically describe and investigate biological processes, impacting our understanding of genetics and healthcare. Computational biology has the potential to become one of the most important areas of scientific research in the twenty-first century.[39]

The potential is either dystopian or exciting. A fusion of digital, physical and biological technologies could enhance the human labour dimension. In such a future, the traditional (and largely artificial) division between arts and sciences begins to dissolve, with important consequences for the way young minds are shaped and steered.

The potential for technological change is staggering and accelerating. The World Economic Forum list of Top 10 Emerging Technologies 2016 at the time of writing includes a diverse range of breakthrough technologies, including batteries capable of providing power to whole villages, 'socially aware' artificial intelligence and new generation solar panels, that could soon be playing a role in tackling the world's most pressing challenges.

> Technology has a critical role to play in addressing each of the major challenges the world faces, yet it also poses significant economic and social risks. As we enter the Fourth Industrial Revolution, it is vital that we develop shared norms and protocols to ensure that technology serves humanity and contributes to a prosperous and sustainable future.[40]

What, though, about the potential for disruption in developing economies arising from labour substitution? It is in everyone's interest to ensure much of the world is not left behind while more developed economies surge ahead. More economic migrants will add to the flood of people on the move already. At present, the skills gap around the world seems to have decreased significantly as new IT hubs are operating in sophisticated ways. This could go into reverse. Automation and new technology are taking away jobs and fuelling growing inequality of income between the rich, who hold the capital, and the poor. Yet there are many hopeful voices suggesting that advanced technology will leapfrog stages of industrial development such as a strong manufacturing base and enable many parts of the world that are ready for it to leverage the Fourth Industrial Revolution. Witness Singularity University in Silicon Valley, which is about the convergence of exponential technologies to solving global challenges.[41] The aspirations are ambitious. The Grand Global Challenges range incudes:

- disaster relief
- food
- energy
- security
- health
- prosperity
- environment
- space
- water
- learning
- governance.

The last one is about equitable participation of all people in formal and societal governance in accordance with principles of justice and individual rights; free from discrimination and identity-based prejudices; and able to meet the needs of an exponentially changing world. Such is the promise of technology for the digital human; indeed a way of helping us to be more human, not less. The unmet needs of half the world can be met more fully as they are integrated into the global economy, connected with goods and services available worldwide that fuel demand.

In summary, it is highly possible that, as Lynda Gratton warns, the future of work will be marked by increasing levels of fragmentation, isolation, inequality and exclusion within societies experiencing the digital economy.[42] Yet there is a future available where a robot carries out a surgical operation with precision and under only the lightest of human supervision.[43] Robotic assistants are an attractive proposition to hospital managers: they tire not, neither do they strike. Whether patients will trust robots with their lives, or who is liable when things go wrong are other questions altogether. Intuitive Surgical, a maker of operating robots, have already had lawsuits claiming defective machines.

In the first wave of automation when the emphasis was on brawn power, factory output did not depend on the workers being happy. In the digital revolution undergirding the wave of automation that is already upon us, it will still be contented and creative cows that give the most milk, not just the robots.

Notes

1 Kelly, K. (1999), *New Rules for the New Economy*. New York and London: Penguin, p. 5.
2 Keynes, J.M. (1931), 'Economic Possibilities for our Grandchildren', in *Essays in Persuasion*. San Diego, CA: Harcourt Brace.
3 Rostow, W.W. (1978), *The World Economy: History and Prospect*. London: Macmillan.
4 Steed, C.D. (2011), *Let the Stones Talk: Glimpses of English History through the People of the Moor*. Milton Keynes: Authorhouse, p. 169.
5 Rubin, I.I. (1975), *Essays on Marx's Theory of Value*. London: Black Rose Books, p. 25.
6 Marx, K. (1975), *Economic and Philosophical Manuscripts: Early Writings*, London: Penguin, p. 325.
7 http://www.bankofengland.co.uk/publications/Pages/speeches/2015/864.aspx/, accessed May 2016.
8 Frey, C.B. and Osborne, M. (2013), *The Future of Employment: How Susceptible Jobs are to Computerisation*. Oxford: Oxford Martin School.
9 Deloitte LLP, 'UK benefiting from automation of work'. http://www.deloitte.co.uk/.
10 http://www.bankofengland.co.uk/publications/Pages/speeches/2015/864.aspx/, accessed May 2016.
11 Smith, A. (1776), *An Inquiry into the Nature and Causes of the Wealth of Nations*, ed. R. Campbell and A. Skinner, Book I, Chapter 5. Indianapolis, IN: Liberty Classics.
12 Smith (1776).
13 Ricardo, D. (1951), 'Absolute Value and Exchange Value', in *The Works and Correspondence of David Ricardo*, Vol. 4, Chapter 1, Section 1. Cambridge: Cambridge University Press.
14 Davenport, H.J. (1964), *Value and Distribution*. Reprints of economic classics. New York: Augustus M. Kelley Publishing, p. 56.
15 Marx, K. (1969), 'Critique of the Gotha Programme' in *Marx and Engels: Basic Writings on Politics and Philosophy*, Part V. London: Collins Fontana Library, pp. 153–174.
16 Brown, A. (2009), *The Rise and Fall of Communism*. London: The Bodley Head.
17 Nikolaus, M. (1973), 'Fragment on Machines', in Marx, K. *Grundrisse*. Harmondsworth: Penguin.
18 Sennett, R. (2008), *The Craftsman*. London: Allen Lane.

19 Crawford, M. (2009), *Shop Class as Soulcraft: An Inquiry into the Value of Work*. London: Penguin.
20 Mason, P. (2015), *Post Capitalism: A Guide to the Future*. London: Allen Lane.
21 Schultz, T. (1963), *The Economic Value of Education*. New York: Columbia University Press and Schultz, T. (1971), *Investment in Human Capital: The Role of Education and of Research*. New York: Free Press.
22 Becker, G.S. (1964), *Human Capital: A Theoretical and Empirical Analysis with Special Reference to Education*. New York: NBER.
23 Schultz, T. (1962), *Investment in Human Beings*. Chicago: University of Chicago Press.
24 Becker (1964).
25 Dutta, S. (2009), 'Innovation. Speaking from Davos', *You and Yours*, BBC Radio 4, 30 January 2009.
26 Jacob Zuma, president of South Africa, reportedly said in 2015 that the value of commodities should depend on 'the labour time taken in production'. *The Economist*, 19 December 2015.
27 'The Third Industrial Revolution', *The Economist*, 21 April 2012.
28 Abramovitz, M. (1989), *Thinking about Economic Growth: And Other Essays on Economic Growth and Welfare*. Cambridge: Cambridge University Press.
29 Ayres, R.U. and Ayres, E.H. (2010), *Crossing the Energy Divide: Moving from Fossil Fuel Dependence to a Clean Energy Future*. Upper Saddle River, NJ: Wharton School Publishing.
30 Debeir, J.-C., Deléage, J.-P. and Hémery, D. (1992), *In the Servitude of Power: Energy and Civilisation through the Ages*. London: Zed Books.
31 Young A., *Tours in England and Wales*. London: LSE, p. 269, quoted in Hobsbawm, E. (1977), *The Age of Revolution*. London: Abacus, p. 68.
32 'Digital Era brings Hyperscale Advantages'. *Financial Times*, 13 August 2014.
33 Pink, D. (2001), *Free Agent Nation: The Future of Working for Yourself*. New York: Grand Central Publishing.
34 *World Economic Forum Gender Gap Report 2015*, 10th edn.
35 *The Economist*, Special Report, 13 September 2014.
36 Rainie, L. and Wellman, B. (2012), *Networked: The New Social Operating System*. Cambridge, MA: MIT Press.
37 'Conversation as a Platform', 'Build' technology conference, San Francisco, March 2016.
38 'The Coming Merge of Human and Machine Intelligence'. now.tufts.edu/articles/coming-merge-human-and-machine-intelligence/, accessed May 2016.
39 Tatarinova, 'Fighting Cancer: How Supercomputing is Helping to Make the Impossible, Possible'. http://www.hpcwales.co.uk/fighting-cancer/, accessed June 2016.
40 Jeremy Jurgens, Chief Information and Interaction Officer, Member of the Executive Committee, World Economic Forum Newsletter, June 2016.
41 http://singularityu.org/, accessed May 2016.
42 Gratton, L. (2011), *The Shift: The Future of Work is Already Here*. London: Collins.
43 Kim, P., (2016), 'Supervised Autonomous Robotic Soft Tissue Surgery', *Science Translational Medicine*, 8 (337), 337–64.

Chapter 5

The creation and conversion of shared value

> You can't singularly maximise profit, or any one thing, in a company or a system and expect that system to thrive.
>
> Raj Sisodia, Shared Value Leaders Summit, 2016[1]

A question of definition

Creating value is what organisations do all day.

In their particular field, it could be the generation of financial value, it could be the creation of wealth through productive processes of manufacture; it could be the generation of added value in schools and colleges or generating non-measurable forms of value in not-for-profit sectors ranging from faith-based organisations to artistic endeavour. All this is well-trodden ground. What breaks new ground here is how the generation of value digs into the motivational drivers of human action.

It is in the self-interest of organisations generally to fathom the conditions that unlock the inner value their participants have so that it can lead to value added and productive environments. These considerations become sharply accentuated as computers take over routine brain jobs and despatch countless people to the dole queue. What we have been noting essentially is that a unit of economic value, of wealth, is created today with far few workers than before. This trend can only increase as people are replaced by algorithms. Will it still be the case that in a world where you can buy so much computer power off the shelf, the competitive advantage of organisations lies in the quality of their employees? At issue in this book is how the workplace can be a productive environment; productive not because of the output per se but because the conditions are in place for people to flourish. Can you have the former without the latter?

The simple proposition being advocated here – that where people feel valued, where felt human value increases, economic value will increase – sounds like a re-run of a tea and sympathy style of management. It is far more than that. What is needed is hard-headed recognition that the two realms are interdependent. The former provides an index for the latter. It is in the interests of economic units or organisations, from companies to schools, to work with such an index, that accumulating value capital of participants will lead to more being achieved and of higher quality, not just quantity.

Human activity in organisations flourishes at its optimum when people are valued and the link between the two is optimised. The value added by the contribution of personnel, whether managers or staff and workers, is related to the productive energies they bring to their task. That in turn is related to motivation and morale. However, there is a problem:

that of the apparently familiar and obvious. To assert, for instance, that 'the sixth principle of naked leadership is that everyone is valued'[2] would, for many, be like apple pie or motherhood. A fruitful starting point to carve out analytical space is the negative factors that drive disengagement or demoralisation and hence to carve out a space for a valuing environment in which our humanity is nourished.

Triple bottom line (TBL) accounting has become increasingly fashionable in recent years in such diverse organisations as management, consulting, investing and non-governmental organisations. The idea is that the performance of an organisation should be measured not just by the traditional financial bottom line but by its social and environmental impact. The new aspect of TBL is that the sum total of a company's obligations to all stakeholders should be quantified on the basis that 'if you can measure it, you can manage it' – the adage of modern business. Norman and MacDonald argued that the rhetoric is in fact misleading, that TBL is an unhelpful addition to the theory and practice of how firms demonstrate their total impact on their world. Indeed, the triple bottom line can become a smokescreen for avoiding social and environmental impact that is truly effective.[3]

The production of value is the *raison d'être* of organisations. Can we make an equation between inputs (the human dimension) and the outputs, the added value that typifies what the organisation is in being for? But what is value?

Keen defines value as 'the innate worth of a commodity, which determines the normal ("equilibrium") ratio at which two commodities exchange'.[4] Value is defined in the *Oxford English Dictionary* as 'the amount of money something is worth'. There is a second definition. Value is also 'the importance or worth of something'.[5] The study of the concept of economic value has a rich history in the economic literature.

These two definitions are conflicted when it comes to how different forms of value cohere. Marketing strives to utilise the 'value proposition', the difference between a customer's evaluation of benefits and costs. In investment decisions, value is crucial for the determination of share marketisation. In economics, value is a measure of the benefit that may be gained from goods or services or the maximum amount of money a specific actor is willing and able to pay for the good or service.

Through the concepts of 'value in use' or 'value in exchange', there are differing metrics for the assessment of value, for example comparing water with diamonds. Marx made much of these distinctions, emphasising the labour that had gone into the production of an exchangeable commodity. His 'labour theory of value' was largely replaced by the prevalence of supply and demand as the twin-sisters that determine price and value. For the Austrian economist Ludwig von Mises, exchange value was always the result of subjective value judgements. There was no price of objects or things that could be determined without taking these market-based judgements into account. There is little meaning in discussing the market value of an item without reference to what that is worth to a given individual or set of individuals. This is problematic. There is such a thing as a property market and range of prices that is independent of particular purchasers though it could be argued that house prices reflect the value to them personally of thousands of individual purchasers!

When it comes to the production of other forms of value, there is a considerable variation as to what this means in practice. How does one compare the value of a work of art with educational benefit or other forms of value that are not tangible? A not-for-profit organisation or faith-based community will try to generate things that are worth something to a great many people but which are less susceptible to market evaluation. There is a whole range of services rendered against which it is far harder to affix price than against tangible goods. The production of value differs between organisations.

- The manufacturing industry – here there are measurable outcomes. Value is added at various stages of production or processing, subject in most instances to Value Added Tax.
- The financial services industry – where the value generated through transaction derives from lubrication of the whole production economy.
- The knowledge industry – educational institutions or those involved in cultural production such as broadcasters attempt to generate results that can answer the question, 'is this activity worth it?'
- The creative arts – where value is sharply dependent on the perceived worth of the artist.
- Community and faith-based organisations – where social value or spiritual impact is vital.

Shareholder (or shared) value

In the industrial revolution, wealth creation came to the fore as a mode of life and way of organising society. 'Value' was primarily about quantifiable output. The foot soldiers of industrial society were those who could be productive through demonstrating an exchange value in the global marketplace. The new world was based on restless output and an unprecedented leap forward in output and productivity to achieve higher rates of output at less cost than your competitors.

The capitalist world economy, as Wallerstein noted, was constructed by integrating a vast set of production processes, the establishment of a single division of labour. It is based on the endless accumulation of capital, upon workers working harder and more efficiently, thus creating greater output. 'Since its outset, the capitalist world economy has had ever more productive activity, ever more "value" produced, ever more population, ever more inventions.'[6] It is based on limitless expansion. It is only by becoming 'competitive' that individuals and groups may obtain what others already have. Until then, unequal incomes remain.

It required the factory approach to systematic ways of working, of mechanical efficiency, the application of bureaucracy and standardisation; all to achieve output, output and ever greater output and boost productivity. As Max Weber described, this technocratic mindset is the essence of modernity. The purpose was to achieve quantity; output on a vast scale, an 'industrial' scale. What is measured can be captured, 'mastered' (I use the term deliberately), then undertaken. The management historian Alfred Chandler documents how the need for vastly more capital, workers and managers spread across the capitalist world economy. The managerialism needed for such growth in scale and corporate power became the pre-condition for business success. As its main drive, the visible hand of managers had replaced Adam Smith's invisible hand of market forces.[7]

It would be misleading to characterise the industrial age as just being about output and quantity. That it was also about quality – through such management approaches as Total Quality Management – attests to the continuing consumer revolution. What counted was not just producing more and more but producing items the customer wanted. This was the chief difference between the command and control economy typical of communist countries (with five-year plans) and capitalist economies that responded far more dynamically and flexibly to what people wished to buy.

In tandem with the industrial revolution there was a consumer and also a financial revolution. It was a vital means of bringing the ever-expanding need for private finance into industry. In turn, this contributed hugely to a vision of capitalism that was closely linked to the charter of personal freedom articulated in the Enlightenment in the days of Adam Smith and Immanuel Kant – the freedom to advance one's own interests by providing goods and services to others. It was not just shareholder value per se that built the modern world.

There is a growing mood that the future of business is not just about meeting traditional needs through traditional customers but lies in some concept of shared value. As articulated in a seminal paper by Porter and Kramer from Harvard Business School in 2011, the new initiative around 'Shared Value' is testament to a growing mood that business needs to be socially responsible; not divorced from its social context.[8] In the wake of a low period for the reputation of capitalism as a way of organising the economy and society, the concept of shared value forced a rethink of the role of business in society.

There had always been many voices urging that the nineteenth-century model of what was often exploitative capitalism (a sharp polarisation between capital and labour) needed serious revision. Workers' rights and health and safety legislation created a framework for a more humane approach. Philanthropy by some was seen as a way of demonstrating that business could be a force for good and that, though its role was clearly to make money, money could also be given away in good causes. Then Corporate Social Responsibility (CSR) took business to another level. There were then numerous positive things that companies were doing. Along with the idea of business acting ethically, such positive stories dramatically increased.

The Shared Value concept, however, took things to another level. Shared Value is different. It is about using the business to meet social needs and strengthen the communities within which business operates. Using a business model to solve problems is self-sustaining. Once the engine of using a business model to generate social impact, it can be scaled. It was about harnessing the dynamism of the private sector to drive change. How businesses can solve problems had not always been possible in addressing the social agenda. How businesses understood their role needed to be thought through, that societal impact was not a separate matter but fundamental to what commercial companies – not just charities – do. Given a business model and a profit, the private sector could generate sustainability and scale-ability through harnessing the potential of business so it is integrated with social impact. Given that the days are over when government income can be generated on a scale that meets social needs, large-scale transformation can only be made possible through this means. As Michael Porter has eloquently argued since, there is a growing disconnection between social challenges and the resources society has to address those challenges.[9] Conversely, there is a direct line of sight between the economic and social. If we can solve a problem like nutrition while generating income, that is transformative. The challenge is for investable and marketable socially enterprising solutions which address unmet social needs in original and innovative ways.

A new lens on the corporate relationship to society could mean the business manuals will have to be rewritten.

Elsewhere, I have argued that 'Marching to a different drum' means that we must have a far wider, more distributed notion of value to address uneven development, accelerated globalisation, economic uncertainty, and entrenched and complex social problems that characterise the capitalism of the early twenty-first century.[10] The bottom line that every manager operating in a commercial environment needs to attend to is more than just financial. Since enterprises cannot do well if they do not do good, it is also about operating within a holistic understanding of well-being, paying attention to 'the common good' (i.e. the social ecology). It is about paying attention to the well-being of staff and workers, about 'the power footprint' with which the organisation influences those it deals with plus the need to attend to issues of quality, not just quantity. If such factors impact the bottom line, it is in the enlightened self-interest of every capitalistic enterprise, let alone other organisations seeking to add value, to attend to them.

To summarise here, it means:

- the financial bottom line
- the social ecology
- the well-being of employees and participants
- the power footprint
- issues of quality as well as quantity – human relationships and the scarce commodity of time.

The value chain differs from organisation to organisation. Increasingly, it will be networked, digitally enabled and integrated into the wider economy. Yet, however defined, the value chain always uses resources and affects the health and well-being of employees. If an organisation is not realising the potential of its employees, it is wasting resources. Building an environment of value is not just about the internalities of an organisation. Whatever the product, the generation of value always has a social impact. The life and times of organisations and of business are always affected by the surrounding community but also its people.

It is that point that particularly concerns us here, the value generated by those participating in an organisation that is a crucial input into an equation.

The equation

To varying degrees, the external value generated in each of these spheres of activity depends on the active engagement of the human participants. Deploying post-doctoral work in the context of client observation inside and outside organisations, we probe here the circumstances within which participants perceive themselves as valued – or not. As we will explore, it is the contrast pole, the negative experiences of being disvalued, that throws particular light on the ingredients for what I shall term 'environments of value'. Environments of value are valuing environments that enable a conversion to take place which is crucial for whether organisations will flourish: the creation of value. The construct proposed in this book is in two parts:

1   That there is a strong association between the sense of inner-world value held by staff or workers as they participate in an organisation AND the added, external value they generate that furthers its purpose.

2   That wise leaders understand it is in the interests of the organisation to optimise those factors (proposed here as essentially threefold) that enable a valuing environment to translate inner value into added value.

It could be a company that learns how to help its workforce to be productive and effective. It could be a hospital that sets up the right conditions within which both patient and staff care can become a reality. It could be a school or place of learning that draws out the potential of students and staff and adds measurable value to its record. Or it could be a not-for-profit organisation, charity and faith community endeavouring to fulfil a social mission through setting up a climate within which customers and clients realise their possibilities and live more fulfilling lives.

How leaders transmute that human capital into value for the organisation is a crucial conversion. This is highly relevant to the concerns of this book and its proposals. There is an assumption that the connection between inner value or sense of worth and external value is not just a word.

The answer to this question has a great deal to do with 'value'. Clearly, as noted, it depends exactly what is meant by that term. There are different forms of value, depending on the output. If what is being produced is a work of art to be sold on the market, value will not be the same as some additional transformation of a product or raw material in a supply chain that will then be the subject of 'value added tax'. That too will be different from 'added value' in a school. In not-for-profit organisations such as charities and faith-based organisations, value is assessed in ways that are akin to influence, effective transformations or 'soft power'.

To be clear at the outset, we will be making a strong correlation between inner, subjective value and the external and rather more tangible value by which an organisation assesses its output. It is therefore within enlightened self-interest for leadership and management teams to act as catalysts for this intrinsic connection. They do after all want more from their workers so as to further the aims and/or profit of the organisation.

The question beyond that is a key issue for organisations of all kinds, whatever the productive task. The insights we will be exploring are fairly well understood, though not necessarily expressed in this way. Why does the producer not always work with what common sense might suggest is the best way to get more out of people? If it is obvious how to create positive cultures that are in the self-interest of leaders and senior staff teams, why would they not put this understanding into practice?

One way of lifting people out of poverty is to boost pay. The minimum wage is a national anti-poverty benchmark to ensure that there is a basic wage. An exploitative capitalism might simply maximise profit by minimising cost, especially cutting corners in pay and conditions. An enlightened business environment, though, is one that recognises there is no deep opposition between ensuring that its staff are paid a basic wage (a social goal) and that they are productive, thus bringing the firm benefit (a commercial decision). This was a strong emphasis in the writings of Warren Bennis, a pioneer in leadership studies and staunch critic of lack of leadership. There is no point in employing knowledge workers if you are not going to use their knowledge creatively!

The well-being of society is inseparable from added value that comes from corporate performance (the former is the context for the latter). Human well-being must be seen in an integrated framework. Another term for this is 'the common good'.[11] Shared value is not just a question of two dimensions converging. A third aspect must also be added to shared value: the well-being that comes from personal, inner wealth. The intersection between society and corporate value needs to be complemented with the human value of its participants. I argue too that the broader understanding of value needed in a digital future needs to include the power footprint of an organisation and also generating quality, not just quantity. This is represented by the following:

- inner value of workers – the value of what they produce (quality and quantity);
- value added for the organisation (returns to capital);
- value for the social context of the organisation;
- power footprint (the effect an organisation has);
- quality of participants' experience (staff and customers).

Human flourishing is deeply rooted in those who feel engaged in feel worthwhile pursuits. When the value that is within us is nurtured through interpersonal relationships or cultivated by social policies, it is released and translates into an added value for tasks we do within organisations and wider society. Put simply, people are more productive when they feel that the value placed on them or that they discover counteracts and transcends social pressures that devalue them. This is why staff retention and productivity go hand in hand with being engaged, to being involved or to negotiating one's own hours.

Evidence for the link between inner and outer value

A growing body of management theory reflects the notion that employees need to feel valued in order to draw out personal value and add value to an organisation. Understanding the circumstances in which people feel valued or disvalued is vital for nurturing the strong association between inner and external, added value. Is there, however, any evidence for the proposition that an enabling environment that translates its input into outputs in this way will generate greater prosperity for the organisation? The following examples suggest that there is indeed an association between the sense of value felt by workers and staff as they participate in the organisation AND the outcomes. What follows must not be overdrawn. It concerns the human dimension, the labour element of capital accumulation.

The notion of organisational culture is cast in terms of 'environments of value' within which value is released. Clearly, there are differing metrics for the assessment of value. Organisational culture is shot through with the human dynamics that wise leaders need to understand. At its most basic, within the environmental conditions of that organisation, low motivation leads to poor performance. By contrast, building the right kind of culture is a vital ingredient of success. A positive climate adds to the bottom line.

'Environments of Value' are those that draw out the value and worth of their participants and translate that into added value. This is the first element of a construct proposed in these pages. It can be constructed as the translation of labour into capital. Two types of value are in the frame here. They seem on the surface to pertain to two different, incommensurable realms. Yet there is no essential dualism between the inner, felt value of human participants in an enterprise and the externalised value that becomes measurable and that contributes to the purpose of an organisation. At issue here is how the workplace can be productive environments; productive not because of the output per se but because the conditions are in place for people to flourish. Can you have the former without the latter?

A theory is needed of the link between how these different forms of value come together. How can workplace environments be productive? As soon as we ask the question, 'what is the way to be a human being and not just homo economicus?' we are catapulted into issues of value. Hard-headed companies do not just endeavour to create a sense of value amongst the workforce because of a social mission such as schools might have. Policies have to create value for the firm. It is a common enough observation in the Western management literature. Even though management practices are culturally constructed, it is well established that low motivation leads to poor performance.

The Global Reporting Initiative (GRI), the largest and most widely used ESG reporting entity (environmental, social and governance factors), has encompassed both the 'value' (financial impact) and 'values' (normative behaviour) perspectives, reflecting its status as a multi-stakeholder association of advocacy groups, non-profits, investors and others. In a related Report by the Harvard University Business School Investor Responsibility Research Centre Institute (IRRCi), Beeferman and Bernstein demonstrated 'The Materiality of Human Capital to Corporate Financial Performance'.[12] The focus for the impact on financial performance had largely been on environmental and governance matters. By contrast, Beeferman and Bernstein emphasised social factors, specifically those involving how companies manage workplace relationships.

> Our survey of the literature on human capital found 92 empirical studies that examined the relationship between HR policies and financial outcomes such as return on equity, return on investment and profit margins. We conclude that there is sufficient evidence of human capital materiality to financial performance to warrant inclusion in standard investment analysis.[13]

Beeferman and Bernstein pointed out that most institutional investors are largely unaware of the extensive evidence that already exists about the materiality of human capital factors. This is understandable given that most of the studies in the field have not been framed from the perspective of investment analysis. Human capital research has been undertaken in hundreds of studies encompassing a multitude of disciplines: numerous studies have been done in the fields of economics, labour studies, human resource management, psychology and sociology, but investment outcomes have been a concern only in a minority of them. Beeferman and Bernstein concluded that 'corporate training and other HR policies, if implemented correctly, can enhance financial performance.'[14]

One of the most forceful statements of this conclusion came in a 2003 report by a Task Force on Human Capital Management (HCM) established by the British Secretary of State for Trade and Industry, which included several high-level executives of prominent British companies. It concluded:

> HCM should not be regarded solely as an internal matter for management. For most organisations the link between HCM policies and practices and performance is

sufficiently central to be a material factor whose disclosure might reasonably be expected to influence assessments of their value and effective stewardship by management. In such cases disclosure increases the value of financial reports and will be important for the effective operation of capital markets.[15]

Creating a culture of organisational well-being is a vital factor in a successful operation. It is linked with such outcomes as productivity, employee retention and, crucially, engagement. Using a metric of employee engagement, based on the Q^{12} survey, which consists of 12 actionable items with proven links to performance outcomes, the polling organisation Gallup discovered that only one-third (32 per cent) of workers in the US could really be said to be engaged at work. The research categorised workers into engaged, not engaged or – worst of all – actively disengaged. People who are engaged at work use their strengths, know what is expected of them and believe their job matters. Gallup did a study of more than 5,000 full-time workers in the US about their engagement in the workplace.

A year later they re-surveyed them using the same questions.

> We wanted to understand how the elements of wellbeing, engagement, and culture complement and influence each other. ... If people had higher wellbeing in year one, they would tend to have higher engagement in year two and a more positive change in engagement in year two.[16]

The evidence is that the link between individual well-being and company well-being is complex. People that have high individual well-being are more likely to see their workplace as positive, productive and engaging. Conversely, if they are struggling or suffering, it rubs off on the workplace and the team. 'When you have an engaging team, you're more likely to have an open and trusting culture,' Gallup found. 'That encourages people to talk openly about wellbeing in ways that positively influence each other's wellbeing.' These positive changes in individual well-being and employee engagement fed further improvements in well-being and engagement, completing a healthy organisational cycle. Distilling the research, Gallup proposed three types of employees:

- Engaged employees who work with a passion and feel a profound connection to their organisation. They move the organisation forward.
- Not-engaged employees who are essentially 'checked out'. They sleepwalk through their workday, putting time, but not energy or enthusiasm, into their work.
- Actively disengaged employees who are not just unhappy but act out their unhappiness, undermining what senior staff and engaged colleagues produce.

Employees who are engaged and thriving also have greater agility and resilience. 'When people are engaged and have thriving wellbeing, their life situations don't weigh them down and keep them from performing,' Gallup observed. 'They see changes as opportunities, not problems.' It is clear that leadership can make a substantial difference in employee well-being and engagement, the two major factors that seem to affect employee performance. Compared with employees who have high engagement but otherwise exhibit low levels of well-being, those who are engaged *and* who have high well-being in at least four of the five elements are 30 per cent more likely not to miss any workdays because of poor health in any given month. They also miss 70 per cent fewer workdays because of poor health over the course of a year.

Case study – Managers blamed for NHS deficits

In a recent hard-hitting report by the UK Audit Commission, the worst deficits in the National Health Service were blamed on inadequate leadership and ineffective management.[17] The Commission's report – *Learning the Lessons from Financial Failure in the NHS* – was in line with subsequent studies; for instance, *NHS Staff Management and Health Service Quality* of 2011 undertaken by a team of independent researchers at Aston Business School.[18] The results, despite coming from a variety of methods, data sets and years, delivered a clear general message about the importance of staff experience for outcomes. In general terms, the more positive the experiences of staff within an NHS trust, the better the outcomes for that trust. This is shown across many different domains of staff experience. Engagement was shown to be particularly important: having significant associations with patient satisfaction, patient mortality, infection rates, annual health check scores, as well as staff absenteeism and turnover. The conclusion was clear. The more engaged staff members are, the better the outcomes for patients and the organisation generally.

It seems clear that it makes sense for companies to be agreeable to employees because it is in their self-interest to do so. It is otherwise a squandering of investment. There is nothing new about this perspective. Since 1914, Lincoln Electric in the US regularly consulted its workers. From his experiences in the Second World War, the boss of Johnson & Johnson vowed to put people before profit. Procter & Gamble has long since delegated power to teams of workers. This is more than paternalism. America's highest-performing companies have all been included in the annual 'Employee Ownership 1000'. Worker-friendly companies regularly out-perform those whose profit margin is the only truth.[19]

Other strands of evidence for the (intuitive?) association between intrinsic and extrinsic value are:

- Indicators of staff well-being in hospitals and MRSA infection[20] (presumably because staff with higher psychological well-being behave differently).[21]
- Clear concern for employees came out highest in a study of eight predictive factors to do with the climate within 42 industrial companies linked to productivity gains (measured by financial value of net sales per employee).[22]
- In the service sector, where staff well-being is higher, they are more likely to 'go the extra mile' and fix problems that affect customer satisfaction.[23]

Positive relationships exist between psychological well-being (PWB) and job performance (a better indicator, it seems, than job satisfaction). An increase of 1 on an ascending scale of 1–5 measuring PWB is associated with an 8.8 per cent boost in productivity.[24]

A large-scale study from nearly 8,000 separate business units in 36 companies showed a significant relationship between scores of well-being on an employee survey and such business-level outcomes as customer satisfaction, profitability, employee turnover and levels of sickness and absence.[25]

The question is: why? What accounts for these associations? What are the conditions in which the inner source of value is translated into the enterprise?

Notes

1 http://www.sharedvalue.org/groups/livestream-shared-value-leadership-summit-2016/, accessed May 2016.
2 Taylor, D. (2003), *The Naked Leader*. London: Bantam, p. 28.
3 Norman, W., and MacDonald, C. (2004), 'Getting to the Bottom of "Triple Bottom Line"', *Business Ethics Quarterly*, 14 (2), pp. 243–262.
4 Keen, S. (2001), *Debunking Economics*. New York: Zed Books, p. 271.
5 *Oxford English Dictionary* (2000), compact edition. Oxford: Oxford University Press.
6 Wallerstein, I. (1990), 'Culture as the Ideological Battleground', in *Global Culture: Nationalisation, Globalisation and Modernity*, ed. M. Featherstone. London: Sage, p. 37.
7 Chandler, A. (1977), *The Visible Hand: The Managerial Revolution in American Business*. Cambridge, MA: Belknap Press.
8 Porter, M., and Kramer, M. (2011), 'Creating Shared Value', *Harvard Business Review*, February 2011.
9 Witness the discussions at the Shared Value Initiative Summit, May 2014.
10 Steed, C.D. (2016), *A Question of Worth: Economy, Society and the Quantification of Human Value*. London: I.B.Tauris.
11 Felber, C. (2015), *Change Everything: Creating an Economy for the Common Good*. London: Zed Books.
12 Beeferman, L. and Bernstein, A. (2015), 'The Materiality of Human Capital to Corporate Financial Performance', The Labor and Worklife Program at Harvard Law School, April 2015.
13 http://www.sharedvalue.org/groups/livestream-shared-value-leadership-summit-2016/, accessed May 2016.
14 Beeferman and Bernstein (2015), pp. 1–66.
15 Task Force on Human Capital Management (2003), *Accounting for People Report*. UK Department for Trade and Industry. http://webarchive.nationalarchives.gov/.uk/20090609003228/ http://www.berr.gov.uk/files/file38839.pdf/.
16 Harter, J. (Gallup's chief scientist of workplace management and well-being), *Gallup Business Journal*, 27 October 2015. Results are based on a Gallup Panel Web study completed by 24,230 national adults, aged 18 and older, conducted 8 October – 13 November 2014, and a Gallup Panel Web study completed by 24,658 national adults, aged 18 and older, conducted 2 December 2014 – 14 January 2015. A subsample of 9,689 working adults, obtained after matching the above two surveys, was used for this analysis. The Gallup Panel is a probability-based longitudinal panel of US adults who are selected using random-digit-dial (RDD) phone interviews that cover landline and cellphones. Address-based sampling methods are also used to recruit panel members. The Gallup Panel is not an opt-in panel, and members are not given incentives for participating. The sample for this study was weighted to be demographically representative of the US adult population using 2014 Current Population Survey figures. For results based on this sample, one can say that the maximum margin of sampling error is ±2 percentage points at the 95 per cent confidence level. Margins of error are higher for sub-samples. In addition to sampling error, question wording and practical difficulties in conducting surveys can introduce error and bias into the findings of public opinion polls.
17 *Learning the Lessons from Financial Failure in the NHS*, http://www.publicfinance.co.uk/news/ 2006/07/nhs-deficits-blamed-weak-management/, July 2006, accessed February 2016.
18 *NHS Staff Management and Health Service Quality*, http://www.gov.uk/government/publica tions/nhs-staff-management-and-health-service-quality/, August 2011, accessed February 2016.
19 Waterman, R. (1994), *What America Does Right*. New York: W.W. Norton.
20 Boorman, S. (2009), *NHS Health and Well-being – Final Report*. London: Department of Health.

21 Robertson, I. and Cooper, C. (2011), *Well-Being: Productivity and Happiness at Work*. Basingstoke: Palgrave Macmillan.
22 Patterson, M., *et al.* (2004), 'Organisational Climate and Company Productivity: The Role of Employee Affect and Employee Level', *Journal of Occupational and Organisational Psychology*, 77, pp. 193–216.
23 Moliner, C., *et al.* (2008), 'Organisational Justice and Extra-role Customer Service: The Mediating Role of Well-being at Work', *European Journal of Work and Organisational Psychology*, 17, pp. 327–348.
24 Wright, T.A., and Cropanzo, R. (2000), 'Psychological Well-Being and Job Satisfaction as Predictors of Job Performance', *Journal of Occupational Health Psychology*, 5, pp. 84–94.
25 Harter, J.K. *et al.* (2003), 'Well-being in the Workplace and its Relationship to Business Outcomes: A Review of the Gallup Studies', in *Flourishing, Positive Psychology and the Life Well-lived*, ed. C.L.M. Keyes and J. Haidt. Washington, DC: American Psychological Society.

Chapter 6

Three ingredients of a valuing environment: Proposing a construct

> Every leader wants to bring out the best in their teams. Those same leaders, without knowing it, are probably doing some things that actually have the opposite effect.
>
> Liz Wiseman, Willow Creek Global Leadership Summit, 2015[1]

We have been considering the way that 'shared value' must come to mean that value is generated and then shared through a creative process in which humans and robotics are working alongside each other. Value is emanating from that blend. Where technological displacement is a major risk, it is not a question of automation streamlining the element but replacing it. There is a more hopeful future where the human dimension is nurtured and cultivated. There is a strong link between organisational culture and profit, specifically between inner value when that is unlocked and the added value for the organisation. It is essentially the relationship in economics between labour and capital.

In many countries, there are skill shortages. Either the labour is not there in sufficient quantity to ensure economies can grow or there is a productivity problem with the efficiency of labour. What organisations get out of their labour per hour is not as great as what could be achieved. What we are arguing here is that, although considerably reduced, the human dimension will continue to be critical in the digital age.

In a time when customers have access to vast amounts of data about a company, its product and its competitors, customer experience becomes increasingly important as a sustainable source of competitive advantage. But success does not just rely on digital engagement and excellence, but on combining a digital-first attitude with a human touch. In *When Digital Becomes Human*, Steven Van Belleghem explores and explains the new digital relationships. Companies can learn to integrate an emotional layer into their digital strategy, combining two of a business's most important assets – its people and its digital strengths – in an era when digital marketing and the management of customer experience are crucial ingredients.[2]

The free market, with its message of globalisation and the primacy of growth and GDP as a measure of happiness, is under siege. The economic crisis that still affects global conditions has not led to any fundamental reappraisal of how to operate the capitalist way of working ... 'working lives are becoming more precarious.'[3] As the Fourth Industrial Revolution takes hold, hierarchies have been flattened, and old command and control structures are no longer seen as the best or the only option. New styles are needed to replace traditional methods. The organisation rising on the digital scene is one powered by talent and valuing the human.[4]

This is borne out by the findings of a recent (2016) study on the expectations of the generation who have now come of age. In some respects, though, the attitude and expectations of millennials has changed as a result of the economic downturn in many parts of the world. The downturn has had a significant impact on the loyalty millennials feel towards their employers. In 2008, 75 per cent expected to have between two and five employers in their lifetime but in this survey the proportion has fallen to 54 per cent. Over a quarter now expect to have six employers or more, compared with just 10 per cent in 2008. Tough times have forced many millennials to make compromises when finding a job – 72 per cent feel they made some sort of trade-off to get into work. Voluntary turnover is almost certain to increase as economic conditions improve; 38 per cent of millennials who are currently working said they were actively looking for a different role and 43 per cent said they were open to offers. Only 18 per cent expect to stay with their current employer for the long term.[5] With technology dominating every aspect of millennials, lives, it is perhaps not surprising that 41 per cent say they prefer to communicate electronically at work than face to face or even over the telephone. Millennials routinely make use of their own technology at work and three-quarters believe that access to technology makes them more effective at work. Yet, technology is often a catalyst for intergenerational conflict in the workplace and many millennials feel held back by rigid or outdated working styles.

Against this background, I propose a new construct with which to understand better what goes on in the life and times of organisations, especially when it comes to change management. How to create positive cultures in which to foster success is a vital issue. Changing the culture of an organisation when the organisation is failing is not just a question of amending one aspect of what it does, such as its public message or branding. The problem may well be systemic. It may well be a case of shifting a micro-culture towards a very different style, not just a brand change – internal, not just external. We explore that it is the role of leaders to build positive cultures within their organisations against the backcloth of empirical factors that generate their opposite.

Rooted in the notion that organisational success or competitive advantage is achieved through its workforce, the proposition for a new construct is this. Human activity in organisations flourishes to best advantage when people are valued and the link between inner inputs and external value is optimised. The value added by the contribution of personnel, whether managers or staff and workers, is related to the productive energies they bring to their task. That in turn is related to motivation and morale.

The construct proposed in this study is in two parts:

- That there is a strong association between the sense of inner-world value held by staff or workers as they participate in an organisation AND the added, external value they generate that furthers its purpose.
- That smart leaders understand it is in the interests of the organisation to optimise those factors (proposed here as essentially threefold) that enable a valuing environment to translate inner value into added value.

'Environments of Value' are primarily the internal environment of the organisation but that system cannot be separated from the interconnected system of the external environment in which it is set. It does of course depend on the forms of value that an organisation generates. When it comes to the production of other forms of value, there is a considerable variation as to what this means in practice. How does one compare the value of a work of art with educational benefit or other forms of value that are not tangible? A not-for-profit organisation or faith-based community will try to generate things that are worth something to a great many people but which are less susceptible to market evaluation.

As we have seen, to varying degrees, the external value generated in each of these spheres of activity depends on the active engagement of the human participants. Economics is about value, how it is generated through work and profits and how prices are determined that reflect what something is worth at any one time. I suggest that there is a different form of value − 'value-in-oneself' − the drive for which is fundamental both to social processes (as I seek to argue elsewhere) and to the success of organisations.

It is hardly new to argue the case for valuing environments as the optimum context for human participants to flourish.

In search of empirical evidence − emotional cognition and reflection as research

The construct is this. *Participants in an organisation flourish when, under right conditions, the inner value they live out in the workplace is converted into external, added value.* Quantification, the incessant default to generate the metrics, does not capture this perspective that is best discerned through its opposite. When the wrong conditions are present, or have been embedded systemically in the culture of how the organisation operates, participants will not be so productive; both quality and probably quantity will suffer. The question is, 'What are those conditions?'

Over a period of some five years, the author had constant and regular opportunities to witness the impact of human devaluation on many subjects. The experience of being disvalued emerged strongly following moments of insight into client reports of their distress. Some of these reports by clients were of their experiences in everyday life; sometimes of difficult circumstances of violence, abuse or self-harm. Nearly half of the experiences of clients were of those in the workplace. Being under stress in organisations gave rise to particularly striking reports of what it means to be devalued.

Whether in interpersonal exchanges or in organisations, not being in a valuing environment gave rise to various reactions. What follows is an attempt to categorise those responses and make sense of them. Client work is a minefield ethically as a basis for investigation and to draw conclusions. Within the guidelines, for example, of the British Association of Counselling and Psychotherapy, ethical issues are vitally important in any journey of reflection as research in client experiences. We do not normally regard clients as impersonal 'subjects' only to be mined for data.

Two research lenses were brought to bear on how to make sense of client reports about the life and times of contemporary organisations. The first was auto-ethnography. The second was a relational constructionist methodology.

Auto-ethnography is an approach to research and writing that seeks to describe and systematically analyse personal experience in order to understand wider cultural or psychological experience.[6] A researcher uses tenets of *autobiography and ethnography to do and write auto-ethnography*, which becomes in effect both process and product.[7] There is growing recognition that research cannot be done from a neutral, impersonal, and objective stance, that it is not value-free. Working with stories and everyday lives, the auto-ethnographer is hearing these analytically, deploying a set of theoretical and methodological tools and a research literature.[8] The methods are those of writing accounts based on participants' stories, fieldwork and notes from *interactive interviews* that provide an 'in-depth' and intimate understanding of people's experiences with emotionally charged and sensitive topics.[9] Various methods allow researchers working with this approach to analyse, categorise and draw conclusions.[10]

The second lens was that of a relational constructionist approach. Research is always a process of inquiry; we are all engaged in research. Within the scientific community, there are various philosophies. The constitutive nature of all forms of inquiry implies that theory and method are not independent; that a method is not necessarily what it is regardless of context. As a process, research is an inquiry into everyday activity, open to complexity and multiplicity of relational processes as opposed to pre-existing social structures and forms of knowledge. In this case, 'reality' is co-constructed though dialogue, iterative discussion in the context of client experiences within various organisations and at the boundary of living persons, organisational entities and workplace environment. It is 'what people do together and what their doing makes'.[11] As Foster and Bochner observe, inquiry embraces the details of lived experience, the reflexive relationship between personal interaction and cultural contexts, and the dialogic and dialectical complexity of relationships and communities.[12] This is a process of 'engaged unfolding' in which collaborative practice comes to the fore. Clients were helping create a social reality through the client–therapist relationship.

What began a period of sustained reflection in client observation was noticing how, in various domains, issues of worth were being constantly generated when people were facing its erosion. On being repeatedly struck by how many clients spoke of experiences of devaluation and how they expressed their indignation in terms of value – 'I'm worth more than that!' – I wanted to examine the role that worth and value play in everyday life. This then is the author's personal journey, working with clients in a way that began to provoke sustained reflection on the usual accounts of the motivational drivers and a likely deficit. More importantly, it is interleaved with clients' personal relationship to the realities of their organisation, interpersonal dynamics and their own responses.

Every attempt was made to inform clients that, while they were sharing their experiences, some points were being noted in a non-attributable way.

There is a danger in seemingly being able to explain things without bothering to try to prove them; it is the classic fallacy known by its Latin tag, *post hoc ergo propter* ('after this, therefore because of this') – arguing from how we act to infer why we act as we do. So, given the difficulties of verifying inter-subjective experience and without empirical tests using survey data, reported experiences about this have to be approached with care. In client observation, I began to look into the statements people made which implied that issues of personal value were being generated along the power lines of human exchanges. The question I set out to answer stemmed from intrigue. Why were client narratives, often of distress arising from experiences within organisations *generating statements about human value or its erosion?*

With client permission, I began to note such statements and gradually attempt to generalise in order to develop theory to explain why it was that human subjects have

responses to being devalued. I began to listen out for client reports to do with 12
perceptions of feeling:

- belittled or put down
- diminished
- bullied
- 'trashed'
- useless
- disrespected
- not noticed or regarded
- not heard
- passed over
- rejected
- discriminated against
- insulted.

Various statements that seemed to be generating such reports were then grouped
together as 'meaning units', to be analysed according to the canons of qualitative
research.[13] This journey was accompanied by post-doctoral research both into the
motivational drivers but also psycho-social processes in the public domain where issues
about the worth of people were generated including experiences in the workplace as
well as forms of distress or of inequality more widely.

The results are offered as a form of knowledge best described as 'emotional cognition'.
The usual way of describing cognition is that it is 'the mental action or process of
acquiring knowledge and understanding through thought, experience, and the senses'.[14]
As usually understood, cognition includes:

1   The mental process of knowing, including aspects such as awareness, perception,
    reasoning and judgement.
2   That which comes to be known, as through perception, reasoning or intuition;
    knowledge.

The ontological assumption behind this act of knowing is that of the self as an independent knower who is making sense of his or her own experience of the world and
translating that sense experience into knowledge. Emmanuel Levinas, the French ethical
philosopher, repositioned cognition as 're-cognition', that it arises from the interaction
between people rather than being the province of the solitary self.[15] The kind of process
through which client work is gently interrogated as to its meaning is set in a relational
context which draws out the extent to which significant knowledge is emotionally laden.
Emotion cannot be separated from acts of knowing. Children become good at subjects
where there is some emotional aspect; where there has been affect as an attachment to
what they know and the emerging field of knowledge in which it is embedded. The
view of the world adopted by social participants cannot be divorced from some degree of
emotional state associated with it. This surely is why opinion, such as about politics, is
laced with emotion, often at a visceral level. It is not an act of cognition purely as a
rational act.

Smart leaders understand and work with the grain of what it means to be written down in some way. Arguably, this is the basis of inequality in its many forms; that social actors are told they must go second class, or in more extreme cases that they are made to feel sub-species. What takes places in the social life of organisations is inseparable from wider social processes and indeed is a mirror upon them.

If these factors encapsulate what makes individuals feel disvalued, it is a prime leadership task to pay attention to them so as not to waste talent and human resources. The contrast polarity then emerges. Leaders need to give attention to attention, to noticing and combining necessary purposeful action with being in listening mode, antennae attuned. Leaders need to build strong cultures of involvement, of participation which breaks through the deadlock of staff disengagement towards active creativity rather than a passivity fuelled by 'being done to'. Leaders need to build work-related environments in which stakeholders are given dignity. If creativity is about having ideas and innovation is about turning those ideas into solutions, then enterprise is about making those solutions sustainable. A dynamic culture within an organisation that is conducive to drawing out the value of those who work within it is vital.

The reason why these factors, obvious to many, are important is not often captured. It is that they dig down into the motivational drivers. The contemporary emphasis on diversity and equality in the life and times of contemporary organisations is testament to growing awareness of countering inequality in the form of unequal treatment. Almost every public sector organisation has a diversity and equality officer of some sort. Yet it begs the question: if environments of value are those that mobilise the worth of participants, what are the inner ingredients of that sense of value and worth that can be aroused and recruited? The motivation to be treated in a non-discriminatory way, to be included in the conversation, runs deep into the human psyche.

Case study

It is my belief that people bully others in response to having been bullied themselves. I worked with a lady who claimed to have been bullied but was stronger now and wouldn't ever let it happen again. This was a shared confidence early on in the working relationship of bullying that we had both experienced. Did she then take advantage of that shared information and decide to bully me, attacking a perceived weakness? I think so, or was she someone who looked to dominate and belittle any showing a passive/submissive personality?

Every day you go to work there is a dark cloud over it when you know that you will be seeing your tormentor that day as the unpredictability of what they will say manifests itself as a tangible fear. If they are off on holiday – there is relief and momentary joy at being able to be yourself without being observed and criticised.

I had been doing the job efficiently and effectively for five years before this new boss arrived. However, they chose to micro-manage every aspect of my job, introducing a system of me having to ask for work all day long. All autonomy was taken away. It only applied to me. Two other people being managed were not treated like this. If anything was pending or unresolved – I was asked to chase it – making a nuisance and a nag with other users who were not able to resolve it – as I well knew – until the next day. Despite my assertive explanations to this boss – it was ignored and I was told that no more work was going to be issued until it was resolved. This impacted on new targets that had been set that were unachievable anyway. I couldn't move forward and plan my work – even though I promised faithfully to follow up on the unresolved issues.

Criticism was levelled at me through loud comments in the office to another so that I could clearly overhear – like 'the filing is in a disgusting state – I learnt my alphabet in primary school – I thought everyone did' 'I know that there was only one person doing the filing that day and it wasn't you or me …' and also directly 'you're supposed to be doing invoicing' to which I replied that I was! The filing I knew full well had been done by the Receptionist but what was I supposed to say? The filing was often disassembled and reassembled by others in the company so we had little control over it anyway.

Additionally I was not greeted in the morning or talked to even though everyone else was. I was excluded from invitation to social events and also on essential work information. If I worked extra to help out when someone was off sick – I was not thanked even though I explained I had done it to help out the team – I was told 'I didn't ask you to'.

I would be sitting there feeling hot and cold – sweating and feeling that my heart was about to explode in my chest. I had numerous headaches. The Receptionist and I would be exchanging looks of dread. At times we even felt at odds with one another as it felt like a blame-game. I began to feel hateful to the person who was making me feel like this.

I feared turning into someone I was never meant to be – full of ill-feeling, snappy and irritated with the family or just tired and withdrawn, my self-confidence ebbing away before me day-by-day. I was told in a review that 'I know I've been treating you like a child but I found it necessary'. I was too shocked to ask why at the time but cited it as a reason for leaving to the Finance Director who was sad to see me go. I also told him that certainly as regards me – nothing could be done to ameliorate the situation – she wasn't going to change.

I was right. The Receptionist handed in her resignation and left before me without working her notice – saying she wasn't going to be treated like that any longer – she had been in tears the day before. I have just received news that my replacement – four months down the line has also resigned for the same reason.[16]

In a subsequent study in group settings, findings from surveys in response to the statement 'I feel valued when … ' or 'I feel devalued when … ' resonated with reports made both in research interviews and ongoing voices of clients regarding 'a valuable self'.

Somewhere along the line, disgruntled employees often report experiences of devaluation. When asked what are de-motivating factors that make you feel valued at work or devalued, a typical list that emerges through client work will include:

- I feel valued when I am recognised or acknowledged as a person, when my achievements are recognised by a significant 'other' person.
- I am often devalued with no challenge and little opportunity to participate.
- I feel valued when I am consulted and management takes us with them.
- When I am valued, heard and taken seriously, when I am not a cog in the wheel, treated with indifference or ostracised.
- I feel valued when given dignity.[17]

These factors boil down to contrasts of three things noted in this chapter, the interplay of indifference, indignity and inequality (denigration) that encapsulates processes of devaluation. It suggests that wise leadership can operate effective management systems or deliver public projects as long as they ensure people are heard, recognised, involved and dignified. The notion of an 'environment of value' is one that stresses a community of valuers. All this can seem to be both obvious and simple. Yet the gap between rhetoric and reality yawns insistently. Part of the perceived problem that received wide exposure at the time of the failure of the Royal Bank of Scotland that led to its being taken into government ownership was a culture of bullying in which authority must not be challenged.[18]

Much cited in business education circles in a previous generation, Dale Carnegie's blend of self-help (of which he was father) and latest psychological theories of motivation, recognised emotional dynamics of professional people. 'We are not dealing with creatures of logic. We are dealing with creatures of emotion', he emphasised. 'Learn what makes people tick!'[19]

Results

Within organisations, these principles emerged as follows:

1   *Lack of purposeful engagement (indifference)* – not being seen (noticed) or heard, not having one's humanity greeted or recognised; being treated passively rather than actively recruited and energies released. The senses of sight and hearing from those with power to propose comes across as being clouded, hence workers feel unnoticed or ignored.

2   *Not honouring our humanity (inequality)* – diminished, not being treated fairly, living workplace life as if of lesser worth than others. Walking away from encounters diminished, so often people walk away from workplace encounters less than they are; dwarfed and belittled (unintentionally or not). Invariably, put-downs are to do with the reactions of the person rather than their actions. Or in creative teams, human potential and consequently the emotional life of professional people fail to be respected. As we will be noticing, the need for significance is fed by having a worthwhile role.

3   *Being invaded (indignity)* – often, human responses that express indignation were to do with indignity. This might relate to overt workplace bullying such as is highlighted at the BBC at the moment of writing, or strong arm tactics that fail to bring people round to the leadership point of view.

The role of **indifference** in organisational culture is, quite simply, that it triggers negative reactions around a sense of value and worth. Fundamentally, as with all negative triggers, the issue is one of well-being, of what it means to us to feel undervalued, or of little worth. The gaze emancipates staff. Changing the tense from what is being done to and for someone passively, seeing and hearing facilitates players to be in active voice. Transformative leaders will scrutinise their scrutiny and look at their gaze; who is noticed and looked upon in a way that, like the sun, daubs them with colour and brings them out. Strategic listening is key to incentivisation.[20] Listening is vital to success in the workplace:

> 'I never felt appreciated there like I do here … I just worked there but here I feel treated as a valuable person.'
> 'Being listened to, having a voice gives you a stake and share in what is going on.'

Someone being 'retired' from a top job after a very bumpy ride evokes a sympathetic reaction, framed in terms of 'seeing'. '*I hope he gets the recognition he deserves.*'[21] The gaze communicates value or disvalue.

In a research exercise in a training group (n=21), participants were asked to complete the following survey question. 'When I'm not listened to, I feel ... '

- rejected
- disregarded
- ignored
- angry
- sad
- useless
- worthless
- unimportant.

By contrast, the practice of being heard led to the following reactions in the same training course:

- accepted
- appreciated
- wanted
- happy
- valued
- hopeful
- included
- respected
- affirmed.[22]

With regard to the second factor in the interpretive grid, **inequality and diminishment,** client reports, for example, voiced:

> 'They make me feel I'm not worth very much', says a lady about the people at work.
> 'If you disagree, you are sidelined and diminished', reports an employee about the boss. Points would be jabbed in his direction lined with comments like, 'do you see?'[23]

Or, if we look at third factor, that of **indignity**, reaction against strategies of invasion; of being dishonoured; of the violation of sacred space that is the essence of violence:

> 'The boss is a bully. The people around the boss have all adapted to be bullies also.'
> 'He's been bullying people for ages. It drives out those who disagreed with him and who challenged his leadership ... subordinate off for six months with work-related stress. He's very good at manipulating people' – a client employee.[24]

Promoting dignity at work is crucial for creating environments of value. 'Dignity is crucial for our well-being and for many reasons is at risk in many kinds of work'.[25] The definition of what constitutes dignity at work is challenged, recognising that organisational culture is constrained by hierarchies and structures. Dignity is only meaningful between people. What bullying is can be questioned: illegal actions, uncivilised behaviour, demeaning and humiliating, insulting and ignoring? Any definition must involve repeated occurrences. Hodson referenced four challenges to working with dignity – mismanagement and abuse, overwork, challenge to autonomy and contradiction of employee interests. Dignity at work results in autonomy, job satisfaction and human well-being.[26]

The concept of indignity is not just about bullying in the workplace. The performance management culture characterised by efficiency can have a dark side. 'It's about power and control', complains someone about the micromanaging tendencies the manager deploys discouragingly.[27] Perhaps this is really a narrative of value, the need to be valued in a competitive environment against the zero sum game of devaluing staff. Where there is hunger for control, only one person can be allowed to win! The point about indignity as a driver of being devalued is that it is not just an *insult* of what people do, cutting you down to size. It is an *assault* on what people are; an infringement of the sacred. When that takes place, what is needed is a long hard look at the fundamental problems that enabled such practice to happen. Many organisations are vulnerable to certain patterns of behaviour becoming the norm. It can easily drift over the line and become abuse. Many of the difficulties are the result of clients' own responses to authority and stress.

The contrast

Invoking the contrast pole assists conceptual clarity by highlighting the psychological formats that create a sense of perceiving oneself as disvalued. Discerning what factors drive a lack of value and worth aids understanding beyond what a direct approach to understanding valuing environments might yield. This is due to the problem of the over-familiar. New conceptual space is opened up by the contrast. As with human transactions that occur on an interpersonal level, reactions of being devalued *need explaining*. Existing psycho-social frameworks are not up to the mark.

Contemporary life can hardly be understood without some concept of the struggle to realise our value. The reason why this is a driving force is that it plugs into the felt worth people have. The world of contemporary organisations is a human landscape that can be read through the lens of human devaluation. Companies, public services and management styles often evoke statements of personal worth by their employees – either because they value them, or the opposite – because they practice devaluation.

Value is a foundational principle of human action. Conveying worth is not merely an aspiration but a dimension of the human operating system; an ineradicable trait. Without a sense of value we are cramped and constrained. Or we wither. With a rising sense of a valuable self, we function at our optimum and offer pathways of hope.

So let us now turn this approach back on its head. What will generate a valuing environment will be to draw out cultures of:

- **Listening, looking and learning** – redressing indifference through attention, learning, noticing, recognition.
- **Involvement** – recruiting active participants in the project that converts passive spectators into commitments and shared responsibility, not being 'done unto', a learning environment in which staff and workers engage in their own development.
- **Dignifying** – giving dignity and ensuring non-invasive 'sacred' space.

So what will it mean for the organisation of the future to be a valuing environment which evokes the value and worth of its human participants?

Notes

1 http://www.willowcreek.org.uk/, accessed June 2016.
2 Belleghem, S. Van (2015), *When Digital Becomes Human: The Transformation of Customer Relationships*. London: Kogan Page.
3 BSA Work, Employment and Society 2016 Conference – Call for Papers. Work, Employment and Society Conference 2016, 'Work in Crisis'.
4 Thompson, P. (1989), *The Nature of Work*. Basingstoke: Macmillan Education.
5 Henretta, D. (Group President, Asia & Global Specialty Channel, Procter & Gamble), 'Millennials at Work: Reshaping the Workplace'. PWC, May 2016, https://www.pwc.com/m1/en/services/consulting/documents/millennials-at-work.pdf, accessed May 2016.
6 Sadruddin Bahadur Qutoshi, 'Auto/ethnography: A Transformative Research Paradigm', *Forum: Qualitative Social Research* 12 (1), 1–13, https://www.researchgate.net/profile/Sadruddin_Qutoshi, January 2011.
7 Ellis, C. (2004), *The Ethnographic I: A Methodological Novel about Autoethnography*. Walnut Creek, CA: AltaMira Press.
8 Holman Jones, S. (2005), 'Autoethnography: Making the Personal Political', in *Handbook of Qualitative Research*, ed. N.K. Denzin and Y.S. Lincoln. Thousand Oaks, CA: Sage, pp. 763–791.
9 Ellis, C., Kiesinger, C.E. and Tillmann-Healy, L.M. (1997), 'Interactive Interviewing: Talking about Emotional Experience', in *Reflexivity and Voice*, ed. Rosanna Hertz. Thousand Oaks, CA: Sage, pp. 119–149.
10 Fine, Gary A. (2003), 'Towards a People Ethnography: Developing a Theory from Group Life', *Ethnography*, 4 (1), pp. 41–60.
11 MacNamee, S. and Hosking, D.M. (2012), *Research and Social Change: A Relational Constructionist Approach*. London: Routledge, p. 1.
12 Foster, E. and Bochner, A.P. (2008), 'Social Constructionist Perspectives in Communication Research', in *Handbook of Constructionist Research*, ed. J.A Holstein and J.F. Gubrium. New York: Guilford Press.
13 Bryman, A. (2016), *Social Research Methods*. Oxford: Oxford University Press.
14 Compact *OED*, 3rd edition, 2008.
15 Sohn, M. (2014), *The Good of Recognition: Phenomenology, Ethics, and Religion in the Thought of Levinas and Ricoeur*. Waco, TX: Baylor University Press.
16 Author's client notes – used with permission and name withheld.
17 Author's client notes – used with permission and name withheld.
18 Hearings before Treasury Select Committee. Paul Moore, 10 February 2009, reported on *Newsnight*, BBC Two.
19 Watts, S. (2013), *Self-Help Messiah: Dale Carnegie and Success in Modern America*. New York: Other Press.
20 Faruqui A., (1997), 'Creating Competitive Advantage by Strategic Listening', *The Electricity Journal*, 10 (4), pp. 64–72.
21 Author's client notes – used with permission and name withheld.
22 Author's client notes – used with permission and name withheld.
23 Author's client notes – used with permission and name withheld.

24 Author's client notes – used with permission and name withheld.
25 Sayer, A., (2007), 'Dignity at Work: Broadening the Agenda', *Organisation*, 14 (4), p. 565.
26 Hodson, R., (1997), 'Group Relations at Work: Solidarity, Conflict and Relations with Management', *Work and Occupations*, 24 (4), p. 562.
27 Author's client notes – used with permission and name withheld.

Chapter 7

Lifting the LID on your organisation

Millennials love employers that mix purpose with socio-professional development and economic opportunity. In the impact investment industry, we notice this because our combination of social or environmental purpose, professional skills development across private, public and civil sectors, and ethos of creating solutions that straddle sectors, attract millennial talent like bees to honey. Millennials frustrate managers and parents. Yet they also offer great promise, as digitally native, entrepreneurial and cosmopolitan world citizens.

Bob Moritz, Harvard Business Review, 2014[1]

In this chapter, we develop the construct offered in this book and probe what are the ingredients for an environment of value in which the value and worth of participants in an organisation is tapped and released.

As I write, a hugely successful UK businessman, Mike Ashley, owner of the retailer Sports Direct, has been hauled in front of a Parliamentary Select Committee on the terms and conditions of UK workers.[2] He was accused of allowing work-house conditions in his formidable sports clothing factory chain. Staff lived in fear of being even a minute late or being fired if they infringed the conditions such as no talking in breaks or being a minute late for work. In one infamous example, a woman gave birth in the toilet. Staff were not allowed to be slightly early for work: pressure was unrelenting.

Although technological displacement will soon make the old jobs obsolete, the skills needed for a new era will have to be those that allow for human imagination and innovation to flourish, the driving force behind economies led by talent. It is governments that create the environment that allows innovation to thrive in order to make the most of the transformations reshaping the world. Innovation is highly prized across the piece, but an innovation that is rooted in a 'think differently mindset', an entrepreneurial mindset.

Take an Internet piece entitled 'Why Intrapreneurs Should be Valued by Corporate Leaders'.[3] It is argued that leaders of established organisations could attract, retain and drive value from employees by relying on traditional levers for success, such as established career tracks, organisational stability, title promotions, etc. However, in our current 'entrepreneur as rockstar' age, these levers lack the pull of days gone by. In the recent Deloitte 2014 Millennial Survey '70 percent of tomorrow's future leaders might "reject" what traditional organisations have to offer, preferring to work independently … in the long term.'[4] To address this issue, mature organisations need to replicate key facets of the start-up and entrepreneurial culture, in ways that can be scaled within a larger corporate context. In response, a diverse range of established organisations such as Pfizer, Target, Exxon Mobil, GE, Intuit, etc., are building and supporting intrapreneur efforts.

In its sweeping effects, the technological paradigm is no respecter of persons. The day is not far off when androids will be doing the work people do. Technology has changed everything and the organisation is inseparable from that. There is a strong tendency in capitalism whereby wage labour previously done by humans will be automated. Work and tasks will increasingly be done by robots. There are two kinds of work – organic labour or emotional labour – and wage labour, or variable capital. Once you have algorithms in practice, algorithms are cheaper than humans. Robots will almost always be cheaper than humans and hence in the interests of entrepreneurs to introduce.

Yet what of the rising generation, who came of age at the dawn of the third millennium, who will shape and share these sweeping changes? As Bob Moritz, US Chairman of PricewaterhouseCoopers wrote in *Harvard Business Review*:

> Sometimes I wonder what my reaction would have been if, as a twenty something starting out at Price Waterhouse nearly three decades ago, I had been magically transported to today's PwC. I would have been stunned by how much had changed. During most of my career at the firm, the rewards system focused more on quantity than quality of work, although clients demanded standards just as high then as the ones they do now. Bigger bonuses and promotions went to those who sacrificed more of their personal lives, whereas our current HR policies primarily reward quality and value the work and life needs of every person.[5]

According to Gallup, 55 per cent of these millennials report feeling unengaged at work, 5 points higher than Gen Xers, 7 points above baby boomers and 14 points more than traditionalists. When they are looking for new work, millennials want to see signs that bode well for their career development. The top five things they consider, according to Gallup, are: opportunities to learn and grow, quality of their manager, quality of management in general, interest in the type of work and opportunities for advancement.

Although those qualities are important to members of every generation, millennials are particularly concerned with some of them. For example, 59 per cent of millennials rate opportunities to learn and grow as 'extremely important' when applying for a new job. Just 44 per cent of Gen Xers and 41 per cent of baby boomers say the same. Exactly half of millennials rate advancement opportunities as extremely important in a job search, compared to 42 per cent of Gen Xers and 40 per cent of baby boomers, according to PWC.[6]

Motivating staff in the digital economy will be a different proposition. This is not just because their needs will change. The organisation of the future will surely look different in a digital era. The 'system' of an individual workplace environment will feature the kind of 'agile technology', the mobile worker. We will return to this subject.

Look, learn and listen (vs indifference)

Learning changes minds; it alters people's mental maps.[7]

We now apply the construct formulated in Chapter 5. If environments of value are those that mobilise the worth of participants, it begs the question: what are the inner ingredients of that sense of value and worth that can be aroused and recruited? The first factor in an environment of value is for leaders to set up micro-cultures which are the contrast pole of not being seen, noticed, recognised or listened to. As we will see when revisiting motivation theory in the light of this construct, acts of seeing and hearing are vital for drawing out participants in organisations. This emerges in client work:

All my ideas and efforts were never recognised; I was never given credit for them … when building a team, listening is crucial.[8]

Anecdotally, where participants experience a sense of being heard, it is more likely to generate positive outcomes. Where participants feel ignored, they are more likely to be disgruntled and engage in further protest or become further disengaged. Recognition is vital. George Davies – former fashion designer at Marks and Spencer – had a celebrated row with a senior manager that reverberated round the City of London at a time when M&S were struggling to recover from years of poor performance. A resignation letter was written, though not acted upon. The row was said to be about the lack of recognition George Davies was receiving for his work to turn the ailing ship around.[9]

An environment of value is an environment in which participants can learn from failure and move on. How organisations deal with failure is crucial. It involves cultures where, rather than the corporate blame-game, reflecting on past performance and knowing how to improve are embedded in practice. This is redemptive. It is also wise.

Smart leadership invites *employee ideas and incorporates them into workplace well-being initiatives*. For instance, allowing employees to choose the well-being activities that are best suited to them based on their individual well-being goals simultaneously promotes clarity about an employee's role alongside a culture of well-being. It does both while honouring each employee's unique talents and interests. In the management literature, this is the emphasis of *Flying High*, the story of the US airline JetBlue. Its founder, David Neeleman, worked hard at understanding what customers really need. Though CEO, he would regularly perform management by working on the ground, walking about and talking with staff and customers about how they could thrive.[10]

Strategic listening is key to incentivisation.[11] Listening is vital to success in the workplace. This is because, as the US church leader and writer on leadership Bill Hybels notes, facts are your friends.[12] Clearly, leaders can help drive learning environments; that is, fostering a climate of experimentation in which people can experiment, though in a prudent way. As Patching observes, 'learning changes minds; it alters people's mental maps'.[13]

Modern business or organisational leadership is a highly complex operation. Establishing a culture of learning from what happens on the ground is crucial to success. Reflecting and adapting is vital to operating in a demanding and multi-layered environment. To ensure that something is learnt from mistakes or things that did not go well, does, however, require that leaders gather together those involved while it is still fresh and distil any learning and that they have equal voice. Approaching such a review without recrimination or playing the blame-game is an environment of value in practice. Being allowed to fail is the path of wisdom by a listening, responsive leadership. Employees need space to work things out for themselves, to make mistakes, review what they have done and to learn.

Case study

The first day of the Battle of the Somme

As I write, there is much scrutiny of the appalling loss of life in the First World War 100 years ago. The British military commander, Sir Douglas Haig, comes under particular criticism. He is variously described as 'the butcher of the Somme' for the epic casualties both at the Somme in 1916 and Passchendaele in 1917; his name is synonymous with the futility of war and incompetent tactics. Revisionist historians have called for a much more balanced assessment. The British Army was on a steep learning curve in its transition towards a mass land force in the field. Haig adapted and when he was given freedom to act in the emergency of 1918, he held firm and broke the German Army.[14] Advocates such as John Terraine and military historians since point out that Haig did visit the troops and would not be averse to comment from all quarters.[15] What is difficult to avoid, however, quite apart from the horrific casualties, is the corporate failure to learn quickly enough. A military historian such as John Keegan stressed that, although the radically new situation demanded a steep learning curve, the British Army was too slow in learning to adapt. After all, it should have been apparent from the ghastly French losses in the Battle of the Frontiers in August 1914 (where the losses were substantially higher than 1 July 1916) that a new type of warfare had arrived; one which rewarded the defence. Other voices argue that the British Army in 1918 was only a highly competent integrated fighting force that won the war precisely because of the willingness to learn and adapt.[16] The debate will rumble on.

It is, however, interesting to juxtapose this debate with the US Army After Action Reviews (AARs). This is an organisational learning process which invites those who were involved in an action to consider (1) what they set out to do, (2) what actually happened, (3) why were the outcomes so different to what was planned, and (4) what was learnt? Harvard University Professor David Garvin, who developed the tool, recommended that one-third of the time is spent on 'what did we set out to do', in order to ascertain goal alignment. Holding off cause and effect (blame) until the end is a state of mind. To help participants recall key events quickly, skilled facilitators often step in.

Peter Senge is the creator of the 'learning organisation' philosophy, which he defines as an organisation 'where people continually expand their capacity to create the results they truly desire, where new and expansive patterns of thinking are nurtured, where collective aspiration is set free, and where people are continually learning how to learn together'.[17]

Organisations have seen the rise of the learning organisation philosophy. The learning organisation sets itself up to provide an environment built on the need for continuous learning. He postulates that organisations learn only through individuals who learn. It is, however, the working team that is the fundamental learning unit in any organisation. The success of a team is never just a matter of adding up individual skills or learning. For example, one cannot just gather a group of football players and expect to get good results. A team of any kind must grow and develop together.

Leaders need to step back and be willing to let someone else facilitate. The US Army works hard to build a climate of openness and candour. It is salutary that most corporate efforts to adapt this model do not foster a living, organic process to identify what went wrong but end up writing a report that stays on the shelf. An essential aspect to such post-mortems is 'Seek maximum participation'.[18]

Listening and watching are powerful ways of learning, of driving a journey of continuous improvement, of adaptation to fast-paced evolutionary change.

There is growing realisation that, in the new game of work, learning beats knowing. In the management literature, an emphasis on constant learning being more important than mastery is a theme. In an example of a popular best-seller, *Rookie Smarts*, Wiseman contends that in a rapidly changing world, experience can be a disadvantage; knowledge and skills become obsolete and irrelevant. Innovation can stop and strategies grow stale. What counts is an unencumbered mind. Learning beats knowing in the new game of work.[19]

Involve and include

Another dimension of a valuing environment is one that involves and includes.

This is to do with honouring autonomy. Autonomy need not mean the individual imprisoned in isolation. The drive towards autonomy is closely linked with the need to be of high value that is built into the human psyche. This is important for how we conceptualise the motivational drivers. Here are a few example of an inclusive approach that endeavours to recruit the interests and talents of participants.

'Opinions count' is a central component of an engaging workplace. Asking employees to contribute well-being ideas is a great way to galvanise them and make them feel they are a part of the well-being movement. Employees also will have excellent feedback about which well-being programmes are working and which aren't – and how they can be revised or new programmes added. *This includes milestones in work review and progress meetings.* Research has shown that engaged employees are much more comfortable than other employees in discussing their well-being goals with their manager.

People need to feel part of the decision-making process. There seems to be growing awareness of the importance of helping people gain greater influence over their environment.[20] Involvement is an exercise in autonomy, to provide direction but also greater autonomy in which people accept responsibility for what they are doing as they are given a clear framework. The balance between direction and autonomy is hard to find.

Involvement is about matching the gifts and talents people might have to the tasks that need to be done. There is much wasted talent; gifts by the million lie underused, amongst women and minorities. One study suggested that the improved bottom line for companies with more women senior executives is not produced through the management of earnings or lower quality earnings. Instead, earnings quality is positively associated with gender diversity in senior management. In other words, involve the whole breadth of talent and gifts that is available.[21]

It is about what is known as 'economic democracy'. When the prospective prime minister Theresa May made a statement about her intentions, she set out plans to change the way big businesses are governed. Mrs May said consumers and workers should have places on their boards – a feature of corporate life in Germany for many years. Outlining her plans to reform corporate governance, she hit out at the way non-executive directors who are supposed to provide oversight of the way firms are run often come from the same 'narrow social and professional circles' as the executive team and 'the scrutiny they provide is just not good enough'. She said: 'So if I'm prime minister, we're going to change that system – and we're going to have not just consumers represented on company boards, but workers as well.' Theresa May also promised to strengthen 'say on pay' rules, giving shareholders more influence over how much executives are paid. This is an example of the importance of 'involve and include' to business in a modern democracy.

As I write these words at the end of June 2016, Wales has upturned the wisdom of sport commentators by storming to victory in a vital match in the Euro 2016 football tournament. The question football pundits across Europe asked was this. What is driving Wales' stunning Euro 2016 success? What do they have that other teams don't? Amongst the reasons Wales have stormed into the semi-finals was that this was a team moving as one. The players were friends, a community. They felt part of something which exhibited camaraderie but one in which players were 'not afraid to fail'.[22]

Famously, Sachiro Honda understood the way a team works. Crucially for this perspective on organisational culture, he treated others as equal. That ethos pervades the Honda way. Employees are associates. They are regarded as people of worth who will generate value to the company. Today, Honda is doing well in a difficult climate.[23]

The success of the British retail giant John Lewis owes much to the co-ownership values of its founder, John Spedan Lewis, who handed control and ownership over to the employees in two trust settlements beginning in 1929. In the US, in 2015 the top 100 employee-owned companies employed more than 626,000 people. America's top five stock market performers have all been included in the annual 'Employee Ownership 1000'.[24]

Collaborative working is the mantra of the age. New generations of leaders have arisen who are committed to changing things and taken on the high value of doing things 'through' and 'with' rather than 'to'. The lonely hero leader is out of date.

Expanding gender participation in the workforce and smashing the glass ceiling is clearly part of this emphasis. Involving half the world at every level of organisation is recognised as the imperative of the previous generation. Everyone has an equal stake in society. Its challenge remains. So too is the focus in successful economies such as Germany to spread economic democracy through worker participation on company boards. The degree to which people have control over their work has been found to impact considerably on chronic stress and is therefore a determinant on health outcomes.[25]

Dignify

The third factor in the typology proposed here is that a valuing environment is one that counters disrespectful, controlling or bullying behaviour. Instead it respects the sacred space of the person in a non-invasive way. The narcissistic behaviour of leaders conditions the former: respectful managers foster the latter.

In the UK alone, it has been estimated that stress costs £13.75 billion to organisations and one in four absences are due to bullying. Perhaps 100 million days of productivity are lost with a cost to the economy estimated at £17.65 billion from a 1.5 per cent reduction in overall productivity.[26]

'Be our Guest' is the title of the staff guidebook to perfecting the art of customer service at the Disney organisation in Orlando, Florida. 'The service standard of courtesy', it is urged, 'requires that every guest be treated like a VIP – a very important, very individual person.' This means more than treating guests how 'we would want to be treated'. It means 'treating them the way they want to be treated, with recognition and respect for their emotions, abilities and cultures'.[27] The importance of value and worth is not just about customer service. It runs through the culture of staff engagement and motivation and into the value added in the company.

Conflict in industry or strikes are not just about pay and conditions; they are a demand for respect. Industrial relations seem to be bedevilled by management practices that fail to engage staff or confer appropriate recognition on workers and their grievance. As in interpersonal life, when grievances are not responded to with appropriate recognition, it becomes an attack on the workers. Comments by two UK leaders experienced in industrial relations perhaps indicates the point. 'Until employers realise that respect is at the heart of modern industrial relations, we will be in conflict.'[28] 'Lack of respect for the workforce, bullying and intimidation by management lie at the heart of this dispute,' declared a UK trade Union leader in an airline cabin crew strike.[29]

These statements seem to be obvious truisms. Yet experience shows that, often, the culture of contemporary organisations – despite being enlightened with management wisdom – does not reflect them being translated into operating principles. Leaders need to pay attention to the signals they send, the environment that is part of the work they do.

What is being conceptualised here are the factors that nourish engagement, whether it is of staff, workers or volunteers. To understand what fosters engagement, it is helpful to discern what drives disengagement. This is fundamentally an issue of enlightened management. If such an association exists and is strong, then it is in the self-interest of leadership, especially at senior level, to use that knowledge and put it into practice. Leadership insight to build positive cultures which can catalyse self-respect or dignity of labour, however that is understood, is vital.

Essential for the future are skills of creativity and empathy in learning environments. These are components for 'environments of value', positive cultures within which such aptitudes flourish. Valuing environments are those which place strong emphasis on the human dimension and will be increasingly important in a world subject to de-personalisation. Although shrinking in the economy as a whole, the human element is enhanced by an engaged and productive workforce, generating value appropriate to the sphere of activity. Value added by the contribution of personnel, whether managers or staff and workers, depends on productive energies they bring to their task. That in turn is related to motivation and morale.

Replete with strong vision, wanting to win, a leader must assert control and establish discipline to achieve common objectives, otherwise anarchy will break out and the organisation will be impossible to lead. An organisation is purpose-driven. Everything matters and points to the top of the mountain, as Alex Ferguson suggests. High expectations that persuade and nudge to achieving something they would not ordinarily manage is vital. A leader must be hard-nosed at times with difficult people. Often staff or workers need to be laid off. A pipeline of new workers must be laid. High-performance teams may need to be built and rebuilt.

Yet, as two generations of management theorists have argued, scoring highly in the area of strong purpose needs to be combined with a strong focus on people. Listening, learning and leading are components of leadership in any walk of life. Respect must be present. This is not about a supposed dichotomy between ruthlessness and love; respect for a leader is critical. Respect is a two-way street. One of the fundamental 'givens' in leadership is 'getting things done through people'.

We are testing the construct to consider briefly the ingredients that drive disengagement or poor morale in an organisation that lead to staff or workers feeling disvalued. What is for debate here is how leaders can build cultures in their organisation that enable inner value and worth to be translated into external, added value. Arising from client and organisational observation, lifting the LID on an organisation requires attention to three ingredients that contribute either to valuing environments within which we flourish, or, when absent, to environments that erode our sense of self and produce disengagement. I suggest this is best approached negatively to begin with so as to provide greater illumination. Factors that drive engagement are illuminated by the factors that drive disengagement.

A paradigm shift in leadership requires a change in the skill set, a change in approach and a desire to grow and develop collectively. Instead of seeking personal power and reward, leaders recognise the value of empowering others and find ways to inspire and influence them through being in relationship. Such a style will be a natural fit with those that came of age around the year 2000. Employers that learn to attract, stimulate and leverage millennial talent will have a fierce competitive advantage in the decades to come. They will see the boundaries of their firms challenged by the continuous flow and interaction between politics, business and purpose that already provides the licence to operate in most sectors of society. As *Harvard Business Review* observed, 'Here is one tip for success: value and reward cross-sector experience and skills-building in millennial talent. You will train powerful ambassadors across the social fabric of society, whether they stay for a summer or years.'[30] The survey made for significant reading regarding motivations in the contemporary workplace:

A community of practice

The terms of debate about what the much cited learning environment means seem to be shifting from issues of information and technology per se to how to draw out human capabilities. How do we evoke the sources of creativity, motivation and problem-solving skills that will flourish and create real value in the digital economy? Leadership and knowledge production do not depend on the 'scientific' management promulgated by F.W. Taylor a century ago[31] but on the way the value of participants translates into a community of practice.

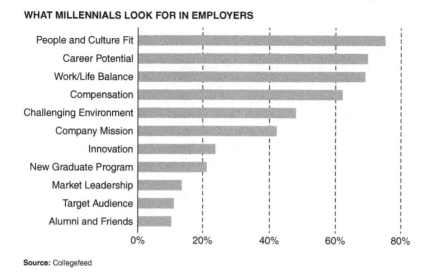

Source: Collegefeed

Figure 7.1

As articulated by Etienne Wenger, an organisation is a constellation of such 'communities of practice' where social learning takes place rather than the individual learner.[32]

With its time and motion studies and emphasis on efficiency above all else, scientific management was a step towards control systems felt to be needed in competitive capitalism. This is not the place to enter into debates in industrial sociology about the historical importance of what became 'Taylorism', which was often strongly opposed by labour.[33] It does seem clear that it became a catch all for 'a broader re-orientation of management'.[34] The attempt to create a managerial monopoly of tight control goes against the need for creative participation by workers, described by Friedman as 'responsible autonomy', getting staff to cooperate with the organisation's objectives so that they act responsibly with a minimum of supervision.[35]

An environment of value is a community of practice, rooted in a theory of learning that starts with the assumption that the primary analysis of learning is neither the individual nor social institutions but the informal communities that people form as they pursue shared enterprises over time. Learning is a form of social participation, the fundamental process by which we learn and become who we are – the intersection of issues to do with community and identity. An environment of value allows for learning as a fundamentally social phenomenon, reflecting our deeply social nature as human beings capable of knowing and participating.[36] Such a social theory of learning brings together meaning, practice, community and identity. It is where we negotiate shared practice and shared objectives through mutual engagement. Identity is a form of competence.

Valuing the human is a working assumption when it comes to various aspects of leadership.

High quality corporate governance. Management style became a topic for debate after research on different styles of leadership in the non-profit-making sector exposed three different styles: autocratic, democratic and laissez-faire.[37] The group was most productive in an autocratic model but if the manager was absent the work stopped. A laissez-faire approach was least helpful in every respect whereas a democratic style was most consistent in quality and output. A competitive workplace situation illustrates the flux between value and power. Today it is recognised that management styles will vary according to the task needed.[38] A collaborative style will work for most of the people most of the time but a task may require a stronger, more directive approach. Leadership is not just about using authority to mobilise subordinates; it is also about giving direction. Henry Mintzberg saw decision-making as the most crucial part of management activity.[39] Corporate governance is about making things happen through structures of support and accountability that promote human welfare as well as delivering the company aims.

Innovation. When dynamism is released, it is associated with creativity. In the wake of the industrial revolution, growth in output and productivity accelerated steadily. In the twentieth century, growth per person in America doubled in a generation though reaching a plateau around 1970 and falling thereafter.[40] Technology is what is left over after the effect of labour, capital and education have been factored out. Sustaining innovation requires a climate in which new ideas can be brought forward and released. What kind of human catalysts are required to drive inventiveness? An environment in which the human is valued enables a confidence that is a rich resource. Within that space, nurturing inner value is translated into adding value through new ideas and dynamism.

Awareness of group dynamics. Relationships are screens on which emotions and thoughts of individuals are projected. This is where the inner world of staff as people is shown up and where they find out most about themselves. It is as true of group relationships as it is of relationships closer to home. Watching the swirl of alliances and personal interaction of groups at work shows who is up or down, who is in and out. Invariably, someone who is on the outside is marginalised because 'they' have not been taking the group with 'us'. In groups, someone may feel unengaged and uninvolved. The usual antidote for those watchful for the signs is to bring them back in from the cold by consulting and listening. A window on commonplace interactions such as these may be to see them as the dynamics of devaluation. Being written down is what the temporary outsider may well have experienced; their return is marked by them feeling valued again. Re-engagement adds value to a group task.

The management of change. The time has long passed when leaders and managers were expected to leave things much as they found them. The successful management of change is crucial to any organisation in order to *survive and succeed in the present highly competitive and continuously evolving business environment*.[41] A rapidly changing external environment and consequent demands means that leaders have to stimulate change in order to adapt. Organisational psychologists have amply demonstrated the stress that upheavals in the workplace can bring to people's lives. The management literature on change is usually situated from the missionary perspective of the change agent, the manager. Reassuring people in the face of perceived threat to their well-being can often depend on the communicator of change not being a threatening figure.

Managing customer relations is another way in which realisation the value of people seems to be growing. Few people will put up these days with poor customer service as competing organisations fuss about that most precious of commodities, a consumer. A customer-centred strategy is allied with a transformation in marketing and service that respects the customer. Increasingly, best practice is seen to be where an atmosphere of respect is held to be crucial.[42] Smart technology means that 'the product' can speak to whoever is handling it. Through such means, including transmitting updates to end-users, manufacturers are emulating other types of business in drawing closer to their customers. Rather than built-in obsolescence (which shaped previous waves of capitalism built on cars and white goods) products could get better over time. It is increasingly realised that the best way to sell their products is to forge personal relationships with the consumer rather than spending huge amounts of money on mass marketing. Retailers have loyalty cards offering discounts and rewards. The business model of Amazon has been built on trying to suggest customer preferences. In Hyundai, the strapline boasts of building connections with customers in this way: 'We promote a customer-driven corporate culture by providing the best quality and impeccable service with all of our efforts aimed at satisfying our customers.'[43] The concept of relationship management is one that has been shaped by larger societal expectations. Otherwise known as 'interactive marketing', it keeps them coming back for more. Cottle estimated that high quality service firms are twice as profitable as others.[44]

In short, the claim to put the value of people at the heart of an organisation has practical implications.

Notes

1 Moritz, B. (2014), 'Keeping Millennials Engaged', *Harvard Business Review*, November 2014.
2 http://www.parliament.uk/business/committees/committees-a-z/commons/.
3 Ferrier, A. 'Why Intrapreneurs Should be Valued by Corporate Leaders: An Introduction', http://www.culturevate.com/intrapreneur-introduction/. The article was originally published in Innovation Management. See more at: http://www.innovationexcellence.com/blog/2015/12/12/why-intrapreneurs-should-be-valued-by-corporate-leaders-an-introduction/.
4 Big demands and high expectations. The Deloitte Millennial Survey. http://docplayer.net/29456-The-deloitte-millennial-survey.html
5 Moritz (2014).
6 Henretta, D. (Group President, Asia & Global Specialty Channel, Procter & Gamble), 'Millennials at Work: Reshaping the Workplace', PWC, May 2016. https://www.pwc.com/m1/en/services/consulting/documents/millennials-at-work.pdf, accessed May 2016.
7 Patching, K. (1999), *Management and Organisation Development: Beyond Arrows, Boxes and Circles.* Basingstoke: Macmillan, p. 226.
8 Author's client notes – used with permission and name withheld.
9 *You and Yours*, BBC Radio 4, 14 November 2007, http://www.bbc.co.uk/radio4.
10 Wynbrandt, J. (2004), *Flying High.* Hoboken, NJ: Wiley & Sons.
11 Faruqui, A. (1997), 'Creating Competitive Advantage by Strategic Listening', *The Electricity Journal*, 10 (4), pp. 64–72.
12 Hybels, B. (2008), *Leadership Axioms.* Grand Rapids, MI: Zondervan.
13 Patching (1999), p. 226.
14 Terraine, J. (1992 [1980]), *The Smoke and the Fire: Myths and Anti-myths of War 1861–1945.* London: Sidgwick & Jackson.
15 Terraine, J. (1963), *Douglas Haig: The Educated Soldier.* London: Hutchinson.
16 Bond, B. and Cave, N. (2009), *Haig: A Reappraisal 70 Years On.* Barnsley: Pen & Sword.
17 Senge, P. (2006), *The Fifth Discipline: The Art and Practice of the Learning Organization.* New York: Random House Business.
18 http://www.usarak.military/, accessed November 2015.
19 Wiseman, L. (2014), *Rookie Smarts: Why Learning Beats Knowing in the New Game of Work.* New York: Harper Business.
20 Miller, E. (1993), *From Dependence to Autonomy: Studies in Organisation and Change.* London: Free Association.

21 Krishnan, G.V. and Parsons, L.M. (2008), 'Getting to the Bottom Line: An Exploration of Gender and Earnings Quality', *Journal of Business Ethics*, 78 (1), pp. 65–76.
22 *Wales Online* http://www.walesonline.co.uk/, accessed June 2016.
23 'High-Potential Employees: Seven Keys to Success', *Industry Week*, http://www.industryweek.com/, accessed September 2012.
24 'Employee Ownership', http://www.nceo.org/articles/employee-ownership-100/, accessed January 2016. See also http://employeeownership.co.uk/case-studies/john-lewis-partnership/, accessed January 2016.
25 Theorell, T. (2003), 'Democracy at Work and its Relationship to Health', in *Emotional and Physiological Processes and Intervention Strategies*, ed. P. Perrewe and D.E. Ganster. Greenwich, CT: JAI Press.
26 Giga, S., Hoel, H. and Lewis D. (2008), 'The Cost of Workplace Bullying and Bullying at Work', Unite the union / Department of Business, Enterprise and Regulatory Reform. http://www.jil.go.jp/english/reports/documents/jilpt-reports/no.12_u.k.pdf/.
27 Disney Institute (2001), *Be our Guest*. New York: Disney Editions, p. 60.
28 Hattersley, R. on *Question Time*, BBC One, 19 December 2009.
29 Woodley, T. Unite Trade Union, *World at One*, BBC Radio 4, 21 March 2010.
30 Moritz (2014).
31 Thomson, P. (1989), *The Nature of Work: An Introduction to Debates on the Labour Process*, 2nd edn. Basingstoke: Macmillan, p. 74.
32 Wenger, E. (1997), *Communities of Practice: Language, Meaning and Identity*. Cambridge: Cambridge University Press.
33 Nadowrny, M. (1955), *Scientific Management and the Unions*. Cambridge, MA: Harvard University Press.
34 Edwards, R. (1979), *Contested Terrain: The Transformation of the Workplace in the Twentieth Century*. London: Heinemann, p. 98.
35 Friedman, A. (1977), *Industry and Labour: Class Struggle at Work and Monopoly Capitalism*. London: Macmillan.
36 Wenger (1997).
37 White, R. and Lippit, R. (1953), 'Leader Behaviour and Member Reaction in Three "Social Climates"', in *Group Dynamics*, ed. D. Cartwright and A. Zander. London: Tavistock Publications.
38 Mintzberg, H. (1989), *Mintzberg on Management: Inside our Strange World of Organisations*. New York: Free Press.
39 Mintzberg, H. (1980), *The Nature of Managerial Work*. London: Prentice Hall.
40 'OECD'. *The Economist*, 12 January 2013.
41 Todnem, R. (2003), 'Organisational Change Management: A Critical Review', *Journal of Change Management*, 5 (4), pp. 369–380.
42 Witness, for example, an announcement by the BBC regarding how they would go about collecting the licence fee using a less threatening series of letters not presuming guilt. TV licence fee collection review, http://www.bbc.co.uk/bbctrust/our_work/strategy/licence_fee/review_collection.html, 31 March 2009.
43 http://worldwide.hyundai.com/WW/Corporate/CorporateInformation/CorporatePhilosophy/index.html/, accessed January 2016.
44 Cottle, D.W. (1990), *Client-centred Service: How to Keep Them Coming Back for More*. Chichester: John Wiley.

Chapter 8

Communities with a purpose: Significance with belonging

> Young people, who are more interconnected than ever through technology and social media, have claimed a key role in shaping civil society; creating a better world for all.
>
> Babatunde Osotimehin, United Nations Population Fund (UNFPA)[1]

Where we have come to in this book is that employers with intelligence, integrity and a concern to create a world with better opportunity for all, regardless of place of birth, are recognising the need to recalibrate the employment relationship. They seek a more balanced set of power relations that do not accentuate insecurity and anxiety nor exacerbate income and power differentials within the workplace. Emblematic employers such as Unilever and John Lewis or the Big Four professional service firms show that it is possible to be commercially successful but still avoid anachronistic and dysfunctional power relationships in working lives. They are not afraid of rebalancing power in favour of their people.[2]

The concept of 'environments of value' is about how to build environments or local cultures in organisations that draw out the value and worth of people in such a way as to invest that in the purpose for which the organisation exists. We propose here that leaders of the future know how to work with the grain of what motivates their people. To develop the circumstances in which people give of their best is therefore to optimise the conditions within which they feel valued.

What we will now address is how the construct offered here might apply to the not-for-profit organisations of the future. Where the reward systems apply to a company in a commercial environment, it might be thought that extrinsic motivations of remuneration are core drivers of turning up for work every day. With his hierarchy of needs, Maslow has of course articulated a very different approach as we will be exploring. How the construct of 'environments of value' applies to not-for-profit organisations may be rather different, though, where salary is often less. People clearly do take a cut in salary to work for charities, faith-based organisations or in civil society. Purpose, significance and belonging – ingredients of a valuing environment – may be shaped differently.

The positive counterparts of the construct we are exploring were to do with:

- L – look, learn and listen
- I – involve and include
- D – dignify.

To develop the construct now, it is important to stress that these ingredients build a sense of significance, the sensation of being somebody, a worthwhile person. Feeling that one is a person of high value is fed by such factors.

Purpose and significance go together. Participants feel that they count, that they matter.

'Significance' relates to questions of purpose. At a popular level, the marketing guru David Hieatt argues that the most important brands in the world make us feel something. They do that because they have something they want to change. And as customers, we want to be part of that change. These companies have a reason to exist over and above making a profit: they have a purpose.[3]

A powerful brand conveys something that it wishes to change but also persuades customers that they want to be part of that change. Steve Jobs at Apple was a prime example of that, as were many innovators who created the digital revolution.[4]

Many derive significance from a sense of belonging, of being part of something.

Typically, belonging seems to involve a sequence of acknowledgement (recognising the person), approval (evaluating the person) and acceptance before a person is admitted to a group and so achieves the need for belonging. With further approval they gain respect, esteem and consequent status, in which they gain power and consequent control. Recognition and respect are the correlates of the factors for being a person of high value. In Maslow's hierarchy, it rates just above health and security needs.[5]

Studies show that when social relationships provide a sense of belonging, people feel life has more meaning. In one experiment, participants were asked to close their eyes and think of two people or groups to which they really belonged. They were then asked about how much meaning they felt life had. This group was compared with two control groups (in total, n=644) where participants (1) thought about the value of other people and (2) the help that others had provided them. Compared with these two conditions, participants who had been thinking about the groups they belonged to felt the highest levels of meaning in life. The evidence was that a sense of belonging predicts how meaningful life is perceived to be. Belonging to a group provided meaning over and above the value of others or the help they could provide.[6]

There are clearly different modes of belonging. Some derive a sense of value that comes from belonging to family, faith community, friendship networks, educational community and social media. For many of working age, it is in the workplace or a high quality organisation where they can build a sense of being part of a web of belonging.

The point about the notion of an environment of value is that it fosters a sense of belonging to a community of practice in which participants do not just feel they are worthwhile people per se, they feel embedded in worthwhile tasks. It is about high value as part of something bigger; not the individual as an agent standing as a subject to which everyone else is object.

This ties in with work from the 1960s and 1970s by Fred Fiedler, Director of the Organisational Research Group in Washington. Fiedler pondered what it is about leadership behaviour which leads to effective group working. Effectiveness was defined, argued Fiedler, according to how well the group performs the primary task for which it exists.[7] Fiedler identified two main leadership styles:

- **Relationship-motivated leaders** derive their major satisfaction from good personal relationships with others. Their sense of value depends on how others regard them. They are sensitive to what their group members feel. Subordinates are encouraged to participate and to offer ideas.
- **Task-motivated leaders** are very purpose-driven, concerned to stay on task, run a tight ship and feel most comfortable working from superiors' guidelines and implementing them.

The ideal leader, Fiedler proposed, aimed at the most appropriate style for each type of workplace context.[8] This will vary. Where a leader has good relations and strong position power, the leadership task is easier. Where in civil society, by contrast, someone might lead an organisation replete with a volunteer workforce or be chair of a parent–teacher association arranging an outing, the technical task-competence might not be so central as the ability to foster good relationships. Leadership performance depends on situational favourableness as much as personal style of the leader.[9]

Building on this work, the UK academic John Adair's Action-Centred Leadership model is represented by Adair's 'three circles' diagram.[10] Adair's three core management responsibilities were:

- achieving the task;
- managing the team or group;
- managing individuals.[11]

Adair was probably the first to demonstrate that leadership is a trainable, transferable skill, rather than it being an exclusively inborn ability.[12] He helped change perception of management to include leadership, for example with his book *Not Bosses but Leaders* showing how executives can become business leaders.[13]

What is crucial, though, is for organisations to be able to draw on the resources of their people in an environment of value. This study is developing a construct that the mobilisation and release of the human dimension in an enterprise depend on:

- the value that participants feel they have in that situation or environment;
- the conditions under which a sense of value and worth is translated into added value for the enterprise;
- that these conditions for a valuing environment in which participants give of their best in a community of practice are essentially threefold:

  a   the opposite of being treated with **indignity** – i.e. given dignity and treated with respect;

  b   the opposite of being treated with **inequality** – i.e. a full measure of humanity honoured and evoked so that participants grow and are not diminished;

  c   the opposite of being treated with **indifference** – being engaged, heard and listened to.

Humans are not only hard-wired to be motivated to pursue high value, we are also relational. It is in constellations with those around us (family or workplace) that our humanity is patterned.

These conditions – whether present or absent – affect the lived experience of one-to-one interpersonal relationships within that organisation – one's fellow workers, the boss, etc. They also shape the pattern and style of the culture on the ground that either makes or breaks aims and strategy. A community of practice or the learning environment (whatever term is used) is the local system, the dynamics of that particular part of the vineyard of the overall company or charity. When workers or staff are in this kind of learning community that draws out the value and worth of its people, that community is developing purpose.

An environment of value is a community of practice that will have purpose at its heart. The purpose is, however, defined differently. There are different kinds of communities and organisations, just as there are different forms of value. The value created by a commercial company is clearly different to that of an arts body. Their purpose is different.

In human relationships, there are close-knit communities such as marriage, family and deep friendships where intimacy is a skill to be acquired. And there are communities with a task. Interaction with purpose fills our days as we trade and exchange with people across our world. Often with commerce, the task is more important than the people. A company exists to fulfil its 'objects'. Yet people yearn to belong. Belonging is available at work, in voluntary organisations, military regiments, in villages, in towns, in cities and in regions and in classes. People belong to the club, to the sports team, the fan clubs, the firm, to trade unions or belong to faith-based groups.

To experience purpose without community is barren food for the human spirit. Belonging has been important to be part of a company. Being laid off affects positioning and place wherewith people anchor themselves. Quickly, it can become an existential threat. Yet a voluntary organisation is different. It does not have the overriding goal of making money, of profit. As long as it is generating sufficient revenue to keep itself afloat, its existence in the world is not tied to the measurable return of finance capital.

There are many voices that have been raised in the last generation about the decline of voluntary association. Supportive social connections have weakened in an era of 'loose connections' to use Robert Wuthnow's phrase.[14] To those who charge that certain kinds of civic engagement may be declining and people are at home watching television rather than getting involved in their communities, Wuthnow argues that innovative new forms are taking their place. A significant change has occurred away from group affiliations and traditional civic organisations; there has been a corresponding movement towards affiliations that respond to individual needs and collective concerns. The need to belong is strong. Many are finding new and original ways to help one another through short-term task-oriented networks.

Similarly the US social scientist Robert Putnam provided evidence that while the number of bowlers in America rose 10 per cent from 1980 to 2000, the number of those participating in bowling leagues declined by 40 per cent. 'Bowling alone' sums up this change in lifestyle. Putnam draws on evidence including nearly 500,000 interviews since 2000 to show that Americans signed fewer petitions, belong to fewer organisations that meet, know their neighbours less, meet with friends less frequently, and even socialise with their families less often. Changes in work, family structure, age, suburban life, television, computers, women's roles and other factors have contributed to this decline.[15] The amount of 'social capital' – the very fabric of our connections with each other – has plummeted, impoverishing our lives and communities.

The application, and indeed the very concept of 'social capital' is open to question here.[16] There is also mixed evidence about the rise of volunteering. The frequency of many types of communal participation has declined considerably since about 1975. Socialising generally, such as eating communally or in families has been falling.[17] Civic involvement has declined considerably. Today's 20- and 30-year-olds are half as likely to join face-to-face groups than their grandparents. Roper surveys in the US show that volunteering has actually increased though this could be the over 65s. The impact of television has been considerable in these trends.[18]

Crucial to note here is that many clearly use communication technologies, such as the World Wide Web, to connect with like-minded people in distant locations. Distance has died. Less formal associations such as support groups are flourishing. People are still connected, but because of the realities of daily life, they form 'loose connections'. These more fluid groups are better suited to dealing with today's needs than the charities and voluntary groups of a past era.

These considerations shape the context of not-for-profit organisations with much greater flexible patterns of working. The future of volunteering is hard to predict as is that of its context in civil society. Civil society is recognised as encompassing far more than a mere 'sector' dominated by the NGO community: civil society today includes an ever wider and more vibrant range of organised and unorganised groups. The Yearbook of International Organisations reported growth from 6,000 in 1990, to 50,000 in 2006 and some 68,000 by 2015: it has details from 300 countries and territories. Approximately 1,200 new organisations are added each year including non-governmental organisations (NGOs).

The 'civil society ecosystem' typically includes:

- NGOs, non-profit organisations and civil society organisations (CSOs) that have an organised structure or activity, and are typically registered entities and groups;
- online groups and activities including social media communities that can be 'organised' but do not necessarily have physical, legal or financial structures;
- social movements of collective action and/or identity, which can be online or physical;
- labour unions and labour organisations representing workers;
- social entrepreneurs employing innovative and/or market oriented approaches for social and environmental outcomes;
- grassroots associations and activities at local level;
- cooperatives owned and democratically controlled by their members;
- religious leaders, faith communities, and faith-based organisations.

When the latter is factored in, faith communities and faith-based organisations run into many, many more thousands internationally. The important point here is, as the World Economic Forum notes, as new civil society actors blur the boundaries between sectors and experiment with new organisational forms, both online and off, roles are also changing: civil society actors are demonstrating their value as facilitators, conveners and innovators as well as service providers and advocates, while the private sector is playing an increasingly visible and effective role in tackling societal challenges. Though the concept should be challenged, renewed interest in the role of faith is identifying powerful sources of social capital.

By being engaged with government, business and international organisations, civil society actors can and should provide the resilient dynamism the world urgently needs. The power and influence of civil society are growing and should be harnessed to create trust and enable action across sectors. The changes that civil society is undergoing strongly suggest that it should no longer be viewed as a 'third sector'; rather, civil society should be the glue that binds public and private activity together in such a way as to strengthen the common good.[19]

Across the board, leadership is needed for turbulent times. Civil society organisations are attempting to find their place in an increasingly networked global context. The baby boomers are educated, socially aware and have high expectations. The generation that came of age at the millennium are now exercising their technology-enabled influence in an interconnected way. When social movements drive momentous change, organised civil society is asking, 'where were we?' and looking to build links to translate spontaneous activity into meaningful change. There is a proliferation of voices online in a way that demonstrates the power of connectivity. This is leading to different forms of public engagement and consultation.

One crucial dimension that civil society leaders must grapple with is that they have witnessed traditional funding streams shrink. Donor criteria have changed including diversification of funding sources, requirements for private sector partners, and stringent requirements to demonstrate impact. Concurrently, new sources of finance are emerging, such as the rise of emerging market philanthropists, social entrepreneurs, and social investment products. New mechanisms to access finance are also emerging, such as crowd-sourced funding and such models as online lending platforms connecting lenders and entrepreneurs. The old charity model is dying but new forms are emerging.

The World Economic Forum identified six critical driving forces that significantly reshape the future context of civil society:

- the level and sources of funding for civil society stakeholders;
- the social and political influence of increasing access to technology;
- the extent and type of citizen engagement with societal challenges;
- the state of global and regional geopolitical stability and global integration of markets;
- the effect of environmental degradation and climate change on populations;
- the level of trust in governments, businesses and international organisations.

Citizen engagement and identification with serious societal challenges determine the public's willingness to volunteer and support civil society activities with funding and political support. This is vital for democracy. As Leopoldo Martinez from the Center for Democracy and Development in the Americas (CDDA) observed, 'civil society is dynamic and essential for the preservation of democracy.'[20] The government and private sector are both deeply engaged in tackling societal challenges. The combination of widening access to data, technology and rigorous monitoring are the hallmarks of a revolution in both economic activity and social development.[21]

What is likely is that the digital future will see many combining occupational skills with community interests in non-profit and voluntary associations. A blurring of roles and overlap of activity by business, government and civil society stakeholders is highly likely. We are witnessing a changing paradigm. In the model we have been used to, government, business and civil society acted in their own spheres of influence. In the network society characterised by new forms of engagement and dynamism, everything is interconnected. There could well be much more of a revolving door between industry, charity and non-governmental organisations. This could perhaps extend to faith-based organisations – often the glue of civil society.

The role of faith-based communities

It is highly likely that a networked future will affect the participation of faith-based communities. Indeed, it is already happening.

The last 20 years have seen a crisis of trust in major public institutions, from politics and media, to banking, to health, social care and education. Alongside this crisis has been a renewed visibility of religion in society, with religions often offering critical but contentious voices, as well as being key but contested contributors to political activism and welfare service delivery. Prominent theorists such as Jürgen Habermas have suggested that religion may hold the key to reenergising the public sphere, that area in social life where individuals can come together to freely discuss and identify societal problems, and through that discussion influence political action.[22] He suggested that there was a political revitalisation of religion at the heart of Western society. Yet religions are just as often seen as disruptive, as engulfed in similar crises of trust, as undermining shared values, or as presenting challenging practices. With societies now becoming more secular, more religious and more plural all at once, claims abound that one group or another is being favoured or presents a threat. This tension is further complicated by contested developments in the understanding of religion: some scholars have broadened the category of religion to include ostensibly secular ideas and practices; others have suggested that religions are acting less like states, with large bureaucracies and loyal citizens, and more like markets that cater to consumers, with belief less likely to be based on dogma than modes of belonging or self-expression; others still suggest that future success for religions will require greater recognition of ethnic minorities, women and LGBT communities.[23]

There is increasing interest in, and prominence of, faith and religious culture in public life, as well as a growing recognition of the contributions these can make to society. Faith communities are increasingly seen as integral to solving global problems and human security needs as influential authorities, trusted partners, service providers, community mobilisers and advocates. The role of faith is also important as a source and voice for values and morality that are widely perceived as lacking in modern, secular society. Several factors drive this renewed interest in new opportunities for faith to engage in civil society and the public sphere, such as increased appreciation of the dynamism and in many cases the growth of individual faith in many parts of the world. Data from the Pew Research Center indicates that more than eight in ten people globally identify with a religious group.[24] The sociologist Peter Berger, writing about the phenomenon of 'desecularisation', claims that 'the world today, with some exceptions … is as furiously religious as it ever was … '. He has admitted to his own miscalculations about secularisation, concluding that the existence of resurgent religiosity in the modernised world has proven otherwise.[25]

Recent years have seen increased appreciation of the resources inherent within communities of faith – people, community buildings, financial capital, and social links. These have the potential to be deployed in the direction of delivering social welfare and community services. This is as true of developing countries, where faith communities are often the primary provider of basic schooling or nutrition, as of the West, where faith communities' infrastructure helps the poor, vulnerable and unwell.[26]

There seems to be increased appreciation of the importance of the role of faith in strengthening social bonds and the resilience of civil society to develop positive resistance to extremist elements. Faith communities are sources of extremism but much more of community cohesion thanks to the engagement of faith communities and organisations at the grassroots of society. Many governments include faith communities in public policy, local governance and the provision of services though the involvement of faith in politics, policy and decision-making remains controversial and requires reflection on boundaries between institutions and between the public and personal. For example, through the UK Government Partnership on Aid with Faith Communities in June 2012, the Church and faith groups signed up to new principles for collaborating with the UK government on aid. The Faith Partnership paper signalled a new stage of understanding and cooperation between government and faith groups on social development. Significantly, the UK Department for International Development's Global Poverty Action Fund (GPAF) – designed to ensure broader reach than 'usual suspects' – awarded two-thirds of their 54 grants to new organisations that had not previously received funding, ten of which were faith-based organisations.[27]

What, however, is the difference between a faith-based group and a company? Indeed, are non-profit organisations so different from either commercial companies or public service providers as to entail separate management models and practices? Is the leadership task a variation of business management? Or is it closer to public administration? Is the task of building an environment of value in which the inner value of people can be mobilised similar in any organisation where the collective dimension moulds the actions and interactions between the human participants?

Leading non-profit organisations

The management of non-profit organisations is usually conceived as being shaped differently because the urge to maximise profit is absent. Not-for-profit organisations vary much in terms of mission, size, mode of operation and impact, particularly in a cross-national sense. Some resemble a commercial company; others are more akin to a publicly funded body.

The lack of an explicit profit motive allows for a range of motivations and causes to come to the surface in non-profit organisations. Non-profits operate in areas that are often hard to operate in commercially: provision for people with disabilities, the socially excluded and minorities; hospices and care facilities for frail older people; international humanitarian assistance; advocacy groups; and local community associations. Indeed, the very existence of the non-profit form is linked to the nature of services they provide and the fields in which they work.[28] Increasingly, not-for-profits are a network, formal or informal. It is worth recalling characteristics that non-profit organisations are generally agreed to have:

- *Organised* – possessing some institutional reality, distinct from entities such as families, gatherings or movements;
- *Private* – institutionally separate from government, distinct from the public sector;

- *Non-profit-distributing* – not returning any profits generated to shareholders or owners or equivalents;
- *Self-governing* – equipped to control their own activities;
- *Voluntary* – some degree of voluntary input in either its activities or its management.[29]

Rather than being seen as trivial and inconsequential,[30] non-profits have become a significant economic force, important political players[31] and a focus of management study in their own right.[32] The rise of the sharing economy especially means that they have to be taken seriously. The complexity of how to lead not-for-profit organisations lies in their sheer variety. For instance, it has been claimed the essence of voluntary agencies lies in their dual functions as both guardians of values of the organisation and provider of the service that they exist to offer.[33] These are organisations that exist around values;[34] another lens is that trust and voluntarism are at the centre of non-profit organisations.[35] Given that some are value-led or value-based, while others operate without any explicit value system, some are at most marginally based on notions of voluntarism, and may involve no volunteers, ambiguity may best describe the essence of most non-profit organisations.[36]

The central issue is that most not-for-profit companies were built around voluntarism, faith, philanthropy, compassion and a concern for the public good. Management seemed both inappropriate and antithetical.[37] The language and values seem to be at odds with those of the private sector. Yet management has been 'discovered' by social enterprises, by charities and even churches.[38] Strategic management is regarded as an essential tool.[39] Effective financial management is now regarded as crucial for the private and voluntary sector alike.[40] Yet not-for-profit organisations cannot fully copy business practices. In the private sector, financial management has tended to view organisations as separate entities that can be measured in terms of inputs, outputs, costs and revenue, assets and liabilities. A non-profit organisation has several bottom lines. The same price mechanisms are not in place that can bring together in numbers the interests of clients, staff, volunteers and other stakeholders and match company goals to actual achievements.[41] The balance of supply and demand, cost and profit or supply to demand are constituted differently and weighed in different scales. The voluntary sector tended to see financial management in terms of cost control. Many non-profit organisations whose purpose is not to maximise profits came to embrace the language, business models, management practices, even the culture of business.[42]

This works both ways. There is much that the private sector can learn from the voluntary sector of the future. This may be particularly true of the thesis of this book, that it is the task of leadership to engender cultures that draw out the inner value of participants. Any non-profit organisation of, for example, 50 employees and 100 volunteers easily surpasses the complexity of managing an equivalent for-profit firm of equal size.[43]

It is not just about life in the corporate jungle. Nancy Lublin, former CEO of Do Something, suggests that learning need not just travel in one direction. Social enterprises can discover from business how best to run their organisations.[44] In *Zilch: The Power of Zero in Business*,[45] Lublin argues that 'not-for-profit' outfits do many things to motivate workers that profit-driven business companies could well imitate – ranging from a flat management structure to leaders pitching in to help get a task done to building long-term relationships with customers and clients rather than a one-off contractual transaction.

Arguably, the reason why these factors are important is because they promote human value as an environment in which people flourish at their optimum.

One obvious way that the private sector can learn from the voluntary sector of the future is the concept of servant leadership developed by Robert K. Greenleaf in 1970. It was inspired by Hermann Hesse's *Journey to the East*, relating a mythical journey involving a band of men. Leo, whom he had known first as servant, was in fact the titular head of the Order, its guiding spirit, a great and noble leader.[46] The servant leader serves the people he/she leads, which implies that employees are an end in themselves rather than a means to an organisational purpose or bottom line.[47] Servant leadership replaces command and control models of leadership, to be more focused on the needs of those participating in a project.[48]

The Alliance for Servant Leadership offers the following guidelines for servant leadership.

- Service as a fundamental goal in the belief that anyone accepting the role of leader should do so out of the desire to be of service to others.
- Enabling environments that empower and encourage service, that recognise the equal worth of every person and that foster the achievement of everyone's full potential.
- Trusting relationships as the foundation for collaboration and service, affirming that all relationships should be based on trust and mutual respect, not power, status or coercion.
- Creating commitment as a way of enlisting everyone's contribution rather than manipulation or some other superficial form of motivation.
- Community-building to create environments in which people can trust each other and work together, recognising that people work best in collaboration, in teams.
- Nurturing the spirit, creating the conditions in which everyone can find meaningful work and satisfaction through their contributions.[49]

In many charity or faith-based enterprises, leaders often have a charismatic, transformational style which inspires others to follow. Yet when leaders want to lead, they give up formal authoritarian control. Following is always voluntary.

The dilemma for servant leadership is that it has paternalistic overtones as it suggests doing things for employees rather than helping them to think for themselves. Treating employees as partners is more respectful and valuing.[50] Employees in a business are not members of a club or citizens at the purest level of community.

Whatever the appropriate leadership style, as public sector budgets are cut back, voluntary organisations are being asked to shoulder more responsibilities.[51] Many used to rely on state support. There is much greater uncertainty. Dependable government support or sources of charity funding have been to a large extent starting to dry up. Some kind of business model seems unavoidable to fund some activities. The prevailing note is of uncertainty – clearly the climate that the private sector is used to operating in.[52]

The human dimension: Working with the construct

For all those comparisons and contrasts between the private sector and not-for-profit organisations including charities and faith-based activity in the public square, leaders are still dealing with people.

The rewards are different. Or are they? We will explore this shortly in the context of the motivational drivers but it seems clear that fundamental to human action is the need for significance. Many participants in an organisation are highly oriented towards having a cause, to what they hope to achieve and how this will make the world a slightly better place.

Recalling Fiedler's work, one major contrast, however, would appear to be that of being people-oriented rather than task-oriented. In a family or social club, the people are all-important. This is a community which is '*for people*', a community simply as a group of people who have something in common; a fellowship or a group of people who come together for mutual support and to fulfil their basic needs. Anthropologists have called this a modality – in effect a people-focused community such as a city. Members of the city do not have to be there. They can move in or move away and in the meantime take up citizen rights such as voting. There are few disciplines in the very loose structure. In this kind of system, members interact personally over time, guided by collectively evolved norms of behaviour.

There are also types of community that are communities with purpose. These are organisations that are more structured, usually more disciplined and which have a task at their heart.[53] These are sometimes referred to as *modalities*. A faith-based community exists on the level of people being the major focus. It also has another dimension though, that of task and purpose. Often, these two aspects are in tension as leaders endeavour to move people towards their mission.

It might be thought that a highly structured commercial environment is completely task focused. Yet much of industry subscribes in principle at least to the notion that people are at the heart of their operation; witness a publicity statement by Modality Systems about 'Advanced Collaboration':

> Advanced collaboration is a facilitator to business transformation, enabling improved communications, better interactions and increased productivity. It can support faster decision making, enhanced customer service, employee engagement and cost savings. Above all, advanced collaboration puts people at the heart of your operations, enabling you to redefine business processes and identify new ways of working.[54]

In contemporary society, leadership is less about issuing directives than building relationships with people. The question is, 'which society?' Leadership styles vary from culture to culture. A style of task-oriented leadership involving giving commands from a distance is more acceptable now in Asian leadership contexts which are more about meeting the group. The structure of not-for-profit organisations generally depends upon a more personal relationship between workers and managers. Making things happen can be more time-consuming than with a traditional bureaucratic or hierarchical model.

There are clearly different levels of thinking about organisations and communities:

- family/club/city
- faith-based/charity
- public sector providers of service
- commercial environments.

At each level, however, belonging is vital. Human participants in an enterprise at any level yearn to belong. They also yearn for significance. These are both ingredients of the sense that individuals may feel of personal value and worth. The dimension of 'belonging' is the collective dimension within which individual worth may be experienced. Putting these two ideas together, we arrive at the following proposition: The need to be a person of value and worth is expressed through SIGNIFICANCE WITH BELONGING. Our sense of being somebody would appear to be needed at every level.

Facework

Faith-based work and that of, say, teachers and doctors have a pivotal role in a Facebook future to exemplify what might be termed 'Facework'. From changing patterns of management[55] to the disbandment of assembly lines in a post-Fordist economy, the reaction against the impersonal has actually been formidable. As the sociologist Daniel Bell remarked:

> in the coming century, the emergence of a new social framework of telecommunications may be decisive for the way in which economic and social exchanges are conducted, the way knowledge is created and retrieved, and the character of the occupations and work in which men engage.[56]

Facework is to do with the recovery of face. This is not just by those on the receiving end of institutional provision; it is to do with the institutions themselves not being seen to wear a human face, being cold places which reinforce the atomisation of everyday life. Lack of face evokes a reciprocal reaction of denial of face in which my personhood is negated. The subject is objectified.

In the wake of austerity and recession, institutional presence is in retreat. Public services are being slim-lined and shrunk to fit a smaller resource base. Relentless public sector reform is here to stay. Facework could be crucial to the redesign of public services to make them environments that are friendlier to human value. Perhaps this is why both the Arab Spring protests and the Occupy movements combined face-to-face with electronic elements, especially social media.[57]

In response to lack of face, contemporary people pursue a vagabond relationship with technology. Technology solidifies systems and considerably strengthens the capacity of public services to deliver. Institutional provision would be unthinkable without the systemic capacities granted by computers. Being seen totemically as a number and subject to management information systems is heavily dependent on the leap forward in capability made possible by the explosion in information technology in a single generation. Reactions of de-personalisation are often associated with automated systems. People want to hear a human voice on the other end of the phone.

As an example, September 2012 saw a storm of protest against UK government proposals to simplify welfare claims. This was a strategy of reduction, lowering the number of benefit options in favour of a single payment. But what raised hackles was the technology that was built into the operation, requiring claimants to claim online. Critics pointed out that this did nothing for the 8 million who do not have online access personally or the even greater number who are computer illiterate. In the eyes of the objectors, the equation seemed to be: automated systems in public service = impersonal response. The lack of human face compounds the reduction and generates a lack of face in its mirror by which I am disregarded and devalued.

One response to the automated systems that characterise modern life is to seek alternative networks and communities. Seeking network through Facebook is an explosive contemporary form of new patterns of apparent familiarity and friendship. It offers face. In a technocratic age, people are as swayed as they ever were by the desire to maintain relationships and build community with other people: at work, in voluntary organisations, military regiments, in villages, in towns, in cities and in regions and in classes. They belong to the club, to the sports team, the fan clubs, the firm, trade unions or a church. It is in belonging and through social interaction where human value flourishes and we do our best work.

Public service institutions can be liberated to offer opportunities for becoming more human. Small communities attempt to do that. Facebook can be seen as an attempt to recreate the intimacy and community that for many is a fading memory. Acres of emails flash across the virtual face of the deep. But the human voices are growing silent. Along comes Facebook and similar networks. These are online communities. How far they offer authentic community or its illusion is another question. The new technology is a site of ambiguity when it comes to human devaluation. Self-absorbed people engrossed in their social media and mobile phones fail to look up and see their fellow humans.

Despite the name, 'facework' is not usually part of the Facebook experience and the distance is not always offset by the potential for web-cams or that small static picture in the corner. But small communities do seem to offer an antidote to the anonymity of urban spaces and often, people value the intimacy and sense of the familiar that comes with small groups. It is about knowledge; knowing and being known. This is possible in community in a way that networks rarely offer. Despite being problematic, networks and online communities do perhaps constitute a wiring up of human interaction that is some kind of remedy to contemporary de-personalisation. How we make online interactions more humane is a major question in a post-industrial age. It is all a far cry from a more regimented machine age. Communities are being redrawn around groups of the like-minded rather than being based on geography. Yet still the need to see 'face' is paramount and it must be doubted if electronic communities will fully satisfy that need.

Place

Face and place live next door to each other. Belonging is a lot to do with notions of 'place'.

The 'place' in which we sit or stand is often taken for granted and ignored in our increasingly mobile society. Differentiating between place and space, Inge argues that place has very much more influence upon human experience than is generally recognised and that this lack of recognition, and all that results from it, are dehumanising.

Working against the dehumanising effects of the loss of place, community and places each build the identity of the other; effects of globalisation continue to erode people's rootedness and experience of place.[58] Politicians who do not grasp either the fears or effects of immigration and free movement of people and jobs simply do not understand why place continues to be important. It may be that globalisation, as it is normally understood, can be regarded as self-destroying when it is considered under the rubric of glocalisation. Globalisation in its literal sense is the transformational process of local or regional phenomena into global ones. It was only with the rise of anti-globalisation movement(s) at the end of the 1990s that the theme of the relationship between the local and the global came to the forefront. As Roland Roberston argues, 'so much stress has been placed in the study of globalisation on what is called either connectivity or interconnectedness; although the introduction of the concept of glocalisation is an important corrective to this.'[59] We are witnessing the return of place.

Theologians are exploring this idea. 'The sense of being lost, displaced, and homeless is pervasive in contemporary culture. The yearning to belong somewhere, to be in a safe place, is a deep and moving pursuit. Loss of place and yearning for place are dominant images.'[60] Seemingly, such forces as fragmentation, mobility and dualism work against our belonging, and work against our richly dwelling in the places we live. Add to these the rise of 'virtual' place and relationships, and our sense of displacement only increases.[61]

The extent to which virtual space offers a collaborative commons that is authentic enough to feed a sense of belonging is a debate in its own right. Social participants might say they 'belong' to a Facebook network. It is a new type of community, not rooted in geography or locality. Arguably, the sense of uprootedness or dislocation is less than from physical place. What is less debatable is that social participants often feel a sense of belonging to the workplace. The very fact that we speak of the 'workplace' is significant. A place of work offers an environment where people often say they belong. It is part of what locates them as individuals in a community and not isolated entities.

Its antithesis – retirement – often brings a profound sense of dislocation for that very reason.

> Our capacity to attract, retain and manage executive talent does not depend on the compensation package, but rather on our ability to create a sense of belonging to an organisation that offers a long-term relationship and a professional development opportunity, and that has a clear conception of itself, of what it wants to be, and of how to achieve it.
>
> Armando Garza Sada, Chairman of the Board of Directors,
> Alfa SAB de CV, Mexico[62]

Future notes

Yet what of the future context in which voluntary and not-for-profit organisations will work? In the highly complex and rapidly evolving connected world, the future of civil society could be one of:

- **Revolving doors** – people migrating more readily between sectors. Agile labour means it is possible to do some work for a charity or creative industry but also hop between private and public. 'The globalisation of talent and technology frees up companies to experiment with new ways of filling critical skills gaps while staying lean. We call this phenomenon agile talent.'[63]
- **Time on their hands** – the future of volunteering is clearly shaped by the extent to which people have time on their hands, possibly through automation making many jobs redundant.
- **Inspiration** – participating in voluntary organisations is also shaped by the extent to which people can be mobilised for purpose, for the great cause that will call forth their passions. In particular, those coming of age at the millennium offer great promise, as digitally native, entrepreneurial and cosmopolitan world citizens.

The leadership for this day and age is the leadership of cross-sector experience and collaboration, able to make the link between private, public and civil society organisations, resources and activities. Harvard professor Joseph Nye calls them tri-sector athletes – individuals and organisations that nimbly cross traditional spheres of influence to translate and broker these different institutional logics into private–public, government–civil and civil–private partnerships and solutions. They are leaders with three distinct sets of strengths who can 'engage and collaborate across the private, public, and social sectors'. Drawing on his cross-sector experience, they can appreciate the needs, aspirations, and incentives of people in all three sectors and speak their language. Tri-sector leaders are distinguished as much by mindset as by experience. They typically have a strong sense of mission but rooted in 'contextual intelligence'.[64] In short, this is significance with belonging.

They will no doubt help to create the organisations of the future. For not-for-profit organisations and faith-based work as much as for the private sector, the culture in an organisation is created by the actions of its leaders. When a culture becomes dysfunctional, leadership is needed to steady the ship. Their challenge is to do things on a human scale which can counter the de-personalisation of remote forces by nurturing places which honour people's humanity and foster their value.

Notes

1 Babatunde Osotimehin, United Nations Population Fund How the Global Goals can unleash the power of young people WEF 24 September 2015 https://www.weforum.org/agenda/2015/09/how-the-global-goals-can-unleash-the-power-of-young-people

2 Hailey, V.H. and Gill, M., 'Power to the People?', https://www.futureworkishuman.org/power-to-the-people/, accessed June 2016.

3 Hieatt, D. (2014), *Do Purpose*. London: The Do Book Company.

4 Isaacson, W. (2014), *The Innovators*. London: Simon & Schuster.

5 Spears, R., Ellemers, N. and Doosje, B. (2009), 'Strength in Numbers or Less is More? A Matter of Opinion and a Question of Taste', *Personality and Social Psychology Bulletin*, 35 (8), pp. 1099–1111.

6 Lambert, N.M. (2013), 'To Belong Is to Matter: Sense of Belonging Enhances Meaning in Life', *Pers. Soc. Psychol. Bull.*, 39 (11), pp. 1418–1427.

7 Fiedler, F.E. (1967), *A Theory of Leadership Effectiveness*. New York: McGraw-Hill.

8 Fiedler, F.E., Chemers, M.M. and Mahar, L. (1977), *Improving Leadership Effectiveness: The Leader Match Concept*, rev. edn. Chichester: Wiley.

9 Babatunde Osotimehin, United Nations Population Fund How the Global Goals can unleash the power of young people WEF 24 September 2015. https://www.weforum.org/agenda/2015/09/how-the-global-goals-can-unleash-the-power-of-young-people.

10 Adair, J. and Thomas, N. (2005), *The Best of Adair on Leadership and Management*. London: Thorogood.

11 'Action Centred Leadership: John Adair's action-centred leadership – a model for team leadership and management', http://www.businessballs.com/action.htm/, accessed July 2016.

12 Adair, J. (2009), *Effective Leadership: How to be a Successful Leader*, rev. edn. London: Pan.

13 Adair, J. (2009), *Not Bosses but Leaders: How to Lead the Way to Success*. London: Kogan Page.

14 Wuthnow, R. (1998), *Loose Connections: Joining Together in America's Fragmented Communities*. Cambridge, MA: Harvard University Press.

15 Putnam, R. (2000), *Bowling Alone: The Collapse and Revival of American Community*. New York: Simon & Schuster.

16 Fine, B. (2001), *Social Capital versus Social Theory*. London: Routledge.

17 Myers, D.G. (2000), *The American Paradox: Spiritual Hunger in an Age of Plenty*. New Haven and London: Yale University Press.

18 Campbell, D.C., Yonish, S. and Putnam, R. (1999), 'Tuning in, Tuning out Revisited: A Closer Look at the Causal Links between Television and Social Capital', *Harvard Education Review*. https://www.researchgate.net/publication/228896075_Tuning_in_tuning_out_revisited_A_closer_look_at_the_causal_links_between_television_and_social_capital/.
19 *The Future Role of Civil Society*.
20 *The Future Role of Civil Society*.
21 Meyer, J., Boli, J., Thomas, G., and Ramirez, F.O. (1997), 'World Society and the Nation State', *American Journal of Sociology*, 103 (1), pp. 144–181.
22 Habermas, J. (1989), *The Structural Transformation of the Public Sphere: An Inquiry into a Category of Bourgeois Society*, trans. Thomas Burger. Cambridge, MA: The MIT Press.
23 Sociology of Religion Annual Conference 2016, British Sociological Association. http://socrel.org.uk/upcoming-events/.
24 'The Global Religious Landscape', 18 December 2012, http://www.pewresearch.org/, accessed June 2016.
25 Berger, P. (1999), *The Desecularization of the World: Resurgent Religion and World Politics*. Grand Rapids, MI: Ethics and Policy Center.
26 *The Future Role of Civil Society*.
27 https://www.gov.uk/guidance/global-poverty-action-fund-gpaf/, accessed June 2016.
28 Hansmann, H. (1996), *The Ownership of Enterprise*. Cambridge, MA: Harvard University Press.
29 Salamon, L.M. and Anheier, H.K. (eds) (1997), *Defining the Non-profit Sector: A Cross-National Analysis*. Manchester: Manchester University Press.
30 Perrow, C. (1986), *Complex Organizations: A Critical Essay*. New York: Random House.
31 Lewis, D. (ed.) (1999), *International Perspectives on Voluntary Action*. London: Earthscan.
32 Drucker, P. (1990), *Managing the Nonprofit Organization: Principles and Practices*: New York: Harper Collins.
33 Kramer, R. (1981), *Voluntary Organisations and the Welfare State*. Berkeley: University of California Press.
34 Hudson, M. (1999), *Managing without Profit*. London: Penguin.
35 Tonkiss, F. and Passey, A. (1999), 'Trust, Confidence and Voluntary Organisations: Better Values and Institutions', *Sociology*, 33 (2), pp. 257–274.
36 Billis, D. (1989), 'A Theory of the Voluntary Sector: Implications for Policy and Practice'. Working paper 4, Centre for Voluntary Organisation, London School of Economics, London.
37 Handy, C. (1988), *Understanding Voluntary Organisations*. London: Penguin.
38 Schwartz, P. (1992), *Management in Nonprofit Organisations*. Bern: Haupt.
39 Oster, S.M. (1995), *Strategic Management for Nonprofit Organizations: Theory and Cases*. New York: Oxford University Press.
40 McKinney, J.B. (1995), *Effective Financial Management in Public and Non-profit Agencies*. West Port, CT: Quorum.
41 Rose-Ackerman, S. (1996), 'Altruism, Nonprofits, and Economic Theory', *Journal of Economic Literature*, 34 (2), pp. 701–728.
42 Kanter, R. and Summers, D.S. (1987), 'Doing Good while Doing Well. Dilemmas of Performance Measurement in Non-profit Organisations and the Need for a Multiple Constituency Approach', in *The Non-profit Sector: A Research Handbook*, ed. W.W. Powell. New Haven, CT: Yale University Press.
43 Anheier, H.K. (2000), 'Managing Non-profit Organisations: Towards a New Approach'. Civil Society working paper, Centre for Civil Society, London School of Economics, London.
44 HRM Today, 29 June 2010, http://www.humanresourcestoday.com/.
45 Lublin, N. (2010), *Zilch: The Power of Zero in Business*. London: Penguin.
46 Hesse, H. (2003), *The Journey to the East*, trans. H. Rosner. New York: Picador.
47 Spears, L.C. (ed.) (1998), *Insights on Leadership: Service, Stewardship, Spirit, and Servant-leadership*. New York: Wiley.
48 Greenleaf, R.K. (2002), *Servant Leadership: A Journey into the Nature of Legitimate Power and Greatness*. New York: Paulist Press.

49 Indiana State University Alliance for Servant Leadership, http://www.indstate.edu/asl/, accessed June 2016.
50 http://www.leadersdirect.com/servant-leadership/, accessed June 2016.
51 Deakin, N. (1995), 'The Perils of Partnership: The Voluntary Sector and the State, 1945–1992', in *An Introduction to the Voluntary Sector*, ed. J.D. Smith, C. Rochester and R. Hedley. London: Routledge.
52 Williamson, O. (1975), *Markets and Hierarchies*. New York: Free Press.
53 Haviland, W.A., Prins, H.E.L., McBride, B. and Walrath, D. (2010), *Cultural Anthropology: The Human Challenge*, 13th edn. Belmont, CA: Cengage Learning.
54 https://www.modalitysystems.com/, accessed July 2016.
55 Waterman, R.H. and Peters, T. (1982), *In Search of Excellence*. New York: Profile Books.
56 Bell, D. (1979), 'The Social Framework of the Information Society', in *The Computer Age: A 20 Year View*, ed. M.L. Dertouzos and J. Moses. Cambridge, MA: MIT Press, pp. 500–549.
57 Gitlin, T. (2012), *Occupy Nation: The Roots, the Spirit, and the Promise of Occupy Wall Street*. New York: Harper Collins.
58 Inge, J. (2003), *A Christian Theology of Place: Explorations in Practical, Pastoral and Empirical Theology*. London: Routledge.
59 Robertson, R. (2015), 'Beyond the Discourse of Globalization', *Glocalism Journal of Culture, Politics and Innovation*, Issue 1.
60 Brueggemann, W. (2002), *Place as Gift, Promise, and Challenge in Biblical Faith*. Minneapolis, MN: Fortress Press.
61 Hjalmarson, L. (2014), *Introduction to a Theology of Place*. CreateSpace Independent Publishing Platform. https://www.createspace.com/, accessed June 2016.
62 *Millennials at Work: Reshaping the Workplace*, PWC, May 2016. www.pwc.com/people/, accessed May 2016.
63 Younger, J. and Smallwood, N. (2016), 'Aligning Your Organization with an Agile Workforce', *Harvard Business Review*, February 2016, https://hbr.org/.
64 Lovegrove, N. and Thomas, M. (2013), 'Triple-Strength Leadership', *Harvard Business Review*, September 2013. https://hbr.org/.

Chapter 9

Environments of value, systems and the organisations of the future

No structure is better suited to solving complex, ill-structured problems than adhocracy.

Henry Mintzberg[1]

The market can be described as 'a complex adaptive, ultra-large-scale socio-technical system of systems that is brittle'. The challenging news for leaders of organisations is that the future will be even more dramatic.[2]

Post-industrial leadership will have to adapt to new times. Industrial leadership models were for their time along with the organisational structures that expressed them. Post-industrial leadership will respond to the growing digital economy where the premium is on connectivity and networking rather than the hierarchical organisational structures we have been used to.

It is worth recalling that when in the early nineteenth century it had become clear that factory life had come to stay, they were by no means the large enterprises that are often associated with industrialisation. Returns from around the UK in 1851 indicated that over two-thirds of firms employed fewer than ten people.[3] Though on a larger scale, even railways and ships were essentially created by the craft method. It was when parts made in one part of a factory or production site were taken mechanically to another that the age of machinery entered into another phase. Machines produced other machines. The assembly line had arrived.

The organising principles of the big corporation as well as the bureaucracies we built to run modern society were about 'plan, organise, command, control and direct'. This was the core of Henri Fayol's administrative theory of management that epitomised the industrial revolution.[4] For Max Weber, bureaucracy was the superior form for well-defined and routinised task environments.[5] Senior managers of factories commanded people to perform their tasks in carefully laid-down ways. Industrial-era leaders treated people as cogs, as interchangeable and easily replaceable as spare parts on a factory machine. After the Second World War when the Allies, and especially the USA, won by out-producing their enemies, industrial leadership models reached their zenith. The factory was the way a corporation or public service bureaucracy should operate. Business schools taught this hierarchical perspective – essentially a continuation of wartime production. Bob McNamara, CEO of Ford before his public service career, epitomised this.[6] CEOs or company presidents, in whom leadership was vested, were the peace-time generals of their age. Leaders are what the leader does – a follower is expected to implement. James Mac-Gregor Burns commented that the leadership approach tended often to be elitist – it projects a heroic figure on the background of drab, powerless masses.[7]

In the concept of the individual rationality, the basis was laid for the major rationalising device for the twentieth-century beginnings of organisational science. The individual mind of the worker/employer/manager becomes a pre-eminent object of study. Knowledge of the organisation is a by-product of the individual rational agency of the scientific investigator.[8] The prevailing belief in rational agency figures in the concept of the ideal manager who acts out the idea that management is a process of planning, organising, coordinating and controlling. Individuals are in charge of the operation and through development of their capacities to think rationally, plan ahead, can generate superior performance. The task of the leader is to create an optimal balance between the organisation and environmental conditions. Strategic styles of management rest on the practice of optimising strategic choice, goal setting and path–goal orientations of leadership.[9] The new administrative science was to be an expression of 'deductive and inductive methods … operational definitions and measurement and evaluation'.[10] In Organisation Theory, organisations are treated as if they are individual entities that exist in their own right as singular, bounded and separate existences.[11]

The factory model was far too much of a straightjacket for the development of collaboration and continuous learning across an organisation. It could not respond to complexity. Models of post-industrial leadership, however, recognise that the level of complexity in the global work environment has increased dramatically. In a fully networked economy, the amount of information distributed is available to almost everyone in the organisation. Following Drucker's emphasis on knowledge workers, the importance of every individual in any organisation to be a fully involved member of a leadership dynamic is better understood. Followers are not the soldier ants for leaders but collaborators or partners. The role of leadership is to help generate transformative change through generating greater levels of effectiveness, not management which makes sequenced change incrementally through efficiency. The task is to create relationships and partnerships that engender transformative change.

Leadership in the post-industrial age is about people working together to create this level of change but in an environment of value built on trust. In this kind of environment, post-industrial leadership is incongruent with the nature of complexity.

> Many management and organisation textbooks have a tendency to look for the real dynamics underlying forces in an organisation or to promote something called 'best practice'. Quite apart from the epistemology of such efforts, I find that organisations are far too complex and messy for these efforts to be successful.[12]

Typically, OB and HR treat person and organisation as separate entities in the relation of subject to object where the former aims to know the latter through rational purposes and relational processes are reduced to input–output dynamics. Relational constructivism is a new psychology in which people are seen to participate in the construction of social realities.[13]

Yet where the call is not so much 'tell it like it is' but 'tell it like it will become', there is no way to close off creational processes of co-construction. Conversational partners tend to glaze over. In post-industrial leadership, post-modern critiques undermine the assumption of a scientifically managed transformation of organisations, the promise of steady growth in organisational efficiency plus long-standing assumptions about effective leadership. The new style recognises that patterns speak before we do. Patterns act.[14]

Although it is no doubt the conceit of every age that it is living through a time of unprecedented turbulent change, it must be beyond doubt that the growth of content, innovation, and technology is faster now than any other era in history. Such rapid acceleration, epitomised by Moore's Law, drives the speed of change in organisations. Peter Senge, author of *The Fifth Discipline*, argues that leaders cannot keep up with rapid change through the traditional top-down control mentality, nor can they do it with no formal structure or processes without an outbreak of anarchy. His solution to this was to create a learning environment, the sort of place where people expand their capacity to create the results they truly desire, where new and expansive patterns of thinking are nurtured, where collective aspiration is set free, and where people are continually learning together.[15]

The landscapes are shifting rapidly. As Alvin Toffler noted a generation ago in his *Future Shock*, the frenzy towards restructuring will give way to a 'new free form of kinetic organisations'. 'We are', he predicted, 'witnessing not the triumph but the breakdown of bureaucracy ... this is the organisation of the future. I call it "ad-hocracy".'[16]

Or Laloux could be cited. His thesis in *Reinventing Organisations* noted how seeing organisations as machines was being replaced by organisations as living organisms. The 'teal' organisation is a self-directed one, having moved away from meritocracy and hierarchy towards teams being liberated to run themselves.[17] These were of their time following a 'demise of size' much hailed by management gurus as major industrial companies were yielding to a far more entrepreneurial economy.

That at least is the story. It is a pleasant story but just as likely to be wrong. A fairy-tale narrative about the inversion of hierarchies that reflects a new cleavage in society is at worst but one reality, at best a pleasant bedtime narrative. Re-enter the corporate superstars. Apple, Facebook, Amazon, Google and the rest are the new giants, created out of nowhere to become the face of oligopoly in a digital age. Just as giant corporates fashioned the steel and oil industries and harnessed both electricity and the engine in the second industrial revolution, today's big businesses gain control of entire markets. The tech firms of our times succeed in this through privileging their own goods and services on their own platforms in a way that strikes everyone else as unfair competition. They generate howls of protest ranging from huge complaints that hard-nosed tax authorities are soft when it comes to the big corporates, to cries of corporate privilege that exacerbates pernicious inequality in society. The new superstars reply that they are merely being successful in combining economies of size with a culture of entrepreneurialism made in America. Business historians such as Alfred Chandler point out that a brief sprint of competition is usually followed by a marathon of consolidation and concentration.[18] Whatever became of Silicon Valley, harbinger of open-ended capitalism and freewheeling business organisations? It was after all a winner-takes-all jungle where only the fittest survive.

Digital technology has transformed the scope, scale and potential of business over the last decade. And those that have harnessed its potential have achieved greater returns and higher engagement with their customers.[19] Today's organisations face change forces from inside and outside the organisation. The complexity of the emerging future will completely recast the relationships between governments, businesses and workers. As we have noted, there is likely to be far more migration between the state, the private sector and civil society. These institutions used to offer a 'job for life' but this disappeared from the employment proposition about the same time as 'mergers and acquisitions', 'global restructuring' and 'downsizing' became mainstream. Organisations are moving towards employing agile talent to extend their capabilities in fast-moving strategic areas. Increasingly, leaders recognise that lean and agile business strategies require new ways of accessing talent to fill critical gaps deploying non-traditional employment and whether the industry can adapt the Uber model to more specialised, and higher-paying, fields such as consulting, engineering, IT and design. All such shifts in both the expectations of employees and obligations of employers have changed the nature of the power dynamics in the employment relationship. The 'Gig economy' is in a dynamic flux.

Growing numbers of Americans no longer hold a regular 'job' with a long-term connection to a particular business. Instead, they work 'gigs' where they are employed on a particular task or for a defined time, with little more connection to their employer than a consumer has with a particular brand of chips. Borrowed from the music industry, the word 'gig' has been applied to all sorts of flexible employment. Some have praised the rise of the gig economy for freeing workers from the grip of employers' 'internal labour markets', where career advancement is tied to a particular business instead of competitive bidding between employers. Rather than being driven by worker preferences, however, the rise of the gig economy comes from employers' drive to lower costs, especially during business downturns. Gig workers experience greater insecurity than workers in traditional jobs and suffer from lack of access to established systems of social insurance.[20]

At the time of writing, Uber have announced they are appealing against a court ruling in the UK that they provide their drivers with basic workers' rights. Judge Anthony Snelson even quoted from Shakespeare's great tragedy *Hamlet* in his withering assessment of the company's defence, saying: 'Reflecting on the respondents' general case, and on the grimly loyal evidence of [Uber regional general manager] Jo Bertram in particular, we cannot help being reminded of Queen Gertrude's most celebrated line, "The lady doth protest too much, methinks".' Uber drivers had won a landmark legal case meaning they can be classed as workers rather than self-employed contractors. Drivers for Uber, specifically, should have 'employee' status, which includes minimum wage and paid time off.[21]

To compete in the future, organisations will need to recruit a global network of outside contractors, outsourcing partners, vendors, strategic partners and other non-traditional workers. Such valuable talent is also increasingly mobile, global and borderless, thanks to the opportunities to work remotely. A great deal more now can be done by individuals interacting with each other directly rather than as market actors through the price system.[22] Increasingly, we will see decentralised action by individuals, working through voluntary forms of organisation. Wikipedia is the current example. There is very little management hierarchy.

We also have the blockchain revolution and its impact on the future or the organisation. This is where a network of peers is motivated to validate transactions, secure the network and achieve consensus about what has taken place. Such new thinking blurs the boundaries of what a company does and how it operates. A sign of decentralised, open services? And what of the human dimension since much of this is technology driven? Until now, the architecture of the corporation invented in the early twentieth century has remained intact. Companies remain companies and most of what a company does occurs within corporate boundaries. How long that continues for is anyone's guess. There will be some activities that are 'mission-critical'. Yet over time, what constitutes corporate boundaries and identity is bound to shift as lines blur between consultants, an agile workforce, customers and external peer communities.

Organism or organisation

Leadership of the future will have to work in a rapidly shifting environment and be used to the dynamic flux as a normal state of affairs rather than the steady state under conditions of equilibrium.

The varied styles needed to lead organisations effectively are increasingly complex because organisations and the environment in which they operate are increasingly complex. Knowing the varied ways organisational cultures work makes us wary of big generalisations.[23]

The idea of complex systems and emergence has come to be in vogue in the last 20 years. Complex systems are not to be confused with management systems which need to be in place to ensure delivery of objectives, bring order out of chaos and promote efficiency. Complex systems are in a different category. They are to do with patterns that form at a macro-level despite huge diversity amongst individuals. Just like the brain somehow brings together a constant flux of countless neurons and cells, complex systems are a dynamic flux of moving parts and information that creates new states. This is a developing model in the social sciences. It provides a different way of theorising the relationship between the individual and society, between human agency and structures. In classic accounts of society or organisations, what took analytic priority oscillated between such factors.[24]

Systems thinking is not new. It was implicit in classic organisational models. The emphasis though was on closed, physical systems. You analysed and then changed an organisation by reference to the internal environment. The system had reached its optimum when equilibrium had been restored and things had settled down (energy converted into heat, as it were).[25] The human element was subjected to technological imperatives. The concept of an organisation being 'dysfunctional' was developed to how show stresses and strains could lead to bad practice but these were still largely within the system.[26] Closed system thinking did not really capture the way that mutual permeation between an organisation and its environment shaped its life and times.

It began to be recognised that the task of leadership was not to tell people what to do but to provide boundary conditions that enabled workers to identify and then to get on with their tasks.[27] Open systems provided a new lens on organisations to explore the relatedness of individuals, the organisation and its environment but also more intangible realities borrowed from psychoanalytic approaches to group relations such as symbolism and projection.[28]

The reality is that organisational culture is manifested through the day-to-day interactions of employees. It does not exist in a filing cabinet on the top floor. The culture of a workplace is constantly being formed and re-formed through interaction; interaction of key players, policies, external constraints and the history of staff engagement. What each brings to the table is in dialogue and often in tension. Crucially, it will affect how staff listen to change and often will stymie the top-down structural changes managers think are necessary. The real issue is to change the culture.

There are major questions that arise from all this talk of emergence and the new participative paradigms. If, in the terms we have been looking at, indifference, indignity and diminishment are embedded and reproduced through cultures of human devaluation, is this to be equated with the old idea of systems based on self-balancing negative feedback to an equilibrium? In a complex system, instead of 'homeostasis' and system stabilisation, rapid change to new positions and states is possible. In the literature on complex systems, emergence seems to be implicitly benign. This must be challenged. Stacey describes a journey of thinking about organisations. From discovering how the idea of chaos in the natural sciences could be applied to management, he went on to think through the notion of complexity and open-ended systems. But he is careful to say that seeing organisations in terms of biological systems is useful but it is helpful only as a metaphor.[29] This is surely right. A self-organising biological system is a guide to thought rather than an exact description of an organisation. But where does the pressure to change come from in a dynamic human system? Arguably, alongside external or internal pressures towards structural change, the pressures towards change can often arise from reactions to being devalued in some way or the need to mobilise better the creative participation of the workforce and translate that into added value for the organisation.

Michael Porter from Harvard Business School suggests that the competitive advantage of a company lies in the way that networks of reinforcing activity are strung together in a way that is hard to replicate. It is the entire system of interlocking activities that constitutes a successful organisation.[30]

Yet in a very real sense, the whole economy will be networked and the system of constantly moving parts within an organisation must be framed as part of a wider field of external forces that impinge on it and interact constantly with it. As Yochai Benkler, former Professor at Yale, observed, the network economy is 'a new mode of production emerging in the middle of the most advanced economies in the world'.[31]

Irresistibly, economic forces are undermining old ways of doing things; reframing organisations and the leadership needed for them to be effective. As has been well said, imagine trying to explain the Internet to somebody living in the year 1200. The frame of reference you would use would be so different that it would be almost impossible to convey how the Internet works, let alone what it means to our society. You are standing on the other side of what would seem impossible to a person from the Middle Ages. The current rate of accelerating change and innovation suggests that we are the medieval ones. Trying to imagine future shock is a paradox, because it is an attempt to envision what is by definition unimaginable today.[32] What can be said though is that the willingness to be relational, to do the emotional labour is the key to better personal and organisational results. We were never taught the importance or the difficulty involved in doing this type of work. This has kept us stuck in our current paradigm, unable to achieve sustainably better results. Organisations must learn how to embrace rapid change while creating the trusted adviser relationships that will enable them to out-care the competition. The question then becomes this. 'How can emotional labour be taught (or caught)?'

Notes

1   Mintzberg, H. (1983), *Structure in Fives: Designing Effective Organizations*. Englewood Cliffs, NJ: Prentice Hall, p. 463.
2   Colville, R. (2016), *The Great Acceleration: How the World is Getting Faster, Faster*. London: Bloomsbury.
3   Checkland, S.G. (1964), *The Rise of Industrial Society in England 1815–1885*. London: Longman.
4   Witzel, M. (2003), *Fifty Key Figures in Management*. London: Routledge. See also Wren, D., Bedeian, A.G. and Breeze, J. (2002), 'The Foundations of Henri Fayol's Administrative Theory', *Management Decision*, 40 (9), pp. 906–918.
5   Mommsen, W.J. (1992), *The Political and Social Theory of Max Weber: Collected Essays*. Chicago: University of Chicago Press.
6   Halberstam, D. (1972), *The Best and the Brightest*. London: Pan Books.
7   Burns, J.M. (1978), *Leadership*. New York: Harper Collins.
8   Gergen, K. and Thatchenkery, T. (2006), 'Organisational Science and the Promise of Postmodernism', in *The Social Construction of Organisation*, ed. D.M. Hosking and S. McNamee. Copenhagen: Copenhagen Business Press, chapter 2.
9   Gergen and Thatchenkery (2006).
10 Thompson, J.D. (1956), 'On Building an Administrative Science', *Administrative Science Quarterly*, 1 (1), pp. 102–111, at p. 102.
11 Hosking, D.M. and Morley, I.E. (1991), *A Social Psychology of Organising*. London: Harvester Wheatsheaf.
12 Ramsey, C. (2006), 'Why Do I Write about Organization in Poetry?', in Hosking and McNamee (2006), p. 17.
13 Sampson, E.E. (1993), *Celebrating the Other: A Dialogic Account of Human Nature*. New York: Harvester Wheatsheaf.
14 Goffman, E. (1982), *Interaction Ritual: Essays in Face to Face Behaviour*. New York: Pantheon.
15 Senge, P. (2006), *The Fifth Discipline: The Art and Practice of the Learning Organization*, 2nd edn. London: Random House.
16 Toffler, A. (1970), *Future Shock*. New York: Random House, p. 125.
17 Laloux, F. (2015), *Reinventing Organisations*. Brussels: Nelson Parker.
18 Smothers, J. *et al.* (2006), 'Alfred D. Chandler, Jr: Historical Impact and Historical Scope of his Works', *Journal of Management History*, 16 (4), pp. 521–526.
19 'Profitable growth in the digital age', http://www.pwc.co.uk/services/consulting/insights.html/, 30 September 2013.
20 Friedman, G. (2014), 'The Rise of the Gig Economy', *Dollars and Sense*, March–April 2014.
21 http://inewstoday.net/2016/10/uber-loses-drivers-rights-ruling/, 30 October 2016.
22 Benkler, Y. (2006), *The Wealth of Networks: How Social Production Transforms Markets and Freedom*. New Haven: Yale University Press.
23 Schein, E. (1985), *Organisational Culture and Leadership*. San Francisco: Jossey-Bass.
24 Walby, S. (2009), *Globalisation and Inequalities: Complexity and Contested Modernities*. London: Sage.
25 Rice, A.K. (1963), *The Organisation and its Environment*. London: Free Association Books.
26 Merton, R.K. (1957), *Social Theory and Social Structure*. Glencoe, IL: Free Press.
27 Rice, A.K. (1958), *Productivity and Social Organization: The Ahmedabad Experiment*. New York and London: Free Association Books.
28 Miller, E. (1993), *From Dependency to Autonomy: Studies in Organisation and Change*. London: Free Association Books.
29 Stacey, R.D. (2003), 'Organizations as Complex Responsive Processes of Relating', *Journal of Innovative Management*, 8 (2), pp. 27–39.
30 Porter, M. (1996), 'What is Strategy?', *Harvard Business Review*, 74 (6), pp. 61–78.
31 Benkler, Y. (2006), *The Wealth of Networks: How Social Production Transforms Markets and Freedom*. New Haven, CT: Yale University Press, pp. xii, 515.
32 'The Future of Organizational Behavior', https://www.linkedin.com/pulse/future-organizational-behavior-phil-johnson/, accessed June 2016.

Chapter 10

The future leadership garden

The illiterate of the 21st century will not be those who cannot read or write; but those who cannot learn, unlearn and re-learn.

Alvin Toffler[1]

Future-proofing our children

We are educating children for a society that will be out of date within 15 years. As we have already noted, almost 47 per cent of US jobs could be computerised within one or two decades according to an Oxford study that attempts to gauge the growing impact of computers on the job market. Released by the Oxford Martin Programme on the Impacts of Future Technology, 'The Future of Employment: How Susceptible are Jobs to Computerisation?' evaluated around 700 jobs, classifying them based on how likely they are to be computerised, from low-risk occupations (recreational therapists, emergency management directors and health care social workers) to high-risk ones (library technicians, data-entry keyers and telemarketers).[2]

It brings us to the concept of 'digital intelligence'. Cultivating digital intelligence grounded in human values is essential for young people to become masters of technology, not just mastered by it. The acquisition of these abilities rooted in desirable human values such as respect, empathy and prudence cultivates values that facilitate wise and responsible use of technology for the leaders of tomorrow.[3]

Digital intelligence, or 'DQ', is the set of social, emotional and cognitive abilities that enable individuals to face the challenges and adapt to the demands of digital life. These abilities can broadly be broken down into eight interconnected areas. Amongst these is **Digital emotional intelligence:** this is the ability to be empathetic and build good relationships with others online.

This chapter discusses briefly four ways in which educators can promote skills essential for the future, skills of creativity and empathy in collaborative and connected environments as being positive cultures within which such aptitudes can flourish. Valuing environments are those which place strong emphasis on the human dimension and will be increasingly important in a world subject to de-personalisation. They are non-threatening learning spaces; an education ecosystem.

Looking at this in terms of 'people should all be valued' or some theory of valuing does not take us very far. Invoking its contrast pole, however, through examining what generates experiences of being disvalued allows us to highlight what promotes well-being. From a process of narrative research rooted in client observation and integrative

8 DIGITAL SKILLS WE MUST TEACH OUR CHILDREN

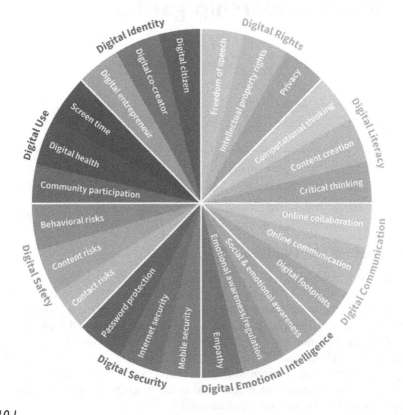

Figure 10.1

counselling in therapeutic contexts, I asked, 'What happens when we turn the idea of being valued on its head? What factors in social life generate reports of being disvalued?, Three types of responses emerged, offering the basis for a new construct:

- indifference – not seen or heard, regarded or recognised; treated as passive;
- inequality – not being treated equally or fairly, the full measure of one's humanity being denied, eroded, diminished or reduced – the politics of *insult*;
- indignity – the invasion of personal space; rejection, the politics of *assault*.

Human action is motivated by the pursuit of value which is eroded in environments where disvaluing takes place in accordance with the three principles outlined above.

Learning is boosted and participant well-being enhanced when this is recognised and opposite factors are engendered, i.e.:

- engagement and empowering through seeing and hearing;
- respecting a full measure of the humanity of participants – teachers and fellow learners alike;
- recognition of a dignity that is both allowed and encouraged.

The concept of promoting environments of value is best situated as a form of critical theory in which the transmission lines of power are seen as engendering human devaluation. As Carr and Kemmis observe, a critical approach must provide ways of distinguishing ideologically distorted interpretations from those that are not.[4] Through this lens, the notion of human value theory highlights the tension between the role that pursuing value plays as against the erosion of value. In short, valuing environments help to nurture the value of their participants. It is in the enlightened self-interest of leaders at all levels, including educational settings, to understand the factors that generate negative cultures so they can be corrected and positive cultures can be developed instead.

To bring about transformative change in which human worth is unlocked, should we change the model? Is education, and indeed the economy, more like a garden than the factory system appropriate to the first machine age? The metaphor of tilling the garden suggests an organic process; creating the conditions in which learners flourish who will be the leaders of tomorrow.

'Ecological thinking', as often described, involves recognition of interconnectedness. This can transform views of learning and knowledge into communal and holistic ones. As we have to find a different way of understanding the interconnectedness of all things, we must extend this approach to our very way of thinking about those things and our conception of what counts for knowledge.[5] 'A firm grounding would be secured for the value of students, of the skills and abilities they can acquire and of the work toward which they are being prepared': a balanced curriculum for the whole person.[6]

It is vital to hang on to a vision of what education is for. Yet there is no escaping the reality that the politically charged issues that swirl around education hugely affect the degree to which learning environments are environments of value. Schools are political battlegrounds, contested places, because underlying educational philosophies reflect different views of the world. Such external contexts and intense national debates shape how far schools can become environments of value.

Against that background, the proposition in this chapter that applies our construct is this. *An environment of value in education is a learning environment where there is a strong connection between inner value and added value for student, school and society.*

Going beyond school reform to transformation requires realisation that the purpose behind school success is to nurture the human spirit, not just use human resources. In education practice, it is widely assumed that the individual has value and worth. Contemporary education is unthinkable without this concept. Take one example, the role of self-esteem and positive identity in learning power:

> The management of these is never simple and never settled, and its state is powerfully affected by the availability of supports from outside. These supports are hardly mysterious or exotic. They include such homely resorts as a second chance, honour for a good, if unsuccessful try, but above all a chance for discourse that permits one to find out why, or how things didn't work out as planned.[7]

Or the need to be alert to what could be termed 'the value dynamic' is implicit in another text for learning assistants regarding a productive learning environment:

> The most important function of a support teacher is to develop a pupil's self-esteem by listening to stressed pupils, helping complete work which would

otherwise be added to a pile of unfinished bits; often just getting to know pupils as individuals.[8]

The question is, 'why does this happen so rarely'? What are the resistances – either individual or societal – to that happening? Whose value are we talking about? Value added to a school rises in the league tables contrasted with the inner value of pupils; the learning environment. There is no real dichotomy here. Inner value that is nurtured as pupils discover potential surely helps to boost the micro-culture of the classroom. In turn, this should translate into added value for school and indeed community as the reputation and esteem of the school rises.

It is to be sure difficult to measure how a sense of being a valuable self translates into achievement. Often this will be a longer-term effect rather than assessment levels noticeably rising from year to year. What seems clear is that the tricky concept of 'potential' has a lot to do with unlocking a route through which inner worth becomes realised. How you get the best out of children is a reflection of a learning environment where they perceive that heady sense of communicated value, which is then translated into outcomes for children. Arguably, schools that are adding value to what they are doing with a pupil, in a way that can be measured, are nourishing and then tapping into a sense of the child's personal value. Anecdotally through classroom practice, the way to unlock potential of disaffected boys is to give them value. But where is the source of such Eldorado gold?

The quest to unlock potential leads some schools to work holistically with families. As the debates of previous generations have highlighted, for example the Coleman Report in the USA, it may be that 'schools bring little influence to bear upon a child's achievement that is independent of his background and general social context'.[9] Then came the idea of school improvement; that it did make a difference what happened in schools. The child should be nurtured as a learner yet is not just a learner but a person. Situations where the home environment pulls the child down may require the school to work with family constellations. Other teachers will keep focused on what happens in the school so that the rules in the home environment are parked outside. When the child enters through the school gates, the clear message is 'this is how you are expected to behave'.

In official guidance, the emphasis tends to be on organisation and control, leadership, monitoring, target setting and behaviour management. Such factors are vital ingredients for educational success but they are means to an end, not the ends in themselves. Raising achievement is much to do with giving learners the power to think. It is about releasing the energies; cultivating creativity and social responsibility and empathy. Crucially, apropos the concerns of this book, creating environments of value promotes achievement in the widest sense, not just as measured by the results of assessment.

Yet school improvement is primarily a matter of giving power to teachers and learners alike, not just control to ensure that homework gets done and to tighten up on behaviour. An evaluative culture in education is only effective if it supports a philosophy and practice of empowerment, for pupils, parents and staff. As Terry Wrigley observes in a fine study of success in the education of Asian and other bilingual pupils in the UK, the ethos of a school is more than ensuring discipline and that pupils keep at it. It depends on the development of the school as a community within the wider community, upon the quality and equality of relationships both within the school and externally.

Anecdotally, parents who did not enjoy good outcomes in their own education can easily project their own low self-esteem on to the school. Displaying the work pupils have produced can help in countering narratives about schools 'never being any good here'. Raising expectations is more than a matter of pressurising pupils to aim higher. It involves addressing narratives that are playing, whether challenging or supporting attitudes within that micro-culture. Wrigley observes that Asian parents are proud to know their children are succeeding. In other contexts, creating a counter-culture to the street environment that boys especially are influenced by must involve engendering a heady thrill of pleasure from what they do at school. If that can be done, it will reinforce self-esteem because the work and the worker will be valued highly. The only sure path to an achievement culture in a school is through collective valuing of educational achievement. It must be embodied in the stories that are told about 'how we do things around here'.[10]

Classroom practice suggests many children do not think their ideas are worth considering because they are not worth very much. Erosion of value occurs regularly through not being on the 'cool table'[11] or being the last to be chosen for a sports team. Value is key to educational processes against a background of being devalued, witness the Challenge agenda in London schools, another initiative aimed at building a culture of learning where pupils feel better about themselves and valued.[12] Learners do their best work when they are treated with respect in the *context* of learning. As with organisational culture, getting the most and the best out of pupils is enhanced by their being valued.

What makes someone play truant? In interviews coinciding with a report on truancy called for by the British government, pupils spoke of the effect of 'teachers talking down to you', 'they think you are bad and then treat you like that'. The environment of the classroom is demeaning.[13]

Contrast this with the work of Vince Tinto, an educational theorist who has faith in community. He wants to create universities as places where students can thrive. Sharing and connecting, he argues, can produce a community of equals. 'The key concept is that of educational community and the capacity to establish educational communities that involve all students as equal members.'[14]

What then are some ways to build valuing environments in education in a way that embeds skills essential for the future? How can we develop learning spaces in which students really do take part in their own formation through creativity and learn to make connections through empathy? We will use the gardening metaphor rather than the mechanistic approach and speak of ways in which young people can be nurtured through the right conditions being in place. In a post-Fordist digital economy, systems of all kinds prevail.

To foster valuing environments that develop skills increasingly at a premium because they recruit the irreplaceable human dimension, teachers do not merely operate systems. The industrial revolution with its emphasis on mass production and mechanical reproduction shaped the education systems of modernity. In the future that is already arriving education needs to be redesigned so as to foster skills that nurture the human. To help grow future leaders, educators become tillers of the soil; gardeners and guardians of tender shoots and do so, I suggest, in four ways.

1 Nurture the professionals – an environment of value is one where teachers are trusted to function, not de-skilled

> If you're not prepared to be wrong you'll never come up with anything original.
>
> Sir Ken Robinson[15]

The notion of communities of practice has been important in education.[16] It is based on shared conceptions of professionalisation and a belief that there is knowledge that new members can learn from. Anything that reduces the status of teachers is unwelcome. Many teachers report that they feel written down by government diktat or by micro-management at local level. The child–teacher relationship is crucial for environments of value. When children perceive that a teacher is not valued or held in esteem as professional (as sometimes happens with regard to those in learning support) it will not feed into their own confidence as learner. It will do nothing for their own sense of worth.

Against that, 'just let teachers teach', we are often told. That way you will have enthusiastic teachers. 'There is too much emphasis on assessments, measuring everything a school does', complains a teacher in reaction to the performativity that occupies commanding heights of policy.[17]

A decentralising agenda has been pursued giving more control to local people to run schools. This comes with a threat to under-performing schools. Schools seem to do better if they have greater autonomy and are less reliant on control. The education revolution in a former era resulted in mass education being available for all. In the twenty-first century, the promise is that good education must be available to all, using particularly the values of private education which appeared to perform much better. To make genuine progress, the relationship between the centre and local autonomy has often needed to be re-set. Long-term, to get the most out of schools, governments will need to meddle less and trust more. In a centralised system, there is little scope for innovation or diversity of practice.

As remarked by one contemporary headteacher, 'pupils taught in an atmosphere of firm respect within careful guidelines fare better than where their self-respect is eroded'.[18] Teachers report the same need to be handled with respect rather than being embroiled in competitive situations and played off against other teachers. The contrast was illuminated by a headteacher in Bristol, explaining how he is able to recruit good teachers to work in a challenging community: 'We have a reputation for valuing our staff. People want to work here.'[19]

Significantly, British schools get no credit for GCSE performance below the D/C grade. Where do pastoral relationships and welfare of pupils feature when what is most important are five GCSEs?

Yet in general, the motivation behind a target-driven education culture was benign. It was intended to ensure that every child should go to a good school in their neighbourhood with strict discipline, inspirational teaching and high standards. Yet too often, it is feared education has become a site of de-professionalisation, assuming teachers will do the minimum and get away with the maximum.

A programme to transform the worst performing schools was particularly successful in London where it ran for eight years, first as the London Challenge and later as City Challenge. Researchers from the Institute of Policy Studies in Education at London Metropolitan University drew on government data to compare GCSE improvement rates for the poorest-performing fifth of schools between 2008 and 2011. These were schools where in 2008 fewer than 32 per cent of pupils achieved five A★ to C GCSEs including English and maths. The analysis suggests that pupil attainment in the under-performing schools supported by City Challenge improved significantly more than it did in other weak schools, including sponsored academies. By 2011, the secondary schools that had been in City Challenge programmes improved their exam results by 4 per cent more than schools, including sponsored academies, that had not. Commissioned by the Department for Education, the evaluation defined the programme's strategy as providing external experts to work alongside existing headteachers to assess each school's individual needs and to set up bespoke support programmes which included mentoring by head-teachers from better-performing schools. Central to the positive outcomes at the heart of City Challenge was a highly supportive and encouraging environment in which head-teachers and teachers came to feel more valued, more confident and more supportive. Expert advisers invited to coach schools were valued for their expertise and for being encouraging.[20]

2 Nurture a much wider and less impoverished view of what constitutes achievement

Creativity and empathy education will, I suggest, be central to the pedagogy of the future because they summon the human dimension that will blend with automation but bring something to tasks that cannot be replicated robotically. Computers will learn to think but lack imagination.

Should not education be an end in itself rather than a means of getting ahead of others and thereby stealing a competitive edge? Is education not simply harvesting the earth for academic success?

Education should not just be aimed at producing pupils as products for a capitalist society; arguably it should help foster creativity and empathy. These values will be at a premium in an age of increasing technological displacement. The arts (and for that matter, sports) can elevate self-esteem; they enable the view that all pupils have potential. Arts especially can generate a sense of creative subversion and restless inno-vation. It is more commonly realised now that human flourishing depends on a range of abilities. A single conception of capability represents an old paradigm. As Howard Gardener has stressed, multiple intelligences are varied but also function in dynamic interaction.[21] That is why interdisciplinary perspectives are often seedbeds for creativity.

As a reaction against the commanding criteria to ensure maximum output from the system, voices in the West protested against a utilitarian approach. Lyotard suggests that the whole of contemporary society is characterised by 'performativity', the reduction of all judgement to a criterion of efficiency of input–output relations.[22] It is feared that education is primarily technocratic; concerned with the means and skills that contribute to the efficient operation of the state in the world market and its social cohesion. An instrumental view of education requires individuals of a certain kind – not autonomous persons but automatons, standardised, governable individuals Foucault describes.[23]

Alongside those concerns have been those of de-personalisation – pupils being treated as people, holistically, not as learners who tick boxes. There was immense pressure to succeed, for exams to prepare and herd pupils through and trying to ensure that absentee records did not allow a school to slip down the league tables. At the same time, it was recognised that schools did not compete on a level playing field between the inner city or areas of deprivation against schools in the leafy suburbs. Hence value added measures were constructed, intended to measure the extra value that schools gave to disadvantaged pupils. Yet critics of school league tables complained that performance was still a dominant rhetoric, mostly recording teaching for the test rather than pupil development.

As one teacher said, 'no one ever says "enough" in the education system. It is always "more, more!" The only response is "must do better" "try harder" messages we have heard from early years!'[24]

Against that backcloth, many voices are urging a much broader concept of what achievement is.

Case study – symposium on education North Devon April 2014

- The school day is so structured there is no time for going 'off on tangents' but this is where self-direction, creativity and free thinking starts!
- Is specialising early a bad thing? It gives the space for a child to indulge themselves in learning and becoming an expert if they wish.
- We have to find ways of measuring engagement, passion and buzz.
- Targets kill creativity.
- Let's have artists in residence in our schools.
- Encourage nurture through home schooling. Be messy!
- Teach children to think. We need to develop thinking skills. Re-introduce philosophy!
- Delay education. Expand 'play'.[25]

Creativity is about creating an environment of value in which students' work is prized and obviously important. The way a learning space is set up help shapes that. Transforming classrooms through displays sends a powerful message that this space is both dynamic and a collaborative place to be.

This is vital. When disguised as working selves, many adults cannot wait to retire. Others, by contrast, could not imagine taking many steps back. There is too much excitement. The things they do are not merely the product of brain or hand; it is an extension of what they are as people. A valuable self is invested in their projects. Their work is part of them and indeed, at one level, it is them!

Education has an important role in helping us to achieve our potential, but the processes by which we assess ability were designed for an industrial age. In a high-performance world, adults can rarely afford to be wrong or to fail. Yet children are infectious learners and learn by experimenting. What is needed is to find a way of releasing and channelling innate creativity and help discover passion.

Opening the doors to creativity can take many forms, most of which are beneficial. Learning an instrument is said to have positive cognitive effects.[26] Doing well in the football team, finding something you are good at with encouragement from teachers bent on developing people, not just teaching for the test – these are environments of value; learning is feeding the child valuing him or herself. Pupils discover that creativity and worthwhile contribution engender a sense of self-worth.

Where pupils are disruptive so as to get attention, perhaps the knowledge system in the classroom seems too much like a conveyor belt, delivered by impersonal forces they can neither see nor relate to, driven by purposes unknown to them. The problem is this. Is there a way of assessing success without the compelling need for measurement? It is often asked, 'Why do we have to measure a child's learning in the first place?' Yet publicly validated examinations will remain as the passport towards recognition by others (especially employers) that students achieve. It is the pass to the system. There seems no way round it – unless, that is, young people are taught to compete not just with others in a highly competitive world but with themselves primarily.

It is an interesting question whether the trend towards automation in the classroom will accentuate performativity and tick-box education or foster opportunities for creativity, if not the social intelligence and empathy which are other key skills for the future that unlock the value of the human. Here is one online voice amidst a plethora of observations about the growth of online education. Will Richardson, educational blogger, argues strongly that the prospect of 'my teacher is an app' does not present us with a disturbing future where technology has taken over the classroom. It opens up myriads of diverse new learning opportunities. A teacher monitors progress made by students online, sees if homework is being done and allows students to go on at their own pace. Learning can be creative and enjoyable, drawing on students' interest in the online world.[27]

A learning environment in which pupils flourish is about the exercise of an imagination which must be stimulated to flourish at all levels. In 2012, just over 30 per cent of white British children entitled to free school meals got five good passes at GCSE. This was fewer than poor children from ethnic minorities. Environments of value in education are about the imagination of aspiration. Where there is a deep lack of faith in education to help their children to get on, parents are less likely to engage with it.

When the job pages of local papers are filled with advertisements for care workers, bar staff and cleaners (important tasks though these are), the horizons of possibility are not expanded. Young people and parents alike must surely be able to see routes into the workplace and better jobs. Education by definition recruits the imagination, drawing out ('educere') towards other options which foster a sense of value and worth, and helps to identify the social factors that distort these. It calls learners to redress factors that have produced disadvantaged and even damaged individuals.[28]

3 Nurture the learner – thinking for themselves

Our pupils are respected as people, not treated as products.
A school brochure, Llandaff Cathedral School, 2008

A valuing environment pays deep attention to the learner. It is not a regimented process. How far pedagogy should be child-led or child-centred is a major issue shaping educational theory and practice. To its cheerleaders, learning from and with children, with the learner in the driving seat for his or her learning, is the optimum and obvious way of enhancing curiosity, requiring that the subject of education should not be an object. To its detractors, person-centred learning can miss the really important point about education; whether or not the child actually learns anything.

Such debates have become storm-centres. It is often alleged, for instance, that the British Office for Standards in Education (Ofsted) marks down classroom learning where there is too much 'teacher-talk'. Those who are insistent that high quality content must be absorbed and embedded complain that this best happens when there is a strong foundation didactically. The teacher MUST talk! There seems to be little doubt that teachers themselves want freedom to teach the way they want to without being prescriptive and regimented. Yet it may also be the case that good research about what teaching style works best is actually rather thin on the ground. It is whether the child learns something and can do something with it that should be the main driver.

In the UK, the education policy agenda moved significantly in the direction of 'personalisation' and then arguably retreated with National Curriculum changes after the 2010 coalition government. The 'Every Child Matters' agenda[29] and the 'New Relationship with Schools' all expressed a clear, public purpose of 'putting the user's experience at the heart of everything we do'.[30] Central to this agenda was choice. The UK Labour government White Paper, *Higher Standards, Better Schools for All*[31] spoke of the need for schools to have the 'freedoms and flexibility to deliver a tailored, choice-driven education'. Parental power was enlisted to help drive up standards on the basis that education was too remote and families needed to engage and register disapproval where justified.

Central to the growing social sustainability agenda is a collective focus on developing the values, attitudes, contributions and achievements of effective, motivated, lifelong learners and citizens, for example the five outcomes of 'Every Child Matters'. At the heart of this agenda is a focus on the value of persons as a matrix of meaning which promotes human flourishing. Indeed, the former Qualifications and Curriculum Authority's statement of values, aims and purposes went on to say: 'we value others for themselves, not only for what they have or what they can do for us'.[32]

In twenty-first century education, what should happen in schools had shifted from being about teaching to a focus on teaching and learning. There came a new focus: education was about boosting learning power so students think for themselves. Teachers should not merely teach children but help them become learners. The 20 years since the inception of the National Curriculum in the UK have seen a growing interest in self-directed learning.[33] Teachers have set about giving to pupils responsibility for their own learning; pedagogy being reconstructed as being not so much teaching as 'facilitating learning' with the aim, as Deakin Crick puts it, of 'developing individuals who are able to understand and participate democratically in their local, national and global communities and thus contribute to a sustainable social world'.[34]

Although problematic, the notion of 'personalisation' is firmly on the UK education policy agenda. There is, I suggest, an implicit assumption behind this notion. The notion of personalisation, over and against de-personalisation, depends on some concept of the value of persons. The concept of personalisation can be explored through the lens of human value, best understood through its opposite, or contrast pole, that is human experiences of devaluation. There are strong implications for learning and teaching and the curriculum.

The personalised learning agenda is one way of demonstrating deep attention to the person of the learner. This is deeply embedded in a particular pedagogical turn, a socially embedded and embodied journey moving from personal desire and motivation to the achievement of verifiable competence. There is a move from the 'personal' towards the 'public', to a 'standardised' outcome, but one which is validated within the personal sphere: the trajectory does not arrive outside it. The learning self must encounter knowledge in a way that promotes a valuing of the human. That is, the encounter must be reflexive and capable of connecting with the life narrative and experience of the learner.[35] Without this engaged encounter, there will be little lasting learning because to be significant, learning needs to be meaningful to the person who is learning. If knowledge is 'out there' as something to be reached towards rather than being generated from within a learner or in the space between learner and what is learnt, de-personalisation takes place. It devalues the humanity of the learner, subordinating the process of learning to outcomes set by the system. The concept of personalisation is simply rhetorical unless it facilitates theory and practice which takes seriously and engages with the value of the human person.[36]

Valuing People, a government White Paper in 2001, stressed that those with learning disabilities are, above all else, 'people'. 'All public services will treat people with learning disabilities as individuals with respect for their dignity, and challenge discrimination on all grounds including disability.'[37] Despite the good intentions of this White Paper and the positive reception to it, a UK Parliamentary Report[38] said that vulnerable adults were still likely to be abused, exploited and suffer lack of respect. It is one thing to sign up to 'valuing people', another to dismantle structures and personal transactions that for generations formed the landscapes of human devaluation.

Arguably, Marxist-type dualism characterised by oppressors and oppressed has failed to build human capital because it has little place for releasing useful energies. The same space that devalues and de-personalises is a site of ambiguity where people can be empowered. Workers in a system can become self-directing, be it in the creation of new wealth, contributing to society rather than being dependent on it or pupils engaging with the curriculum. Gaining publicly validated qualifications at the end of sequenced learning offers empowerment because it feeds a latent source of valuing oneself without which pupils are short-changed. The notion of human value relates to the process of *knowledge creation*. It is precisely because we re-order the way the self encounters knowledge in a way that allows learners to become authors of their own thoughts and experiences that there can be integration between value-driven narratives of the self and learning about human value which happens in a curriculum adopting 'a charter to educate rather than a mandate to train'.[39]

The call for personalised learning is to recruit students as active learners, as independent problem solvers. When teachers and students have a tick-box approach to education, the message is being sent that the only thing that is valued is that which can be quantified and measured. In an age of austerity, to utilise the talents of the socially deprived is not a luxury. There is real tension between external pressures to succeed in ways that can be measured against working from instinct and interest. The alternative is to create open-ended opportunities to develop interests. This is far more fitting for a global society that makes rich use of people's talents and which arouses their passions.

A better-educated citizenry requires new ways of fostering knowledge. Knowledge is key but it is not the acquisition of a body of learning that is likely to be superseded before the ink is dry. Twenty-first century learning does not depend on ink and much less on print media. New technology is driving an emphasis on self-directed learning and at the heart of this is an interaction with knowledge in which the learner is engaged. From this interactive and active stance, new forms of value can emerge. Arguably, the technology that often seems to represent distance – 'humans against the machine' – can allow each child to learn at different speeds through adaptive computer programmes. This constitutes moving from a one-size-fits-all approach towards a more personalised approach. Massive Open Online Courses are restructuring the landscape of higher education. Now, schools are following suit through ed-tech programmes. Clearly, improvements in technology can bring school improvement.

4 Nurture human connections – introduce learners to each other

> I call therefore a complete and generous education that which fits a man to perform justly, skilfully and magnanimously, all the offices both public and private, of peace and war.
>
> John Milton (1608–1674)

Environments of value are those that stress empathy education; the power of human connection that must be mobilised as a key education dimension for the future. Consider this statement:

> We have no culture of thinking or learning about the environment, about our economy, about our society at the same time. So at the heart of the curriculum, just as at the heart of everything else we do, we must be making those connections so that pupils who leave school, indeed who leave university and go into the workplace, are able to make decisions understanding the economic, social and environmental consequences together.[40]

The question is – what sort of subjects can make those connections? Theorists agree for the most part that the only entities that can develop concepts of value in general are beings capable of feelings, emotions and beliefs.[41] Perhaps the kind of human subjects that are best placed to negotiate twenty-first century dispositions may be those who have developed the reflexivity that can make connections between their own narratives and those of the world. The interest in UK Co-operative Trust schools reflected these concerns; the values that lie at the heart of the Co-operative movement – such as self-help, taking responsibility for one's actions, democracy, solidarity, justice and equality – are embedded within every aspect of school life. Many faith schools had similar aims.

In education in the West, much more is being done to promote diversity and inclusion in schools.[42] There is a great deal of distance yet to be covered. Categories that imprison the human are often counter-poised to the need for emancipation, promoting the value of people against the way they are disvalued. This lies at the heart of the Critical Research paradigm.[43] A leading proponent of this turn, the Brazilian educator Paulo Freire argued that a 'Pedagogy of the Oppressed' was needed; not knowledge parcelled up for those who do not know but a curriculum to foster liberated subjects. '"Empowerment" is much more than an individual or psychological event. It points to a political process by the dominated class who seek their own freedom from domination.'[44]

As Freire showed, every human being, no matter how impoverished or illiterate can develop a sense of self that will enable them to be more than passive objects responding to uncontrollable change. This is highly relevant to the potential for de-personalisation in the wake of the digital economy. The critical paradigm followed on from the Frankfurt School of social theory of the 1930s in which the emphasis is on emancipation, unmasking knowledge generated just to keep existing systems in place.[45] Empowerment means children become aware of the systemic structures that can oppress.

Language learning is one route towards empathy of other cultures. In Western societies, that is often very challenging as students inhabit a world where the great majority of computer language and operating systems are in English and where digital translation is easy (though not necessarily accurate). Students need to see the purpose of what they are doing; this is one prime area where purpose-driven education makes sense, i.e. some immersion into culture maybe through VR (virtual reality). A question for political leaders tackling extremism as well as leaders in tourism is this: why are advanced-country populations so prone to xenophobia? It is not as if they have never been exposed to other cultures. The holiday tourist traffic runs in both directions. The problem lies in *how* we travel. Nowadays, we are more likely to have quick, superficial experiences than to immerse ourselves in a culture. But, as modern game theory teaches, a one-time interaction is very different from ongoing contact. Continual exchange is needed to foster trust. Tourism companies respond to the risk of terrorism by minimising contact with locals. Tourism no longer means deep encounters with vastly different cultures. It is possible to imagine settings in which visitors and their hosts interact in a more personal way. Airbnb, for example, can provide a much more engaging experience than a hotel or, worse, a cruise ship.[46]

Despite the fact that the vast majority of countries have signed and ratified the UN's various international human rights Conventions, millions of people around the world do not enjoy the rights that these Conventions set out. While enshrined in the Universal Declaration of Human Rights (UDHR) in 1948, the ways in which the right to education is protected, promoted and ultimately exercised at the national level vary considerably. For example, according to the Right to Education Project, 63 million children don't have access to basic education, 150 million children currently enrolled in school will drop out before completing primary education and at least two-thirds of these students are girls. The right to education is emancipatory. Education 'creates the "voice" through which the value of the human is claimed and protected'.[47] In short, it gives the power of Protest.

By the 1990s a range of education programmes had developed to counter gender and ethnic inequalities in education.[48] Crucial in the UK was the Macpherson Report (1999) into the murder of the black teenager, Stephen Lawrence. Its recommendations included amending the National Curriculum to value social diversity, the duty of local authorities and schools to develop strategies to prevent and address racism.[49] 'Equal opportunities' in schools and local authorities became fashionable throughout the 1980s and 1990s. It embraced the following ideas:

- developing an understanding of how cultural diversity and racism affect pupils' learning and can lead to inequalities;
- developing an awareness of how the curriculum syllabus can exclude the experience of women, disabled groups and ethnic minorities;
- developing an ethos in school where pupils and staff have self-respect and respect for others.

Along with a concern about performativity, value added policies, school improvement, the constant need to drive up standards and how to foster effective citizenship, these issues have become part of the mainstream culture of schools.[50] Such practices as 'Circle Time' have become widespread.[51]

Pedagogy has a relational dimension to it: children are never groups of self-contained entities. For this reason, the primary objective of the school must not only be to emphasise traditional goals for the achievement of specific knowledge and skills, but also the development and practice of the social relations characterising this culture. The benchmarks always focus on core subjects – never those social and emotional aspects of learning! It follows that more attention needs to be paid to the Social and Emotional Aspects of Learning (SEAL) but clearly it is not enough to emphasise social and emotional competence. The cultures and mindset underlying these practices must be nurtured.

Children are precious and certainly not robotic. In an era characterised by the rise of the robots, the capacity to build relationships is vital. The more whole we are, the more we can give to society. Team building must become a vital ingredient of learning environments because children learn best when they feel secure with others. Twenty-first century learning is a social task, not just a solitary pursuit. Becoming a global citizen and lifelong learner surely means that students learn to cooperate with others in collaborative tasks and learn to make human connections.[52] It means too that through modern technology, they can make contact with learners across the globe. Where environments of value are fostered, the politics of mutuality are embedded. Respect and equality can take root.

The question is whether contemporary education helps foster a sense of being a responsible member of global society or does it regard students as passive recipients or consumers of information? Crucial to this is encouraging them to talk together, to cooperate together on tasks and to seek out other learners in the global society that is the only one there is.

In closing, we have identified four factors within a school that help or hinder it being an environment of value, a productive learning environment where the inner value of students is unlocked and cultivated and where there is a strong connection between that inner value and added value/benefit for the pupil, school and society:

1   Nurture the professionals – an environment of value is one where teachers are trusted to function, not de-skilled.
2   Nurture a much wider and less impoverished view of what constitutes achievement.
3   Nurture the learner – thinking for themselves.
4   Nurture human connections – introduce learners to each other.

The very approach that students must learn to navigate, restlessly changing educational landscapes so as to release and unlock human worth, must pay deep attention to such themes. At a fundamental level, these skills and attitudes are to do with addressing how indifference, indignity and inequality play within and around schools. These are factors we are exploring that compress and dampen the felt value of pupils and teachers as co-participants in the education project. Every school in any country would sign up to the idea that pupils are to be cherished and valued. But the factors that make for the opposite must be clearly understood. Where pupils are valued – all of them, not just bright ones – indifference and non-engagement and indignity are counteracted. Similarly, where teachers are properly supported and trusted to function, their engagement is enlisted and they do not feel they are viewed with indifference in a factory process. They will not feel diminished but given professional opportunities to flourish in a way that has a knock-on effect. The third and fourth factors are also fundamentally about different forms of value and worth. Creativity and empathy are vital approaches needed to help unlock value and potential. These are not separate silos.

The notion of 'environments of value' proposed here stresses various factors that engender value by helping learners discern their opposite. It helps to develop ideas of school culture that emphasises school relationships and community rather than the dominance of instrumental technocracy.[53] The UK Royal Society of Arts (RSA) produced a report in 2014 entitled 'Schools with Soul' that concluded spiritual, moral, social and cultural education (SMSC) is neglected. Schools are sidelining education in personal values and cultural understanding because of examination pressures and the need to respond to new government initiatives. An overcrowded curriculum and increased pressure to achieve better exam results have pushed out wider values.[54]

As students are treated holistically, the capacity to write them off is lessened and they are more able to flourish. Educators and observers alike will say that this is common sense and commonplace; of course children and staff should be valued. But to put this into practice, wise educators will surely need to understand and know how to counteract the factors that make for disvaluing. Only in this way can useful energies be released and human flourishing take place in schools and colleges. Only by getting to grips with the reasons why participants describe why they might become devalued will education be released for its mission and the future leadership garden be cultivated.

Few would argue against the proposition that spiritual, moral and cultural education should help students develop the attitudes and skills they need to become engaged citizens. Schools have always had a civilising mission. Yet for learning environments to be places where human flourishing takes place, it is important that this can be clearly communicated in the teaching content of what is propounded but also in the way pupils interact informally with people and conduct the everyday affairs of both classroom and school. After all, for a dozen years at a formative stage of their development, children spend almost as much of their waking time at school as at home – some 15,000 hours.[55] Socialisation into a school culture means it can be caught as well as taught. 'The implicit curriculum – what is received through the total impact of what happens in schools – includes the messages conveyed by the ethos of the school and the total approach to pupils.'[56] Visions for a twenty-first century learning environment will evoke the politics of contestation; visions of what constitutes the good life about which there are many differences of perspective. There is only one society – it is global.

It is the link that brings together inner worth and externally measured achievement for students and their teachers alike that fosters environments of value as the landscape shifts and the Fourth Industrial Revolution unfolds. It is this that will enable schools to fulfil the aspiration of W.B. Yeats. Education is not about filling empty buckets but lighting fires! That insight will be vital to grow future leaders.

Notes

1 Toffler, A. (1970), *Future Shock*. New York: Random House, p. 407.
2 http://www.futuretech.ox.ac.uk/, accessed January 2014.

3 Park, Y., Chair, Infollution ZERO Foundation, World Economic Forum, https://www. weforum.org/agenda/2016/06/8-digital-skills-we-must-teach-our-children/, 13 June 2016, accessed June 2016.

4 Carr, W. and Kemmis, S. (1986), *Becoming Critical: Knowledge and Action Research*. Lewis: Falmer Press.

5 Code, L. (2006), *Ecological Thinking: The Politics of Epistemic Location*. Oxford: Oxford University Press.

6 Jones, S. (1997), 'Recovering the Person', in *Agenda for Educational Change*, ed. J. Shortt and T. Cooling. Leicester: Stapleford, p. 67.

7 Bruner, J. (1996), *The Culture of Education*. Cambridge, MA: Harvard University Press, p. 92.

8 Lovey, J. (1995), *Supporting Special Educational Needs in Secondary School Classrooms*. London: Fulton, p. 285.

9 Coleman, J. (1966), *Equality of Educational Opportunity*. Washington, DC: US Government Printing Office, p. 325.

10 Wrigley, T. (2000), *The Power to Learn: Stories of Success in the Education of Asian and Other Bilingual Pupils*. Stoke on Trent: Trentham Books, p. 9.

11 According to research by Brené Brown at the University of Houston, http://www.brenebrown. com/, 2012.

12 http://www.ofsted.gov.uk/resources/london-challenge.

13 *Women's Hour*, BBC Radio 4, 30 December 2011, http://www.bbc.co.uk/radio4.

14 Tinto, V. (1997), 'Classrooms as Communities: Exploring the Educational Character of Student Persistence', *Journal of Higher Education*, 68 (6), pp. 599–623.

15 https://www.ted.com/speakers/sir_ken_robinson.html/, accessed March 2014.

16 Lave, J. and Wenger, E. (1991), *Situated Learning: Legitimate Peripheral Participation*. Cambridge: Cambridge University Press.

17 Author's client notes – used with permission and name withheld.

18 *The Moral Maze*, BBC Radio 4, 26 January 2009.

19 *PM News and Current Affairs*, BBC Radio 4, 13 January 2008.

20 *Evaluation of the City Challenge Programme*. Department for Education, DFE RR215.

21 Gardener, H. (1983), *Frames of Mind: The Theory of Multiple Intelligences*. New York: Basic Books. See also Davis, K., Christodoulou, J., Seider, S. and Gardner H. (2011), 'The Theory of Multiple Intelligences', in *The Cambridge Handbook of Intelligence*, ed. R. J. Sternberg and B. Kaufman. Cambridge: Cambridge University Press, pp. 485–503.

22 Lyotard, J.-F. (1984), *The Postmodern Condition: A Report on Knowledge*, trans. G. Bennington and B. Massumi. Manchester: Manchester University Press.

23 Marshall, J.D. (1999), 'Performativity: Lyotard and Foucault through Searle and Austin', *Studies in Philosophy and Education*, 18 (5), pp. 309–317.

24 'Another World is Happening', RSA sponsored symposium on education, North Devon, 9 April 2014.

25 'Another World is Happening'.

26 US studies report that in 1996, pupils experienced in musical performance scored 51 per cent higher on the verbal part of their SATs scores and 39 per cent higher on the mathematics part. Students studying music at a university between 1983 and 1988 exhibited higher reading scores than any other students (sample size, 'n'=7,500). A comprehensive review of empirical evidence by The Future of Music Project showed that music instruction aids reading, language (including foreign languages), mathematics and overall academic achievement. Campbell, D. (1997), *The Mozart Effect*. London: Hodder & Stoughton, p. 179. See also Peretz, I. and Zatorre, R. (2003), *The Cognitive Neuroscience of Music*. Oxford: Oxford University Press.

27 http://willrichardson.com/post/12686013800/my-teacher-is-an-app/, accessed March 2014.

28 Probyn, E. (1996), *Outside Belonging*. London: Routledge.

29 Green Paper (2005), *Every Child Matters*. London: DfES.

30 Gilbert, C. (2006), *2020 Vision: Report of Teaching and Learning in 2020 Review Group*. London: DfES.

31 Schools White Paper (2005), *Higher Standards, Better Schools for All*. London: DfES.

32 http://www.qca.org/values/, accessed 2009.

33 Dickinson, L. (1987), *Self-instruction in Language Learning*. Cambridge: Cambridge University Press; Holec, H. (ed.) (1988), *Autonomy and Self-Directed Learning*. Strasbourg: Council of

Europe; Little, D. (1991), *Learner Autonomy 1: Definitions, Issues and Problems*. Dublin: Authentik.

34 Deakin Crick, R. (2009), 'Inquiry-based Learning: Reconciling the Personal with the Public in a Democratic and Archaeological Pedagogy', *Curriculum Journal*, 20 (1), pp. 73–93, at p. 5.

35 Millner, N., Small, T. and Deakin Crick, R. (2006), *Learning by Accident*. Bristol: ViTaL Partnerships.

36 Steed, C. (2009), 'Inquiry-based Learning: Personalisation or the Rehabilitation of Human Value', *Journal of Curriculum Studies*, 20 (4), pp. 465–475.

37 White Paper (2001), *Valuing People*. London: Department of Health.

38 *Valuing People*. House of Commons, Joint Committee on Human Rights, 2008.

39 Hadden, J.E. (2000), 'A Charter to Educate or a Mandate to Train: Conflicts between Theory and Practice', *Harvard Educational Review*, 70 (4), pp. 524–537.

40 Parkin, S. (2008), Forum for the Future, https://www.thefuturescentre.org/user/634.

41 Santayana, G. (1955), *The Sense of Beauty*. New York: Dover Press.

42 Pring, R. (1984), *Personal and Social Education in the Curriculum*. London: Hodder & Stoughton.

43 Aronowitz, A. and Giroux, H.A. (1991), *Postmodern Education: Politics, Culture and Social Criticism*. Minneapolis, MN: University of Minnesota Press.

44 Freire, P. (1996), *Pedagogy of the Oppressed*. London: Penguin, p. 27.

45 Habermas, J. (1987), *Knowledge and Human Interests*. Cambridge: Polity Press.

46 James, H., Professor of History and International Affairs, Princeton University 'The Future of Tourism', World Economic Forum, June 2016, in collaboration with Project Syndicate.

47 http://www.savethechildren.org.uk/2012/12/education-a-voice-for-human-rights/.

48 Gillborn, D. and Mirza, H.S. (2000), *Educational Inequality: Mapping Race, Class and Gender*. Ofsted. London: HMSO.

49 Macpherson, W. (1999), *The Stephen Lawrence Enquiry*, CM 4262-1. London: HMSO.

50 Bourdillon, H. and Storey, A. (2002), *Aspects of Teaching and Learning in Secondary Schools*. London: RoutledgeFalmer, Open University.

51 Mosley, J. (1996), *Quality Circle Time in the Primary Classroom*. Wisbech: LDA.

52 Gardner, H. (2011), *Truth, Beauty, and Goodness Reframed: Educating for the Virtues in the 21st Century*. New York: Basic Books.

53 Newmann, F. (1996), *Authentic Achievement: Restructuring Schools for Intellectual Quality*. San Francisco: Jossey-Bass.

54 https://www.thersa.org/pdfs/reports/schools-with-soul-report.pdf/, accessed June 2016.

55 Rutter, M. *et al.* (1979), *Fifteen Thousand Hours*. London: Open Books.

56 Watson, B. (1993), *The Effective Teaching of Religious Education*. London: Pearson, p. 19.

Chapter 11

Listen to the music (and help change the song): Wise leaders and transformative change

The workplace and workforce are going to change pretty dramatically as we look forward. The entire concept of work is going to become more flexible. The skills needed in the workforce are going to be less about IQ and a little bit more about EQ [Emotional Quotient/ Intelligence], because if you think about it, a lot of IQ knowledge is going to be available at our fingertips through hand-held devices and the computer and technologies that we have at our disposal.

Deborah Henretta[1]

Concerns, not demands

Organisational culture emerges through what the workplace means for them, expressed through the stories staff tell and the songs they sing. To achieve transformative change, wise leaders need to understand the narratives and develop new ones; to listen to the music and change the song.

In complex, turbulent times, human interaction at all levels becomes very 'shouty'. When faced with conflicted demands, participants tend to scream and shout at each other and the potential for deadlock is high. Another approach is learning to relate at the level of concerns not demands. As with business negotiations, political and social movements follow personal life in that they can be understood in two dimensions. The melody must be followed; the ongoing story of the events of our time. But there is also the news behind the news, the resonances or harmonic dimensions playing under the surface.

With a plural society, however tempting it is to hold staunchly on to identity, there is no alternative to engaging at some level with difference. Increasingly, the alternative is sectarianism. As we have been noting, there is only one society and it is global. The world is becoming hyper-connected. Through increasing access to the Internet, social media and mobile phone technology, the power of the individual as a virtual citizen is on the rise. The scale of social networks – Facebook has more than a billion users while SinaWiebo boasts 400 million – and the speed of information transfer have shifted the paradigm of citizen expression. Non-hierarchical communication structures are one result. The industrial era factory stood for de-personalised endeavour in workshop and assembly line. The curious ambiguity at the heart of the Internet is that what it takes away with one hand, through distance and robotic remoteness, it gives on the other – thus enabling interaction over a wider field.

In the Fourth Industrial Revolution, the inputs needed for an organisational environment will shift: to deliver value, different skills will be needed. Indeed, if we come to think about value more broadly than just the financial bottom line, that it is about quality and not just quantity, then as well as the technical skills needed to navigate the new world, factors that promote quality will be at a premium. As a former UK Education Secretary of State observed:

> The economy is changing at an unprecedented pace. Every day, jobs are being lost in professions we used to regard as careers for life. Artificial intelligence, robots, 3D printing and driverless vehicles will impact on sectors as varied as the legal profession, transport and construction. The UK's future workforce will need technical expertise in areas such as design and computing, plus skills which robots cannot replace – flexibility, empathy, creativity and enterprise.[2]

'Flexibility, empathy, creativity and enterprise' are the seedbed through which leaders of the future can be grown. In this book, we are probing how organisations become places where the human spirit is nurtured and sustained and the leadership that goes with it. In the post-industrial economy, what was prized was scientific and technical knowledge but also the ability to empathise with people. The service economy was more relational; teacher–pupil, doctor–patient, managers–staff. Coming transformations in the fourth wave of industrialisation point even more to the importance of skills that have not been needed. There will be a strong premium on creativity and empathy, not just formal skills. Though technology will soon make old jobs obsolete, skills needed for a new era will have to be those that allow for human imagination and through that, innovation to flourish; the driving force behind economies led by talent. The World Economic Forum's 'The Future of Jobs Report' found that over a third of skills that are considered important for today's workforce will have changed by 2020.

Creativity and empathy

We have been looking at creativity and empathy as vital to develop future leaders. Schools are the place where the foundations are laid. Professional development at all levels needs to embrace creativity and empathy to unlock the human dimension in an enterprise. This is vital for executive education for transformative change in such areas as global leadership, addressing the culture of an organisation and for negotiations generally. The purpose is straightforward. It is to generate a creative environment where people are relating at the level of concerns and interests – one where they are continually learning together, expanding their capacity to create the results they truly desire, where new and expansive patterns of thinking are nurtured and where collective aspiration is set free.

Fundamental to this happening also is the capacity to be reflexive, to engage with one's own story and discern fresh possibilities.[3] This is where creativity and empathy education come together very fruitfully as key skills to future-proof our children and growing future leaders. They are far less susceptible to technological displacement. Moreover, creativity and empathy education are central to positive cultures that foster the value of the human. As Albert Einstein remarked, 'I do not teach my pupils. I only create the conditions in which they can learn'.

Creativity – creativity might be thought as the next barrier to fall as robotics learn to script texts and perform creative tasks. The difference is that though there is pattern recognition, there is no meaning attached to the symbols. They are not signifiers of

Top 10 skills

in 2020

1. Complex Problem Solving
2. Critical Thinking
3. Creativity
4. People Management
5. Coordinating with Others
6. Emotional Intelligence
7. Judgment and Decision Making
8. Service Orientation
9. Negotiation
10. Cognitive Flexibility

in 2015

1. Complex Problem Solving
2. Coordinating with Others
3. People Management
4. Critical Thinking
5. Negotiation
6. Quality Control
7. Service Orientation
8. Judgment and Decision Making
9. Active Listening
10. Creativity

Source: Future of Jobs Report, World Economic Forum

Figure 11.1

anything. It is the human dimension that brings true creativity because it comes from and generates meaning. As I write these words, I have been to see a local school's production of *Fiddler on the Roof*, with its powerful evocation of Jewish life in Czarist Russia. The news has come through that *12 Years a Slave* has triumphed at the Oscars with 'Best Picture' for its harrowing tale by Solomon Northup of what it was like to be a slave in mid nineteenth-century America. Creativity is not just about innovation and the capacity to think in new ways; it can arouse empathy by the route of imagination. Eyes that now see may, under the right circumstances, lead to a mind and heart that are now open. Narrative is fundamental to this reflexive process.

Creativity guru Sir Ken Robinson challenges profoundly the way we are educating our children. He is a vociferous champion of a radical rethink of our school systems, to cultivate creativity and acknowledge multiple types of intelligence. We have been educated to become good workers rather than creative thinkers. Students with restless minds and bodies – rather than being hailed for their energy and curiosity – are ignored or even stigmatised with costs and consequences. This has implications for leadership development. 'We're educating people out of their curiosity' is the message of his books and talks. With such titles as *The Element: How Finding Your Passion Changes Everything*, he argues that when people arrive at the Element, the point at which natural talent meets personal passion, they feel most themselves, most inspired and achieve at their highest levels.[4]

An emphasis given to creativity in the curriculum was justified by the British exam watchdog of the day, the Qualifications and Curriculum Authority, in terms which satisfy both the personal and the public concerns for which an elected government rightly claims responsibility: 'creative pupils lead richer lives and, in the longer term, make a valuable contribution to society'.[5]

In Venezuela, the Simón Bolívar Orchestra is a source of national pride, like football stars in other Latin American countries. Called 'El Sistema' by its members, the programme has celebrated 30 years of making classical musicians out of half-a-million young Venezuelans. In the process, it has transformed the lives of many underprivileged and at-risk youths. Reports indicate a marked increase in learning generally.[6] Being 'good at something' seems to increase the student's capacity for valuing him or herself. As Giddens remarks, 'where humans cannot live creatively, chronic melancholic or schizophrenic tendencies are likely to result.'[7]

Empathy – Learning empathy is in everyone's interest. In May 2015, the international travel company Thomas Cook acknowledged the insensitivity and lack of compassion they had shown in response to a tragic incident in Corfu nine years before. Two children had died, succumbing to carbon monoxide poisoning; a faulty hot water boiler, which was in an external outhouse at the hotel where they were staying with their family, had a number of faults and this was the source of the lethal carbon monoxide. Earlier, in 2013, the travel giant had been cleared of any fault in the deaths of the children from West Yorkshire and awarded damages from the hotel. The travel representative for the location declined to apologise. A spokesperson for the company had said, 'What happened in Corfu was a tragedy, and the thoughts and sympathy of everyone at Thomas Cook will always be with the family and friends of Christianne and Robert Shepherd.' This was compounded by the company demonstrating poor judgement in the statements it had made at the inquest into the children's deaths. A jury at an inquest into the tragedy found that Thomas Cook had 'breached their duty of care'. The tour operator then faced a backlash from both consumers and the media after it was revealed that the company was awarded millions of pounds in compensation from the owner of the hotel for its costs when it was awarded the damages. Acknowledging this, Peter Fankhauser, the chief executive of Thomas Cook, has admitted that mistakes were made in his and the company's handing of the deaths of the two children.[8]

Empathy and awareness of others is certainly a very important part of forming alternatives to violence. Marcus Aurelius suggested that to become world citizens, we must not simply amass knowledge but comprehend the motives and choices of people different to ourselves, in short, to be sensitive cross-cultural interpreters.

> Stoics propose that the process of coming to recognise the humanity of all people should be a lifelong process, encompassing all levels of education – especially since, in a culture suffused with group hatred, one cannot rely on parents to perform this task.[9]

As Nussbaum observes, the problem with engaging with people different to ourselves from a position of superiority or proselytising is that learning rarely travels in two directions. Education must invite our pupils to imagine or know someone like them and to enable them to know themselves. This failure of knowledge entails a failure of the kind of love our faith asks all people to have for one another. Becoming an educated citizen means learning many facts and mastering techniques of reasoning. But it means too learning how to be a human being capable of love and imagination. Otherwise we continue to produce human beings who have difficulty understanding people different from themselves, whose imagination rarely ventures beyond the local.

Seeing the world from another's perspective is an attitude or a skill that enables someone to relate well to others in many different contexts and probably in the main sphere delineated above. An attitude of empathy in private relationships will presumably be reflected in an ability to see other people's viewpoint in the workplace or within the community. In other words, empathy will build shared understanding and attitudes that celebrate diversity.

Eagleton observes that you do not need to leap out of your skin to know what another person is feeling. You may need rather to burrow more deeply into it. A society which has suffered colonisation, for example, has only to consult its own local experience to feel solidarity with another such colony.

> I do not understand you by ceasing to be myself, since then there would be nobody to do the understanding. Your understanding of me is not a matter of reduplication in yourself what I am feeling, an assumption which might well raise thorny issues of how you come to leap an ontological barrier between us.[10]

There are problems with empathy. We are not in possession of our own experience. We can be mistaken about what we are feeling, let alone thinking. Someone else might understand me better than I understand myself. The process of stimulating reflexivity about oneself and others goes wider than empathy. Empathy does not after all imply that you value someone else as fully human – one could empathise with a dog! Neither does it imply that you will resolve problems non-violently. Understanding is not a form of empathy. I do not understand a chemical formula by empathising with it. Nor am I incapable of sympathy for a slave because I have never been enslaved myself, or unable to appreciate the sufferings involved in being a woman because our gender is different.

The starting point to resolving conflict is becoming comfortable with asserting one's needs and respecting the needs of the opponent. There are undoubtedly practical skills to be learnt in mediation. But what could be developed more, I suggest, is a functional understanding of the conflict scenario in which participants recognise what they and others are trying to achieve and act out through it. It is not just reflection on one's own needs and emotions but includes those of another.

Global leadership

Focusing on the themes of human interaction by going under the surface 'noise' will be especially vital for leaders of the future functioning in a global context. To find out what concerns are important to those of other cultures and perspectives is crucial for conflict-resolution and to build understanding.

Continuing tensions coupled with problems such as the environment that are bigger than any one nation highlight the need for healthy responses to diversity or attitudes of international cooperation. With so many businesses in high-octane global competition, commercial companies often perceive leadership as their key challenge. Establishing leadership and management teams that ensure sustained growth in a fast-moving environment is vital. Yet the call will be out for social and not just company leaders, those who lead with social purpose to drive forward ideas and change to help solve the challenges of the twenty-first century.[11] They will be those that are couched in values and wisdom rather than status and the power that motivates many senior leaders currently. They will be those that connect life and leadership, vision and reality, heart and head. They will be those who have the know-how to create and nurture the enabling environments we are exploring in these pages. They will be those who gain wisdom; not just technocratic competence for 'smart leadership' in a digital era.

A new type of society is emerging. Amidst vast changes to do with the rise of China and the world looking east, a fully networked world economy that now has Africa plugged in, heated environmental debate and a highly politicised form of Islam, something else is reshaping global society. In today's increasingly interdependent and rapidly changing world, understanding the transformations of the twenty-first century that are characterised by uneven development, accelerated globalisation, economic uncertainty, entrenched and complex social problems requires an academic approach that is interdisciplinary and focused on both innovation and commercialisation. It requires imaginative leaders.

According to the Global Leadership Survey, HR currently is focusing heavily on two skills that they are not rating as critical leadership skills for the future: *Building consensus and commitment* and *Communicating and interacting with others*. HR is either overemphasising these with their current focus or undervaluing their future skill criticality, failing to recognise them as foundational skills. On the opposite side of the illustration, two skills that were noted as most critical (*fostering employee creativity and innovation* and *leading across countries and cultures*) are not being focused on. These two skills were identified amongst the most critical in our last forecast, but HR still doesn't focus on them in their leadership development programmes. As a result, leaders have not improved.[12] To facilitate transformation in the organisation and its culture, leaders must be able to perceive a problem and recognise the skills needed to influence the organisation. Over 13,000 leaders worldwide indicated that their leadership development offerings did not prepare them to lead their organisations for the future. In particular, when asked about the primary reason that leaders fail, they ranked a lack of leadership skills (such as facilitating change, building a team, coaching) and interpersonal skills (such as building relationships, networking, communication) at the top of the list. The respondents to the Global Leadership Forecast survey listed the major shortfalls in today's leaders and in leadership development programmes:

- There are not enough opportunities on the job for leaders to learn what they need to know or practice.
- Leadership development programmes do not use enough methods to teach skills and provide opportunities to practise the skills.
- Confidence in leaders is declining.
- Most of the world's leaders are not high quality.
- More than one-third of all leaders fail.
- Leaders lack basic skills.
- Quality of development programmes has declined.
- Leadership development programmes are poorly executed and send inconsistent messages.

Transformative change and the culture of an organisation

Attuning themselves to the underlying themes of human interaction and trying to grasp the different standpoints from which people respond is important also for change management.

We are charting how issues of human value play out in the organisations that shape work and wealth. The life and times of contemporary organisations are replete with instances where they were let down by their culture. Whether that was the immediate workplace environment or that of the various stakeholders, the 'culture' was often cited as a reason for failure. As I write this, the business news carries a report by Lord Myners into the functioning (or its lack) of the Co-operative Group in the UK. In his review, Lord Myners fired a heavy salvo at what he saw as a 'culture of entitlement' which exists amongst a 'small but highly active' proportion of the Co-op's 8-million-strong membership. And he accused them of 'hiding behind values' to 'stifle criticism and protect self-interest'.[13] There is a fundamental question raised by this statement. Management and organisational leaders may be able to set out the principles that foster productive environments, for example those developed in this book. The real point though is, 'Why are they not doing it?' Whether or not the criticism of Lord Myners was fair, acts of stifling criticism (protection against threat to power and position) and also self-interest are so often the spectre at the feast and real brakes on progress.

It is illuminating to notice the reasons why there are fundamental problems with an organisation or an institution that can allow a negative climate. Special interest advocacy is invariably resistant to change, especially when clad in objectivity. When different entities or businesses are brought together either unsuccessfully or at least the going gets very heavy, media reaction can be one of retrospective observation that this was a case of organisations with 'different cultures'. The sense of near fatalism in such reports highlights the strength and dominance of 'culture'. It is revealed in statements about 'who we are'; but not just 'official' versions. Culture shows up in what is said at grassroots level about 'how we do things round here'. The 'who' question cohabits with the 'how' question.

Getting to yes: the bottom line and the skill of negotiation[14]

As I write these words, the UK is embarking on a strong recruitment drive to build expertise in trade-deal negotiations in the wake of 'Brexit'. Leaving the European Union and doing a deal with many countries separately requires an expertise that the British government has not had since 1973. There are few people that have experience of the complex tugs of war that reaching such deals has to involve 'if Britain is to leave the negotiating chamber with its pockets unpicked'.[15]

Henry Kissinger wrote that the usual process of negotiation, coming in with many and reducing demands until both parties arrive at the bottom line that they are prepared to accept, does not enhance understanding and is often self-defeating. Negotiation is one of the most important skills in business. 'No other skill will give you a better chance of optimising your success and your organisation's success'.[16] At its optimum, however, the art of negotiation depends not just on a negotiating position but on the human factors of the negotiators. Who we are and what we bring to the table is crucial to ensure a win–win success everyone can live with. As *Harvard Business Review* drew out, this is vital so as to set the stage for a healthy relationship long after the ink has dried, to make promises both sides can keep and to gain adversaries' trust in high-stakes talks.[17]

On occasions, a bottom line signifies the worst possible outcome that a negotiator might accept. The bottom line is meant to act as the final barrier where a negotiation will not proceed further. It is a means to defend oneself against the pressure and temptation that is often exerted on a negotiator to conclude an agreement that is self-defeating. Although bottom lines definitely serve a purpose, they also regrettably foster inflexibility, stifle creativity and innovation, and lessen the incentive to seek tailor-made solutions that resolve differences. In contrast to a bottom line, a BATNA (Best Alternative To a Negotiated Agreement) is not interested in the objectives of a negotiation, but rather to determine the course of action if an agreement is not reached within a certain time frame. According to the Negotiation Academy, it is a gauge against which an agreement is measured; it prohibits a negotiator from accepting an unfavourable agreement or one that is not in their best interests because it provides a better option outside the negotiation.[18]

What follows is offered as a proposal for executive education to develop the creativity and empathy that will be increasingly important and to do this concurrently.

Two metaphors

Narrative – Learning to read and interpret the texts and stories is a vital leadership skill. As I write, Donald Trump has just accepted the nomination to be Republican candidate for US President. Commentators are hovering between various narratives that are on offer. Is this about a vision of America that is dystopian, dark and declining? Or is the narrative one of a hopeful future albeit with some problems that need to be fixed? The key to an effective model of reflexive learning is to nurture the capacity to imagine, to envisage alternative futures or the situation of those who are different.

Narrative and music can hold a mirror to each participant and shift perspectives. Some great leaders, for example Abraham Lincoln, have been great storytellers. 'Lincoln was a master of the art of storytelling and he used that purposefully and effectively when he was President of the United States.'[19]

Narrative imagination and the use of story is key to developing reflexive learning to provoke awareness by people about their own violence and the violence of others. Stories are powerful, encoding meanings. To paraphrase Carl Rogers, that which is most personal is most general. We dream in stories, think in stories and so often structure our understanding of the world around narratives. One only has to observe the way young people find adverts memorable to realise that narrative has enormous potential for encoding knowledge and meaning. Narrative imagination does not appeal at the level of 'knowing that' or even 'knowing how' (skills) but 'knowing in relation' in the way we know someone. The usual method of knowing and learning is by distancing from the object of study, standing outside it and putting it under scrutiny. With story, we are drawn in and involved at some level.

Narrative imagination is used a great deal in Religious Education where it is essential in the development of religious concepts. Much religious language is inspirational and metaphorical rather than informational. 'Imagination extends the possibilities of knowledge ... Imagination can be the means by which we can come to understand reality ... Imagination is the capacity to make links and see links.'[20] I propose, though, that narrative imagination through story is the key to developing critical reflection and discovery moments in the context of leadership generally. Such stories can be:

1   real life
2   fictional
3   either, but where alternative endings can be imagined and expressed by students.

To provoke discovery moments, some stories might be told where endings are left unfinished and the audience is invited to complete alternative endings. Stories involve metaphor, 'a fundamental mechanism of mind that allows us to use what we know about our physical and social experience to provide understanding of countless other subjects. Because such metaphors structure our most basic understandings of our experience, they are "metaphors we live by".[21]

Stories are crucial. They encode meanings. When resistance to change sets in, a narrative has got off the ground. Ken Parry notes that leaders are often noted for providing a compelling vision that inspires followers to act to fulfil the vision, often by telling stories. From the notion that leaders tell stories, stories themselves operate like leaders. People follow the story as much as they follow the storyteller or author, hence the story becomes the leader. First, within the context of organisational development, leadership development can move from 'people' development to the development of the narratives that resonate within organisations. Decoupling leader as person or position, from leadership as process helps to illustrate stories as leaders.[22]

Music – Recent Western cultures are very much dominated by visual sense and visual metaphors.[23] An auditive and musical culture remains hugely important, however. Listening to the deeper themes playing in human interaction enables a meeting of hearts and minds that facilitates transformative change. The metaphor of music points to developed listening to a high level.[24] This can be found in the aesthetics literature.[25]

Two types of musical genre provide instructive contexts in which to reflect on leadership lessons. Koivunen points to symphony orchestras as unique relating processes: 100 musicians play together, trying to maintain the same rhythm and balance. Communication is largely non-verbal, through cues, body language and craft.[26] Listening and an auditive culture are closely connected. As Gadamer observed, 'anyone who listens is fundamentally open'.[27]

The second type of musical genre that has potential for executive education in leadership is jazz. Management scholar and jazz musician Frank Barrett shows that the world's best leaders and teams improvise. They invent novel responses and take calculated risks without a scripted plan or a safety net that guarantees specific outcomes. They negotiate with each other as they proceed, and they don't dwell on mistakes or stifle each other's ideas. In short, they say 'yes to the mess' that is today's hurried, harried, yet enormously innovative and fertile world of work. This is exactly what great jazz musicians do. Barrett argues that the improvisational 'jazz mindset' and the skills that go along with it are essential for effective leadership today. A new model for leading and collaborating in organisations is suggested by how, like skilled jazz players, leaders can master the art of unlearning, perform and experiment simultaneously, and take turns soloing and supporting each other. Organisations must take an inventive approach to crisis management, economic volatility, and all the rapidly evolving realities of our globally connected world. Leaders today need to be expert improvisers. *Yes to the Mess* vividly shows how the principles of jazz thinking and jazz performance can help anyone who leads teams or works with them to develop these critical skills.[28]

If all behaviour has a purpose, what themes are playing that we should be tuning into? Could there be a reflexive learning approach in which leaders might start to form some insights into their own challenging behaviour and what needs they are trying to meet through it? Stimulating narrative imagination (whether by case study, story or role play) probably has potential to evoke discovery moments more powerfully than didactic approaches alone.

- *Discovery moments* – seeing ourselves/seeing the Other through exploration.
- *Attitude and value shifts* about society and relations with others – vision.
- *Acquiring alternative skills* and behaviour, doing something else – action.

This is an approach which allows for deeper-level transformation because it facilitates self-awareness by individuals as they reflect on their situation, actions and reactions. This process goes beyond acquisition of skills or attitude changes into the area of self-understanding and insight from within. It is an approach that is not invasive, not imposing something on people but is consistent with their freedom. It is not attempting to change people but to facilitate self-change as alternative options and futures can be envisaged and acted upon; an inherently educative process in that it is stimulating discovery of oneself and of others.

Humans relate at the level of demands. They do not relate at the level of concerns. By learning to tune into the themes that are playing in one's own violence or the violence of others, it may be possible to stimulate sufficient reflexivity to be open to such alternative futures and to develop unexpected options. To be practical at this point, here is one such proposal for a short preventative course on these lines about resolving conflict that is not just skill-based but stimulates reflexivity.

Listen to the music (and change the song)

The aim is to help leaders approach the culture that they are dealing with in their organisation and to understand better the drivers of motivation and how what goes on underneath the surface noise is often about underlying themes they need to tune into. Think of jazz, where developing the music involves someone taking the lead, often with a discordant interruption that then signals change – a new tune or theme to the piece.

There is too much shouting. The noise rarely leads to harmony. Leaders need to understand narratives of change and how narratives get going. Harmony is of course double-edged. It may be an excuse to keep the status quo and not challenge vested interest where people have a disguised stake in keeping things as they are. Nevertheless, to go beyond the shouting and polarised, often violent, defaults, bridges of understanding can be built.

Henry Kissinger remarked that when he joined the White House staff as America's National Security Adviser, he found the political or international culture far too focused on immediate demands. Whether that insight was translated into negotiation style is another question but going to the bottom line and underlying concerns that drive the agenda is an important and fruitful approach.

What would happen if organisational leaders or leaders at national level learnt to aim quickly at a meeting of minds and hearts, to grasp what is important to those contesting political agendas AND WHY? What could be different if political and organisation leaders really understood the worldview of those they were dealing with?

Political and social movements follow personal life in that they can be understood in two dimensions. The melody must be followed; the ongoing story of the events of our time. But there is also the news behind the news, the resonances or harmonic dimensions playing under the surface. Arguably, the underlying resonance of social discontent is: 'we're not going to be suppressed or exploited, we will rise up and claim our inheritance … we are equal!'

A musical metaphor suggested itself, echoing Giorgi's descriptive phenomenological method.[29] A performance often contains an underlying theme that plays recurrently. Dietrich Bonhoeffer, the German theologian murdered by the Nazis in 1945, wrote from prison of 'a kind of cantus firmus to which the other melodies of life provide the counterpoint … where the ground bass is firm and clear, there is nothing to stop the counterpoint from being developed to the utmost of its limits'.[30] The 'cantus firmus' will often persist amidst other themes that are detected underneath the surface 'noise'. Listening for the themes playing in the background of life, often the recurrent themes under the main presenting theme, offers a fruitful approach to tuning into people's concerns struggling to find and maintain value.

We use the word harmony in music. You need differences. Music would be boring if on one note. Respecting the other, respect differences. In playing a duet, you must learn to follow the other person's part as well as your own. With jazz, someone takes a lead for a while and the team has learnt to function as one.

Most people don't get beneath the top melody – or maybe the overall rhythm. To listen to serious music and get the most out of it, you must seek for more than the top line. In every conversation and dialogue; behind every demand and negotiation there are underlying themes to be tuned in to that, if heard and recognised, will bring break-through in understanding. What if negotiators in situations of conflict began to tune in to the underlying concerns their opponents had and both sides were not repeating their demands but began to hear the underlying concerns?

The working title of this idea for a course is 'Listen to the Music (and change the song)'. It is about how organisational and political leaders at all levels of society can learn to tune in to the underlying themes playing in the background of human interaction.

A course in executive education based on this idea

Developing this as a social enterprise can involve six sessions or a training day interspersed with music:

1   Tuning in – the art of effective listening; what themes are we picking up under the surface?
2   Motivational drivers – what tunes people in or out leading to engagement or disengagement?
3   Global leadership – the themes of human interaction on the global stage.
4   Change management in organisations – the factors that feed negative cultures and how to bring about transformation so different songs can be sung, different stories told.
5   Negotiation – applying this idea to the process of 'getting to yes' and 'win-win' solutions.
6   Handling disharmony – creating the song or symphony.
7   Writing the narratives – storytelling and creative writing to explore different narratives.

In summary, what is needed is an innovative approach to global leadership and change management geared to leadership in both organisational and political cultures. How we bring transformative change is a crucial question in a landscape that is continually shifting, making relationships between leaders and followers more fraught and less satisfactory.

Simple sets of ideas on how the world works and what leaders should do in response are no longer adequate. The age of algorithms is sweeping away middle-class jobs, putting a premium on creativity and empathy which technology cannot replicate. Utilising both these skills, this chapter advocates two metaphors – that of music and story. One is story; understanding the way narratives get going and how myths are formed. Organisational cultures are reflected in the stories that are told about 'how we do things round here', or 'who we are'. With music, tuning into the deeper themes playing in human interaction, so often there are fears, anxieties, hopes and dreams. Refusing just to meet on the surface opens a space to meet and relate at the level of concerns, not demands. Leaders of organisations will so often encounter resistance rooted in deeper-level concerns. It is vital for negotiation to understand what is going on under the surface. Some issues will clearly be unresolvable, arising from mutually incompatible views about life.

Notes

1 Henretta, D. (Group President, Asia & Global Specialty Channel, Procter & Gamble), 'Millennials at Work: Reshaping the Workplace', PWC, May 2016. https://www.pwc.com/m1/en/services/consulting/documents/millennials-at-work.pdf accessed May 2016.
2 Baker, K. (2016), *The Digital Revolution*. http://www.tes.com/, accessed May 2016.
3 Author's unpublished Doctor of Education thesis, 'Reflexivity and Human Violence', June 2005.
4 Robinson, K. (2006), *The Element: How Finding Your Passion Changes Everything*. New York: Barnes and Noble. See also his *Out of Our Minds: Learning to be Creative*. New York: Wiley/Capstone.
5 http://www.qca.org.uk/.
6 https://www.guardian.co.uk/musicblog/2008/.
7 Giddens, A. (1991), *Modernity and Self-Identity: Self and Society in the Late Modern Age*. Cambridge: Polity Press, p. 56.
8 TTG Digital, 21 May 2015, http://www.ttgdigital.co.uk/.
9 Nussbaum, M.C. (1997), *Cultivating Humanity: A Classic Defence of Reform in Liberal Education*. Cambridge, MA: Harvard University Press, p. 66.
10 Eagleton, T. (2000), *The Idea of Culture*. Oxford: Blackwell, p. 49.
11 Mary Marsh, Founding Director, Clore Social Leadership Programme. http://www.cloresocialleadership.org.uk/, accessed June 2016.
12 http://www.ddiworld.com/DDI/media/trend-research/glf2014-findings/critical-leadership-skills_glf2014_ddi.pdf/, accessed June 2016.
13 http://www.co-operative.coop/MynersReview/, 7 May 2014.
14 Fisher, R. and Ury, W. (1997), *Getting to Yes: Negotiating an Agreement without Giving*. In New York: Random House Business.
15 'Building the Brexit team'. *The Economist*, 16 July 2016.
16 Gates, S. (2010), *The Negotiation Book: Your Definitive Guide to Successful Negotiating*. Chichester: John Wiley & Sons.
17 *Harvard Business Review on Winning Negotiations*. Cambridge, MA: Harvard Business School Press (2011). https://www.hbr.org/.
18 Venter, D. (2016), 'BATNA explained', The Negotiation Academy. http://www.negotiationtraining.com.au/articles/next-best-option/, accessed June 2016.
19 Phillips, D.T. (1992), *Lincoln on Leadership*. New York: Warner Books, p. 22.
20 Watson, B. (1993), *The Effective Teaching of Religious Education*. London: Pearson, p. 56.
21 Lakoff, G. (2003), *Metaphors We Live By*. Chicago: University of Chicago Press.
22 Parry, K.N. and Hansen, H. (2007), 'The Organizational Story as Leadership', *Leadership*, 3 (3), pp. 281–300.
23 Welsh, W. (1997), *Undoing Aesthetics*. London: Sage.
24 Levin, D.M. (1989), *The Listening Self*. New York: Routledge.

25 Koivunen, N. (2003), *Leadership in Symphony Orchestras: Discursive and Aesthetic Practices*. Tampere: Tampere University Press.
26 Koivunen N. (2006), 'Auditive Leadership Culture: Lessons from Leadership Culture', in *The Social Construction of Organisation*, ed. D.M. Hosking and S. McNamee. Copenhagen: Copenhagen Business Press, chapter 5.
27 *The Gadamer Reader: A Bouquet of the Later Writings*, ed. Richard E. Palmer. Evanston, IL: Northwestern University Press, 2007.
28 Barrett, F. (2012), *Yes to the Mess: Surprising Leadership Lessons from Jazz*. Cambridge, MA: Harvard Business Review Press.
29 Giorgi, A., and Giorgi, B.M. (2003), 'The Descriptive Phenomenological Psychological Method', in *Qualitative Research in Psychology: Expanding Perspectives in Methodology and Design*, ed. P. M. Camic, J. E. Rhodes and L. Yardley. Washington, DC: American Psychological Association, pp. 243–274.
30 Bonhoeffer, D. (1953), *Letters and Papers from Prison*. London: SCM Press, p. 66.

Chapter 12

Leadership with spirit: Wisdom and the black box of power

The fear of failure isn't worth it if we want to solve problems.
Barbara Bush, Shared Value Leaders Summit, 2016[1]

Many excellent people are frustrated with how hard leadership is. The complexity of such rapidly shifting sands means it is about to get a lot harder!

As Robert Colville points out in *The Great Acceleration*, Amazon has a model, 'The virtual flywheel', of creative destruction – the turmoil of change is becoming too fast for humans.[2] Communities evolve rapidly and the pace of change and innovation grows in the global marketplace.

Against a backcloth of mediocrity and mendacity, there is a rising crescendo of voices calling for organisations to change their behaviour. We are beginning to see a fundamental shift towards quality and not just quantity. A growing number of individuals and organisations are learning how to become more patient, committed, connected, engaged, trusted and emotionally intelligent. There are significant challenges associated with these shifts in behaviour but the need and the results outweigh the emotional labour required. It takes wisdom.

Recent emphases in leadership development have been on emotional intelligence[3] or the concept of 'flow'.[4] Wisdom, though, receives less attention. Wisdom is surely about being more effective in inspiring extraordinary performance and results through leading others in positive ways, i.e. transformative leadership.

Wise leadership goes beyond what might be termed 'smart leadership'. Smart leadership adapts to the technologically driven complexity that is reshaping the world. Smart leadership knows intuitively how to navigate into uncharted waters and come up with new products, new services and new horizons. Smart leadership, as with a smartphone, is highly sophisticated and able to duck and weave around many stakeholders and a highly complex environment. Yet although technocratic and appropriately skilled for new times, most smart leaders have a functionalist paradigm. It is pragmatic – 'what works for you'. It is only a step away from amorality – working out what is moral and right by what you can get away with and judging the rightness of actions by people's reactions. It is thinking like this that has led young bank traders to bring the whole banking system into disrepute.

The contrast between smart leaders and wise leaders is likely to be of increasing importance in a world where everything is 'smart'. 'Smart leaders steer their organisations to victory, but wise leaders are needed to keep them on top in a dynamic world', suggests Prasad Kaipa, Senior Research Fellow and Executive Director Emeritus at the

Center for Leadership, Innovation and Change, Indian School of Business in Hyderabad, India. 'Just being smart may not be enough in the long run'.[5] Being 'smart' in these terms means leaders are more aggressive, always looking for what is the next opportunity but while looking at the big picture, do not pay sufficient attention to how that vision gets executed. 'Wisdom', however, means being cautious and careful, paying attention to operational excellence, paying attention to the supply chain, paying attention to the execution of the problem, making sure it gets done impeccably, it gets done on time, under budget to the highest satisfaction.

Kaipa, who worked at Apple, proposed that Steve Jobs, in his first period at Apple, was very much a smart leader. 'When he came back for his second stint, he was beginning to demonstrate, in certain areas, wisdom. He did act with wisdom to start the Apple stores. He did act with wisdom when he began to respect Jony Ive and his designs, and he began to work closely with him. And he also began to demonstrate wisdom when he allowed Tim Cook to become CEO.[6]

Self-awareness is part of Kaipa's overall strategy, where leaders find a 'North Star'. Smart leaders make New Year resolutions and set quarterly milestones, charting progress against ambitious plans and goals. Wise leaders, however, take a different approach: they root themselves in a noble purpose, align it with a compelling vision, and then take action – not just for that year, but for the rest of their lives. That noble purpose becomes a North Star, giving direction when the path ahead is hazy. One of the issues is that smart leaders keep using the same formula even when the context or the situation or the market has changed, and what was smart becomes ineffective. 'Without self-awareness, it's very hard to move out of your smartness.' 'I think the essential pieces of awareness, and through that self-awareness, grows a depth of something that goes beyond smartness,' says Roger Lehman, Affiliate Professor of Entrepreneurship and Family Enterprise at INSEAD.[6]

Similarly, Cranfield Business School have developed a model of wise leadership, developing leaders who can act with integrity in challenging environments.[7] Wise leadership can address the emotional and political elements of the leadership role:

- The ability to read the environment and current situation skilfully;
- The ability to manage what is personally carried in the leadership role.

Ten commandments for the wise leader in highly complex times

In the continuing, increasingly complex, and changing challenges of the twenty-first century, the need for effective leadership is greater now than ever. If the contrast between smart, leaders and wise leaders is likely to be of increasing importance in a world where everything is 'smart, what then marks out 'the wise leader' in the context of the issues raised in this book? Wise leadership is essentially transformative leadership, aiming at profound change, not merely a shake-up of structures.

1 **Wise leaders nurture environments of value** – wise leaders strive to generate working environments where the inner worth and value of staff and participants can be translated into their projects. The day of the leader as lonely hero is past. Within the argument in these pages, wise leadership discerns and is concerned about the ingredients that contribute either to disengagement or recruiting people's passions.

Transformational leadership is the ability to raise others to a higher level of morality; a level where people expand their capacity to create the results they truly desire, where new and expansive patterns of thinking are nurtured, where collective aspiration is set free, where people learn together.

2 **Wise leaders are emotionally intelligent** – such leaders try to understand how new forms of organisation in the future require leaders to devise new ways of operating to manage the emotional needs of followers – individuals and groups. The wise leader has deep listening skills that are attuned to the emotional needs of those they work with, knowing how to use metaphors and stories to listen to the underlying themes in human interaction. The scientific theory-first approach to management assumes a world independent of context and seeks answers that are universal and predictive. However, like all social phenomena, business is context dependent. Analysing it is meaningless unless you consider people's goals, values, and interests. So often executives fail to do just that. 'The world needs leaders who will have to see what is good, right, and just for society while being grounded in the details of the ever-changing front line. Thus they must pair micromanagement with big-picture aspirations about the future.'[8] Wise leaders create informal as well as formal contexts for participants to construct new meaning through their interactions. They know that different styles are appropriate on different occasions. 'We may need to be tough in driving a legal outcome but empathetic to a colleague who is struggling or when delivering bad news.' Wise leaders are relational coaches and rare; formal reviews replaced with ongoing conversations.

3 **Wise leaders act with responsibility** – the context for organisations is the wider environment within which the immediate environment of value in the organisation is set. The concept of 'shared value' as we have seen is that to do well, business must 'do good'. Business does not function in isolation from its setting as part of society. It is embedded, not free-floating. The notion of 'responsible leadership' is defined by Maak and Pless, two of the most prolific writers in the field, as 'a values-based and principle-driven relationship between leaders and stakeholders who are connected through a shared sense of meaning and purpose through which they rise to higher levels of motivation.'[9] As Karen Blakely points out, responsible leadership is content-led. It belongs with a motivation to contribute something to society.

4 **Wise leaders are shaped by purpose** – they have a huge ability to focus and drill down to what is vital while being attuned to what is going on externally. Wise leaders can quickly grasp the essence of any situation or problem and intuitively fathom the nature and meaning of people, things and events. As Flyvbjerg points out, instead of trying to emulate the natural sciences, we should have ensured that management asked questions such as 'Where are we going?' 'Who gains, who loses, and by which mechanisms of power?' 'Is this development desirable?' 'What should we do about it?'[10] Wise leadership sets purpose above targets – not content with tick boxes or taking the credit but transformative change. This has been a recurrent theme. As Dwight Eisenhower observed, 'the first great need is for integrity and high purpose'.[11] If that was any part of the mood music of the baby-boomer generation, millennials expect to derive a sense of purpose from their jobs. When professional and personal lives were more cleanly separate, a pay cheque was enough. But with the erosion of the wall between work and play, a shift in focus from pay cheque to purpose is required.

5 **Wise leaders are ethical leaders** – some companies give business a bad name by ignoring or flouting the new norms around ethics and responsibility. Wise leaders are ethically attuned. People are angry about the visible lack of values and ethics in business. The media frequently provide examples of how organisations fail to act with integrity and make unethical choices but it is important to know how executives and leaders at all levels manage NOT to fall into such situations when personal and organisational values conflict with expedient. Wise leaders create an organisation able to act with integrity when under pressure to deliver results that may conflict with organisational practices, relationships and culture that form the context for these decisions.[12] The particular environment in the organisation may engender different actions and behaviours in a variety of contexts. In the workplace, how we behave is situational. An environment of value is one where an inner guidance system and instincts may work out differently but there is a common thread of honesty and integrity running through all actions and policies. It is one where the participants in the organisation are also spurred to act ethically. As the great religions and principles of morality have demonstrated amply over the centuries, acting ethically is not acting pragmatically, looking around to see what others consider acceptable and making a decision relative to them. It is not 'what you can get away with' (situation ethics or even amorality). Wise leaders make it relative to themselves as it will affect other people. It is attuned to the need for everyone to be heard equally. As one participant in a conference put it, ethical leadership is 'directed by respect for ethical beliefs and values and the dignity and rights of others. It is based on the concepts of trust, honesty, openness, consideration, fairness and engagement.'[13]

6 **Wise leaders pay attention to both values and value** – The concept of 'values-driven leadership' has gained enormous traction in recent years. The Centre for Values-driven Leadership seeks to create a more ethical and sustainable business model for the future, to help leaders grow personally, interpersonally (through teams), organisationally (building flourishing companies) and globally (transforming business and society).[14] At heart here is the relationship between two dimensions – VALUE AND VALUES. The theme of this book has been about the need for an extended version of value (singular), namely the value and worth of people that can, under the right conditions, be catalysed into worthwhile goals for the organisation. The other dimension though is values (plural), namely the ideals and practices that reflect what is important to them. How do I do things in accordance with my own values and do these actions promote the value and worth of participants in the enterprise is a question that wise leaders surely ask.[15] How leaders manage personal values is an important issue. In seminal work by Hambrick and Mason, individual leadership orientation is shaped by personal values as much as psychological characteristics.[16] Wise leaders ponder what their legacy will be when they move on. In one schema, values-driven leadership pays attention to six values that appear in combinations in various styles leaders tend to adopt.[17]

Grounding	Family	Management	Relational Awareness	Systems Awareness	Expansion

To be a values-based leader, you must be willing to look within yourself through regular self-reflection and strive for greater self-awareness. You must have balance, which means the ability to see situations from multiple perspectives and differing viewpoints to gain a much fuller understanding. Self-confidence is vital, accepting yourself as you are, recognising your strengths, your weaknesses and striving for continuous improvement. Then there is humility, genuine humility – never forgetting who you are or where you came from. It keeps life in perspective, especially as you experience success in your career. Thus argues Harry Kraemer, author of *From Values to Action: The Four Principles of Values-Based Leadership.*[18]

There is an intrinsic connection between values-driven leadership and the concerns of this book. Indeed, Kraemer goes on to argue that humility helps you value each person. As Hybels points out, 'admit your mistakes and your stock goes up!'[19] Values need 'heating up' according to which value it is both wise and strategic to emphasise at any one time.

Valuing environments that tap into the value and worth participants in an organisation experience under certain conditions discussed here are perhaps a subset of the growing emphasis on values-driven leadership. How you work with and develop the felt value of actors in the organisational matrix has a lot to do with what leaders deem to be important priorities or guiding principles. What it takes to do a leader's job, i.e. translating skills into action, is as much the application of values as competencies.

In the leadership literature, there is much greater acceptance than there was in the heady days of 'scientific management' that the prime task of a leader is to create cultures: micro-cultures that allow the right objectives to be realised under the right conditions. Leadership and management are not just a set of professional competencies but the translation of the guiding values of an organisation into practice in a way that connects with the values of the workforce. The obvious ways this perspective shows up are with respect to the ethical stance of a leader, the management of people and change management. But arguably there are no competencies, actions, policies or interventions in an organisation that are neutral about values. The construct in this book proposes that human beings are motivated by the pursuit of a high value for themselves and their group that is 'value' (singular) not just 'values' (plural). Working with the grain of this quest – what might be termed 'human value theory' – is an important task of values-driven leaders as so many 'values' are about how people flourish.

7 **Wise leaders show flexibility of approach** – an approach that is wise surely goes beyond the polarity between top-down and bottom-up styles of leadership. Both approaches will be relevant in different circumstances. A top-down approach sets conditions and initiates review and planning to help shape purpose. A bottom-up 'dialogic' approach recognises that involvement with others is not a wise preference, it reflects a deep truth about the world. Top-down change has been all-pervasive – witness notions of 're-engineering' the company, 'total quality management' or 'vision and values'. Coming more to the fore in recent years has been more of a 'bottom-up self-directing approach'. Yet the contrast between the dialogic and monologic approach cannot be itself a polarity. Wise leaders surely demonstrate flexibility in shaping radical change by combining both strong leadership AND a commitment to learning. They are both forthright and they listen; giving clear direction while creating space for others to use their initiative, ambitious for the organisation and recognising

their own limits.[20] Wise leadership recognises the need to switch modalities between 'Thinking Fast and Slow'.[21]

8 **Wise leaders are self-aware when it comes to power** – the power relationships between people in an organisation are a vital area for success. As Michel Foucault has highlighted, power is a fluid concept that is not just exchanged through formal power structures but is dynamic, constantly present where people interact. Wise leaders are all too aware that senior managers are motivated by power as much, if not more than, by money. As we will note in the Postscript, this is much about another form of value – the high value that comes in this case through status and grand significance. Wise leaders are therefore reflective practitioners when it comes to their own power needs and the inner need to take the credit or be narcissistic. Group-based discrimination and oppression dynamics have outlined the role of power in affecting individuals' and groups' relationships in many ways. Social psychology has examined ways in which the study of power is central: (a) intergroup relations and (b) organisations. Social dominance theory has attempted to integrate these two approaches. It considers the relationship between different levels of analysis as they pertain to hierarchies. However, 'to date this theory has not incorporated insights about interpersonal power, which is also important in the authority structures and operations of organisations'.[22] Many hierarchy-enhancing contexts appear to encourage the preference in high social dominance bosses towards using harsh tactics.[23] Corporate life develops many individuals who are aberrant self-promoters; those with a narcissistic personality in combination with anti-social behaviour.[24] Arguably, the career of Henry Ford shows that only secure leaders give power to others.[25]

9 **Wise leaders are not off balance** – in a high-octane, high-performance corporate environment, there must be room for a better work/life balance in order to nurture more positive qualities than those that have guided both organisational behaviour and that of individuals. Anecdotally, one-third of US professional people work a 50-hour week but some work far in excess of that and many elite lawyers work 70 hours a week routinely. The 'know-how' to deploy the right word on the right occasion to different audiences and the right time to act is not cultivated by situations of high stress or busyness but being able to take time to be a more rounded individual and 'having a hinterland', as a former UK politician put it. This is empowerment from the inside, maintaining a perspective that spirals up, not downwards.[26] A popular and recent management book advocates 'less push, more pause, better results'.[27] Reflecting changing attitudes, recent research points to a strong perception amongst millennials that work/life balance and diversity promises are not being kept. They are looking for a good work/life balance and strong diversity policies but report that their employers have failed to deliver on their expectations; 28 per cent said that the work/life balance was worse than they had expected before joining, and over half said that while companies talk about diversity, they did not feel that opportunities were equal for all.[28]

10 **Wise leaders lead 'with spirit'** – though management is invariably a highly technical exercise, wise leaders cultivate a spiritual dimension that connects them with a larger vision and dimension about their purpose in life and what success means. The culture gets speedier and more superficial. Yet common values, customs, meanings and purposes are what bind communities and organisations together. To allow complexity and quality to shine through takes wisdom and not just competence,

attuned to a larger dimension outside ourselves, the room of the 'spirit' against which we measure our lives. 'Spiritual intelligence' is the wisdom by which we balance meaning and values and place our lives in a wider context.[29] As Charles Handy wrote in his *The Hungry Spirit*, there is a quest for purpose in the modern world that takes us beyond capitalism. 'We would all like to find a purpose bigger than ourselves because that will raise us to heights we had not dreamt of.'[30] A business best-seller, *The Monk who sold his Ferrari* tells the story of Julian Mantle, a super-star corporate lawyer whose physical collapse arising from 'an out-of-balance' lifestyle brings on a spiritual crisis that forces him to confront his life and seek out ancient wisdom from the East that releases peace, purpose and passion.[31] Other versions are available. From a mainstream Christian perspective, Engstrom provides a model of dynamic and effective leadership that is key to the success of any organisation.[32] Drawing on biblical models as well as organisational management research, Thomas provides a model of leadership that promotes life not self-image, is driven by compassion not obsession and is rooted in relationships not systems.[33] It is attuned to love, a word featuring in management literature still less than wisdom![34]

As Christian leadership writer Bill Hybels wrote in 2015, 'last week I read 1st Corinthians 13 with my leadership lenses on and here's how it read ...

If I cast vision with the tongues of men and angels and have not love, I'm a noisy gong or a clanging cymbal.

If I have the gift of strategic planning and financial forecasting and have not love, I'm bound to make the future of my organisation cold-hearted and cynical.

If I solve problems, engineer change and allocate resources at a world class level, but fail to love my colleagues, I denigrate my workplace and devalue those who deserve better from me.

Love is patient and kind.

Love is not envious of others' success.

Love does not keep track of others' mistakes.

Rather, love engenders openness and trust, vulnerability and candour, hope and optimism.

There remain three: faith, hope and love.

But the greatest of these is love.

It always will be, gang. So, here's my final challenge on this point: don't hesitate a single additional moment in showing and expressing genuine concern and love to your teammates.

Tear down these professional veils that keep your heart cold and closed off from your co-workers.

Get personal.

Say the affirming or the encouraging words.

Or, write them.

Or, send the message by smoke signal if necessary.

Doing so will humanise and ennoble workplaces and create a powerful, caring, high performance culture, you just watch. And need I remind you one more time that this all starts with the senior-most leaders in every organisation. The quality of your loving senior leaders will set the tone for the entire organisation. Please, please, please get this right.'[35]

Notes

1 http://www.sharedvalue.org/groups/livestream-shared-value-leadership-summit-2016/.
2 Colville, R. (2016), *The Great Acceleration: How the World is Getting Faster, Faster*. London: Bloomsbury.
3 Goleman, D. (1996), *Emotional Intelligence*. London: Bloomsbury.
4 Csikszentmihalyi, M. (1991), *Flow: The Psychology of Optimal Experience*. New York: Harper & Row.
5 http://www.prasadkaipa.com/about/about_kaipa_group.php/, accessed June 2016.
6 Lee, A. (2012), 'The Wise Leader', http://knowledge.insead.edu/leadership-management/the-wise-leader-2320#xfFjVCUxLScGedKl.99/, accessed June 2016.
7 http://www.som.cranfield.ac.uk/som/dinamic-content/research/documents/wise_leadership.pdf/, accessed June 2016.
8 Nonaka, I. and Takeuchi, H. (2011), 'The Wise Leader', *Harvard Business Review* 89 (5), pp. 59–67.
9 Maak, T. and Pless, N.M. (2009), 'Business Leaders as Citizens of the World', *Journal of Business Ethics*, 88 (3), pp. 537–550.
10 Flyvbjerg, B. (2011), *Making Social Science Matter: Why Social Inquiry Fails and How it Can Succeed Again*. Cambridge: Cambridge University Press.
11 Eisenhower, D. (1989), *Great Quotes from Great Leaders*, ed. P. Anderson. Oak Brook, IL: Lombard (now Great Quotations Publishing Company).
12 James, K. T., and Arroba, T. (2005), 'Reading and Carrying: A Framework for Learning about Eemotion and Emotionality in Organizational Systems as a Core Aspect of Leadership Development', *Management Learning*, 36 (3), pp. 299–315.
13 Peta Wilkinson, Enham Trust, The Business Collective, Ethical Leadership Conference, June 2016. http://www.thebusinesscollective.co.uk/, accessed June 2016.
14 http://www.cvdl.org/, accessed June 2016.
15 Lew, D. (2013), 'What Does Values-driven Leadership Actually Mean?' http://www.dionnelew.com/what-does-values-driven-leadership-actually-mean/, accessed June 2016.
16 Hambrick, D.C. and Mason, P.A. (1984), 'Upper Echelons: The Organization as a Reflection of Its Top Managers', *Academy of Management Review*, 9, 193–206.
17 Hyatt, K. and Ciantis, C. De (2012), 'Values Driven Leadership', *Integral Leadership Review*.
18 Kraemer, H.M. Jansen Jr. (2011), *From Values to Action: The Four Principles of Values Driven Leadership October 2012*. San Francisco, CA: Jossey-Bass.
19 Hybels, B. (2008), *Leadership Axioms*. Grand Rapids, MI: Zondervan, p. 72.
20 Biney, G. and Williams, C. (1995), *Leaning into the Future*. London: Nicholas Brealey.
21 Kahneman, D. (2011), *Thinking Fast and Slow*. London: Penguin.
22 Aiello, A. *et al.* (2013), 'Framing Social Dominance Orientation and Power in Organizational Context', *Basic and Applied Social Psychology*, 35, pp. 487–495.
23 Altemeyer, B. (1996), *The Authoritarian Specter*. Cambridge, MA: Harvard University Press.
24 Gustafson, S.B. and Ritzer, D.R. (1995), 'The Dark Side of Normal: A Psychopathy Linked Pattern Called Aberrant Self-promotion', *European Journal of Personality*, 9, pp. 147–183.
25 Maxwell, J.C. (1998), *The 21 Irrefutable Laws of Leadership*. Nashville, TN: Thomas Nelson.
26 Maxwell, J.C. (1993), *Developing the Leader within You*. Nashville, TN: Thomas Nelson.
27 Poynton, R. (2013), *Do Improvise*. The Do Book Company.
28 Deborah Henretta (Group President, Asia & Global Specialty Channel, Procter & Gamble), 'Millennials at Work: Reshaping the Workplace', PWC, May 2016, https://www.pwc.com/m1/en/services/consulting/documents/millennials-at-work.pdf, accessed May 2016.
29 Zohar, D. and Marshall, I. (2000), *Spiritual Intelligence*. London: Bloomsbury.
30 Handy, C. (1997), *The Hungry Spirit: Beyond Capitalism – A Quest for Purpose in the Modern World*. London: Hutchinson.
31 Sharma, R. (2004), *The Monk who Sold his Ferrari*. London: Element.

32 Engstrom, T.W. (1976), *The Making of a Christian Leader*. Grand Rapids, MI: Zondervan.
33 Thomas, V. (1999), *Future Leader*. Cumbria: Paternoster Press.
34 Parry, K. and Kempster, S. (2014), 'Love and Leadership: Constructing Follower Narrative Identities of Charismatic Leadership', *Management Learning*, 45 (1), pp. 21–38.
35 Hybels, B. (2015), '*The Intangibles of Leadership*', Global Leadership Summit. http://www.treymcclain.com/wp-content/uploads/2015/08/2015GLSNotes.pdf/.

Postscript

Motivational drivers and human value theory: Maslow revisited

> We have a reputation for valuing our staff. People want to work here.
> Headteacher of Bedminster Down School, Bristol, explaining how they are able to recruit good teachers to work in a challenging community.[1]

In these pages, we have been exploring the proposition that leaders of the future will need to learn different skills for the organisations of the future. They will need to be tillers of the soil, gardeners, who know how to cultivate environments in the workplace that foster the value and worth of people.

This will be vital so that organisations can be humane places that draw out the value and worth of participants to be translated into their various projects. A construct has been offered to demonstrate the claim that there is a close association between inputs and outputs when it comes to the human dimension of an operation. The construct to be tested here is that people are motivated by inner necessity to engage in things that are of worth. The pursuit of high value is a key motivational driver.

In closing, the book must become something else: a lens on motivation and the drivers of human behaviour. That is bound to arise. What is it about us that in a valuing environment, we flourish; in the absence of an environment of value, we wither? How deep does it go? Does it tap into a fundamental driver that we maintain a pursuit to be of high value and worth in many contexts? How might this be described? What account could be given of how needing a high-value environment in order to thrive relates to the psycho-dynamics of human action and interaction? How might this be categorised?

This particular aspect of our construct is offered in sketch form only, yet a claim such as that cannot be proposed without reference to the usual categorisation of the motivational drivers of human action.

For those that came of age at the millennium, recent research on motivation suggests that development and work/life balance are more important than financial reward: this generation are committed to their personal learning and development and this remains their first choice benefit from employers. In second place they want flexible working hours. Cash bonuses come in at a surprising third place. Millennials are attracted to employer brands that they admire as consumers. In 2008 88 per cent were looking for employers with Corporate Social Responsibility values (CSR) that matched their own, and 86 per cent would consider leaving an employer whose values no longer met their expectations.

Fast-forward three years and just over half are attracted to employers because of their CSR position and only 56 per cent would consider leaving an employer that didn't have the values they expected. Millennials are also turned off by some entire sectors – 30 per cent of Swiss respondents said they would not work in banking and capital markets. While salary may not seem to be their main consideration (and only 4 per cent said they would prefer to have higher wages and no benefits), that doesn't mean that they don't care about it.[2]

> If I'm working on something I enjoy and am passionate about, I will be motivated.
>
> Young male worker, USA.[3]

The unique characteristics of millennials demand a different strategic approach to the recruitment and retention of employees. Millennials are looking for more in life than 'just a job' or a steady climb up the corporate ranks. They want to do something that feels worthwhile, they take into account the values of a company when considering a job, and they are motivated by much more than money. Millennials are attracted to employers who can offer more than merely good pay. The biggest draw for millennials, though, is the opportunity for progression – 52 per cent said that they felt this made an employer an attractive prospect.

Motivation has been a key issue in management for a hundred years ever since Frederick Winslow Taylor put forward the notion of scientific management.[4] Workers do not enjoy their work naturally. They need close supervision and control. An overall job should be broken down into numerous small tasks. Each worker should do one task. Business leaders such as Henry Ford saw the potential. Productivity and profit would rise dramatically. This formal and closely supervised control recognised that workers would adapt to the logic of the assembly line because they would be bribed with the extra pay that would follow in the wake of the productivity boost. Study of workflow was a claim to be scientific, holding the key to the future of work. Although widely adopted in Russia and elsewhere, the problem was that workers lost their sense of connection to the production of goods. They feel disenfranchised with the monotonous and unfulfilling work they were doing in factories

Managers have often turned to psychology for insights into motivating their staff and workers. The motivational drivers can be summarised as follows.

Incentive theory – People pursue courses of actions and behaviours because of rewards, for example monetary incentives. Operant conditioning that associates actions with outcomes is relevant to this approach but the emphasis is that the greater the perceived rewards, the more strongly people are motivated to pursue those reinforcements.

Drive theories – Unmet needs generate certain tensions; for example, the feeling of hunger drives the need for food. However, that is physiological and it does not answer why people might eat when they are not hungry.

Instinct theories – Fundamental instincts shape courses of human action akin to migration in birds. Nineteenth-century psychologists such as William James categorised such instincts as love, modesty, shyness, attachments, anger, shame or fear as hereditary drives. This approach went out of fashion in the twentieth century, though evolutionary psychologists still study the effects of genetics on such phenomena as violence.

Arousal theories – Goal-directed behaviour tends towards the increase or reduction of levels of arousal – whether it is too high or too low.

Expectancy theories – When we are thinking about the future, we formulate different expectations about what we think will happen. Vroom suggested that individuals choose work behaviours that they believe lead to outcomes they value. 'An individual tends to act in a certain way based on the expectation that the act will be followed by a given outcome and on the attractiveness of that outcome to the individual'.[5] Human action tends towards positive outcomes and therefore to make that possible future a reality. This leads people to feel more motivated to pursue such outcomes which are, however, differentiated. Outcomes with a direct personal interest have a high valence while a more indirect benefit has lower valence. Expectation is correlated with instrumentality: the greater the belief that one can influence goals, the higher the expectancy.

Equity theories – Proposed by J. Stacey Adams, this theory views motivation as being based on equity or fairness. This theory tries to explain the fairness of financial incentive plans. According to theory of pay a person looks at the relationship between what he/she puts into work and what he/she gets out of it in comparison with that of other workers.

Herzberg's theory of motivation – An attempt to motivate workers through human relations, pleasant working conditions and improved benefits does not work. The only true way to motivate workers is to upgrade their jobs through promotions. Much cited in the literature about organisational health, Frederick Herzberg argued for a two-factor theory of motivation. **Motivators** are those factors that directly motivate employees to work harder. **Hygiene** factors are those that demotivate an employee if absent but would not directly motivate employees to work harder. Businesses should motivate employees by adopting a democratic approach to management and by improving the job through:

- Job enlargement – workers being given a greater variety of tasks to perform (not necessarily more challenging) which should make the work more interesting.
- Job enrichment – workers being given a wider range of more complex, interesting and challenging tasks. This should give a greater sense of achievement.
- Empowerment – delegating more power to employees to make their own decisions.

Theory X motivation – Social psychologist Douglas McGregor in his thesis suggested that leadership strategies are influenced by a leader's assumptions about human nature.[6] McGregor offered two contrasting sets of assumptions made by managers in industry. Theory X, which is congruent with industrial leadership models, is the traditional way of looking at the workforce. Theory X is an approach that assumes that people would rather play than work. Theory X postulates that most people do not like to work and will avoid it when they can and that most people need to be coerced, controlled, or threatened with punishment to persuade them to work. The contrasting set of assumptions, known as Theory Y, is more in line with post-industrial leadership models we have explored in this study which contend that individuals are self-motivated and self-directed.

David McClelland's needs-based motivational model – David McClelland pioneered workplace motivational thinking, developing achievement-based motivational theory and models, and promoted improvements in employee assessment methods, advocating competency-based assessments and tests, arguing them to be better than traditional IQ and personality-based tests. His ideas have been widely adopted across the piece. The three types of motivational need in 'The Achieving Society'[7] were:

- Achievement motivation (n-ach) – this driver is about seeking achievement, realistic but challenging goals, and advancement in the job. There is a strong need for feedback as to achievement and progress, and a need for a sense of accomplishment.
- Authority/power motivation (n-pow) – this driver produces a need to be influential, effective and to make an impact. There is a strong need to lead and for their ideas to prevail. There is also motivation and need towards increasing personal status and prestige.
- Affiliation motivation (n-affil) – a driver towards friendly relationships and is motivated towards interaction with other people. The affiliation driver produces motivation and need to be liked and held in popular regard. These people are team players.

These needs are found to varying degrees in all workers and managers, and this mix of motivational needs characterises a person's or manager's style and behaviour, both in terms of being motivated, and in the management and motivation others.

Humanistic and psycho-dynamics – Human subjects have cognitive reasons to pursue certain actions. Maslow's theory of hierarchy of needs moving with graduated steps from security towards 'self-actualisation' is one such, as is Freudian theory, amongst other psycho-dynamic approaches that focus on drives towards libido (creativity) or death.

Much cited in management literature, Abraham Maslow (1908–1970) argued for a model of **growth motivation** (in contrast to deficit motivation characteristic of much psychology). After basic needs that must be met (conditions of work) we progress to higher needs – job fulfilment, successful relationships, values, beauty and a capacity for genuine love. Self-actualising individuals, he said, enjoy a reasonable feeling of worth and respect.[8] People attend to basics first and progressively deal with more complex needs later. Maslow noted two versions of esteem needs: a lower one and a higher one. The need for the respect of others is lower – the need for status, fame, glory, recognition, attention, reputation, appreciation, dignity, even dominance. The higher form involves the need for self-respect, including such feelings as confidence, competence, achievement, mastery, independence, and freedom. The negative version of these needs is low self-esteem and inferiority complexes. Maslow agreed with Adler's proposal that these were at the roots of many of our psychological problems. These needs were, Maslow contended, important for survival. Even love and esteem are needed in order to survive.

Maslow objected to criticism that he had merely invented the self-actualiser syndrome – the great souls characteristic of perhaps 2 per cent of the population. But the objection was not easily dismissed. He never presented data to prove that his lists of characteristics of self-actualisers were accurate. It was deemed to be obvious, or that every healthy person he knew was motivated in this way. His opinions were not validated in the normal scientific method. He admitted he had read about the great souls and distilled how they met their needs.

But the main reason for revisiting Maslow is not so much the methodology of study but the unit of study. Maslow seems to be positing the needs of a self-contained individual, a human actor on his or her own. It is not a relational model of personhood. Human beings are inherently social. The hierarchy of needs reflects a particular cultural moment, the US of the second half of the twentieth century, an individualist culture where middle-class people worry about their personal needs more than any collective needs. What about staff being concerned about colleagues or employees being tense on the shop floor or in the office because their children are having problems?

A more relational view of motivation was developed by Elton Mayo (1880–1949). Mayo argued that workers are not just concerned with money but are motivated more as they have their social needs met in the workplace. Mayo introduced the Human Relation school of thought, which emphasised managers taking more of an interest in the workers, treating them as people who have worthwhile opinions and realising that workers enjoy interacting together.

Mayo's ideas were put to the test at the Hawthorne factory of the Western Electric Company in Chicago. Two groups of female workers were studied for the impact on levels of productivity when such factors as working conditions or lighting were varied. It seemed that whatever the change in lighting or working conditions, productivity levels remained the same. What counted was the human dimension in the workplace, an environment characterised by:

- **Better communication** between managers and workers (Hawthorne workers were consulted over the experiments and also had the opportunity to give feedback).
- **Greater manager involvement** in employees' working lives (Hawthorne workers responded to the increased level of attention they were receiving).
- **Working in groups or teams** (Hawthorne workers had not previously worked regularly in teams).

Mayo's solution was a paternalistic one. Businesses should reorganise. Team working should become the 'norm'. Personnel departments should ensure that managers be far more proactive in looking after employees' interests. This was a different approach to Maslow who was of the view that the psychological needs of employees should be addressed.

According to a 2013 survey of 2,185 UK National Health Service employees across 250 trusts, a substantial majority of National Health Service (NHS) staff felt undervalued and were considering changing job.[9] A second survey looking at the level of staff motivation in the NHS was conducted in early 2015 across 3,204 NHS employees across the UK.[10] Respondents were based in over 250 NHS trusts and included employees at all levels within the NHS from cleaning and administrative staff to midwives, nurses and doctors. The second survey revealed continued failures in workforce recognition and deepening strain and dissatisfaction amongst NHS staff. It was clear that the NHS risks a mass exit of highly skilled staff if this issue is not addressed. Seven out of ten staff were feeling 'unappreciated' or given 'not enough praise' for their work. This figure remains unchanged from 2013. **Over half of the NHS workforce were ready to exit their job.** This will create additional pressure to fill vacant posts and to train new intakes. Skills shortages are evident as the NHS recruits from a global talent pool – for example, overseas recruitment of nurses has more than quadrupled in a year.

Productivity comes through people. Peters and Waterman showed that companies in pursuit of excellence regard ordinary members of their organisation as the source of quality and productivity.[11] They treat workers as people.

Clearly, motivation, the driver of human behaviour, has been much studied in the psychology around management literature. For example, John Adair, in his book *Effective Motivation*, identified eight basic rules for motivating people.[12] Adair suggested that 50 per cent of motivation comes from within a person and 50 per cent from his or her environment, especially the leadership style they experience. Motivation tends to be categorised according to whether it is external or internal motivation.

External motivation – Behavioural economics is demonstrating that rewards such as incentives and compensation schemes are not the best way of short-term goals and encourage political behaviour. Banks have been caught trying to use bonus culture to drive performance in a way that backfires on them. These are downsides to relying on external motivation. More pay should lead to higher performance. This is the underlying assumption behind compensation schemes. But Earlie found that higher bonuses did not increase performance. This was then established as being valid for the US as well as India. Is this because of stress in a higher-paid job? In the period before bonuses are handed out, there is a great performance anxiety.

Intrinsic motivation – How do we cultivate an environment of intrinsic motivation? Creating an environment that makes people want to join up, the culture, the setting we create helps drive motivation. *The Soul of a New Machine* has by now the status of a classic chronicle of the new computer age. Tracy Kidder recounts the feverish efforts of a team of Data General researchers to create a new 32-bit superminicomputer. As Robert Persig, author of *Zen and the Art of Motorcycle Maintenance*, commented on the cover of one edition, 'all the incredible complexity and chaos and exploitation and loneliness and strange, half-mad beauty of this field are honestly and correctly drawn.'[13] What kind of environment was this? It accords with ideas of intrinsic motivation that people feel they must have challenging work, meaningful work that gives them something. If their actions will have a great impact, that is important as it digs into the need for significance that accrues in a valuing environment. Humans derive value in a variety of ways. Significance is key to this quest.

It will be recalled that the three main ingredients of a valuing environment that can release the value and worth of people can be categorised as follows:

- Look, learn and listen (in contrast to indifference);
- Involve and include (in contrast to unequal treatment);
- Dignify (in contrast to the indignity of invasive conditions or being set aside).

The driver towards a high value plugs into the sense of a valuable self that humans need in order to flourish. We are investigating how far organisational life generates issues of value and coming up with some theory that helps explain it. The core proposition to be explored in this proposal can be summarised like this. Humans are motivated to pursue a high value for themselves, both in everyday exchanges and in social life. Workers will be motivated if they have a task environment which focuses on employees to own the work that is theirs. They respond to being given some level of autonomy and can design their own steps how they get there. It helps too if they can pursue a range of skills and if they have an opportunity to work on a whole task. People do not seem to be motivated by repetition

The client who is experiencing a panic attack may say something like, 'I know I can do this but I'm on the firing line, I am observed.'[14] The stress highlights the dilemma. They cannot react easily from a position of relative worth in comparison to others. They themselves are under threat.

After taking office, the prime minister of Malaysia, Mahathir Mohamad, abruptly reversed his country's long-standing pro-UK stance. From then on, Malaysia had a new policy – 'Buy British last'. It was only after he had been invited to a 'peace-meal' at Downing Street by Margaret Thatcher that Mahathir relented. What he had wanted all along was respect. He refused to be treated as a colonial client grateful for the smallest word from anyone with an assumption of superiority.[15] In short, he sought to be properly valued.

What would it mean to say that the impetus towards high value is fundamental? Should the inner world be re-configured?

In contemporary life, value is accorded to individuals and groups in a way that is unrelated to inner value or 'value-in-oneself'. What someone is worth is awarded to social participants on the basis of the wage economy (economic value), identity badges (status value such as ownership or appearance) or identity boundaries (social value; being the right sort of person).

The hypothesis is this. We have an inbuilt psycho-social need to be worthwhile people engaged in worthwhile projects and therefore active in garnering worth from our world. These considerations constitute a signpost that the impetus for being of worth is deeply rooted. The signpost is downwards. Yet there is a lacuna. Mainstream psychology has, for the most part, still to regard the struggle to realise our sense of a valuable self as being a major content area in its agenda. The impetus towards high value is not usually seen as embedded psycho-dynamically within the psyche.

The dog that didn't bark

> An officer is a miserable creature. Each envies his colleagues, bullies his subordinates, and is afraid of his superiors: the higher up he is, the more he fears them. I detest the idea of having inscribed on my collar how much I am worth, as if I were a sample of some goods.[16]

The writer is the young Sigmund Freud, complaining to his colleague and mentor Josef Breuer about compulsory national service in the Austrian army, in a 'filthy hole working on black and yellow' as he put it, black and yellow being the Austrian colours. It is intriguing to ponder what would have been the outcome of pursuing this line of thought and bringing the struggle to realise our value into Freudian psycho-dynamics. The reaction – against how much he is worth being inscribed on his collar – is a strong one. He detests it. It is the Protest.

Libido came first. The theory of drivers of interpersonal and social processes was given contemporary shape by Freud giving primary importance to the sexual drive. Psycho-analysis, and with it, the twentieth-century edifice of talking therapy, was based on the idea that surface phenomena were insufficient on which to build a theory of human behaviour. *The Interpretation of Dreams* marked the beginning of the psychological century. Through exploring the logic of dreams, Freud had proposed to investigate the inner workings of the human mind. From this starting point in 1899, Freud constructed nothing less than a biology of the mind that signified a revolution in the way we saw ourselves.

The archaeology of the drives, the dark underworld of conflicted human emotion and, above all, human sexuality became ingredients of the new orientation in our thinking.

Amidst the myriad of remedies put forward and practised to relieve the human condition there was, however, a strange omission. The dog that didn't bark in the night seemed to be missing in the classic accounts of human motivation. The experience that Sigmund Freud had in the Austrian army was not taken up as part of his new conceptual architecture; the interplay of value/devaluation not adopted as a mechanism in the psychopathology of everyday life. It seems unlikely that you can explain the dynamic of human value and its counterpoint – devaluation – within existing frameworks. Yet private as well as public worlds demonstrate that humans are not just interest-led. We are motivated by the desire to pursue our value and protest when it is breached. What the energy is for this is a question with profound consequences.

The impetus to be valued and to feel valuable, the need to feel one is worth something is central to what it means to be human. Organisational or interpersonal approaches that give value to people rather than devalue them tap into an aspect of the human psyche that responds to a sense of worth. Understanding how valuing or disvaluing is communicated is a vital insight in many areas of social life and it is this we are noting in this book. Grasping the dynamics of what makes for disvaluing people or groups is particularly rich in offering a lens through which to make sense of responses. Equality has various dimensions – equality of resources, of working and learning opportunities or of power relations. But amongst the strength of reaction against the forms inequality takes, the demand for respect and recognition is significant.

Arguably, the common root is the inner need to be valued. What seems beyond dispute is that we have an impetus to feel worthwhile. How far that is grounded in being someone of worth is a question to be asked and a challenge.

The dominant pursuit of value-in-oneself may seem obvious yet it is not up there amidst the panoply of mental driving forces that form the seedbed of psycho-dynamics. Neither is it a regular topic in social psychology. After all, one could have a sense of self in which identity subsists, without that being grounded in value and worth. The two categories are not coterminous. Are we psychologically structured so as to require a strong sense of value within which to live and move and have our being and do our best work? What would it mean to say that human subjects are formed amidst a dynamic struggle for human value against a constant litany of devaluing factors? What does it mean for human action that we seem compelled to live as if we had high value or we wither in its absence?

But what degree of valuing is achievable for human functioning? Freud said he could catalyse neurosis into ordinary unhappiness as a pessimistic norm. Unlike Freud, who had studied people with emotional problems, Abraham Maslow argued that psychology should also include the study of healthy personalities. Maslow described what he thought healthy personalities should be like. Self-actualising individuals enjoy a reasonable feeling of worth and respect and do not for long have crippling feelings of inferiority or worthlessness.[17] In the terms of this book, we are motivated to pursue our value. How much value is the psyche endeavouring to realise? This is difficult to answer as it is both personally and culturally dependent. The drive is to establish a stasis of a valuable self. That will assume various shapes, often expressed as a status quo of respect, dignity and significance. A valuable self is accrued through significance (a contrast to diminishing), being seen and heard (attention as a contrast to indifference) and assertion of sacred space (in contrast to indignity). Such are the strategies of the pursuit of value in everyday life.

The proposal is that the impetus towards being of high value and the response is a fundamental driver by an energy that is embedded in our psyche. It is, in short, a motivational driver. But what would it mean to describe that need in those terms?

To suggest that the pursuit of high value is a strong motivational driver in society necessarily obliges us to note how motivation theory configures the drivers. The history of psychology is replete with projects to categorise mental structure. One thinks of Freud's endeavour to re-classify the drives into those aimed at self-preservation and those aimed at sexual satisfaction (subsequently elevating aggressiveness into a rival to libido in his 'Beyond the Pleasure Principle').[18,19] Once the structure and mode of the unconscious had been explored, psycho-analysis could attempt to provide a picture of the whole mind. The primary instincts were described as sex instincts, the aggressive instincts but also the ego ideal that served to protect the conscious self from unwelcome intrusion from below.[20] Freud's contemporary William James described an instinctive theory of motivation – an inborn pattern of behaviour around play, shame, anger, fear, shyness, attachment, modesty and love. That was its limitation; the theory was descriptive rather than explanatory. The incentive theory of motivation had a strong running. External rewards provided incentives for behavioural learning. Though the drive theory of motivation seemed successful, achieving certain goals to assuage unmet needs did not account for why, for example, we might eat even when we are not hungry.

Amidst the complexities of the interior world, the unconscious activities of the mind should include the desire to be valuable, to count and be of worth. Distorted neuroses may be a lot to do with blocked attempts to extract significance and value from our world. Repression may or may not be a factor in disguise of pathways towards fulfilment but rejection is an experience that bites people to the core. Core challenges reveal the strength of unconscious influences in human action as the subject is often in the grip of forces that are past all understanding.

Humans derive value in a variety of ways. Significance is key to this quest. Here is a client who takes things personally, to whom any action is an insult if not worthy. It is a personal slight – another category of mistake. It was not the action but their very selves being threatened. An absolute sense of worth is under fire. What is the fuel causing magnification of a slight in such a way that it sits in judgement not just over a fragmentary action or speech but instead over our whole being? Sometimes people get into attack-mode, developing a sharp capacity to ascend from the particular to the general – 'this is typical!'

Social processes or organisational practices that give value to people, either through engagement or listening, are those giving a positive environment that cultivates the welfare of staff or customers and communicates 'I am worth listening to!' Clients often report being devalued and disgruntled in the workplace. 'I was not just re-cycled, I was binned, they got rid of me'[21] as if the self is now a waste product. Issues of value are not just an aspiration; they are key narratives in human functioning. It is often observed that the whole purpose of making money is to put yourself on a pedestal.

What statement about worth is implied in a professional lament such as this: 'I don't feel I'm doing a worthwhile job'?[22] To sum up, the impetus to realise our worth is a neglected topic in the content area of social psychology or psycho-dynamics. It is a 'taken-for-granted' assumption that has yet to be factored into theory.

Arousal theories did not seem to be comprehensive either, accounting for human action in terms of feeding states of arousal. Humanistic theories come closest to the theme of this book, especially Maslow's famous hierarchy of needs in which the primary motivator shifts from 'lower' level satisfaction towards the drive to self-actualisation.

Albert Ellis, founder of one of the early approaches to CBT known as Rational Emotive Therapy (RET), declares that all human beings have extrinsic value to others and intrinsic value to themselves though he did question whether humans really do have an intrinsic worth.[23] But humans end up confusing the two and classify ourselves as being 'worthy' or 'good' on the basis of assumed value to others.

Disaffection manifesting itself in a negative culture within an organisation will generate an issue of value – not the value of assets, product or service initially but of the people involved. The reaction of police in the UK is relevant, who, in reaction to whether pay should be backdated to the previous September said that refusal to do this in order not to breach public pay policy was 'absolutely disgusting, showing the whole feeling of how we are valued by the government … totally devaluing the work we do on the ground … People feel extraordinarily undervalued, they feel very undervalued in terms of their worth.'[24] Although monetary value was the focus, that quickly keyed into a personal or collective sense of worth.

Despite the bad news, there are numerous instances where organisations have nurtured the link between human value and the economic value of the enterprise.

Employee surveys such as that of the Top 100 Companies or Best Companies Guide generate considerable data about the UK's best companies to work for based on what their workers really think. The Best Companies Guide is based on findings of over 500,000 employees in nearly 2,000 organisations; 92 per cent of employees in the so-called 'three star organisations' report that they are 'actively engaged' compared to a national average of only 33 per cent.[25] Year-on-year statistical analysis shows that there are eight main factors driving whether or not employees are engaged:

- Leadership – good management that results in a happy and productive team.
- My Company – how much people value their company, how proud they are to work there and whether or not they feel they can make a difference.
- Personal growth – how far the job is challenging, skills are being used and that managers recognise a career is not just work; it is an education.
- My Manager – seven out of ten people who leave are leaving their manager. Relationship with the manager is probably the most important factor of all.
- My Team – getting on with co-workers. Team spirit increases productivity.
- Giving something back – investing in people, the community and wider society.
- Fair Deal – being fairly paid in relation to others.
- Well-being – stress, work pressure and not encouraging a long-hours culture.

These winning factors are on to something that is about human motivation more than mere organisational success. They relate to employee engagement precisely because they key in to factors that arouse personal value. The link between disengagement and devaluation is a strong one.

Motivated by power

Much of this, despite the high-profile instances where there is corporate failure, seems fairly obvious. The important question is this, however. WHY IS THIS NOT HAPPENING? What are the institutional/personal/cultural reasons why best practice does not get translated into reality? Leaders of twenty-first century organisations surely need to understand and reflect on the reasons why pressure within their micro-culture is generating precisely the opposite of what would be hailed as an ideal.

Organisations at all levels are vulnerable to certain patterns of behaviour that become embedded as the norm. Practices can easily drift over a line and become abusive. It is surely not sufficient to study the factors that make for the life of people or organisations to be valued and thence to flourish. Organisational failure, and indeed the failure of politics, is often about cultures where manipulative patterns such as these have become normal:

1 **'I want what you have'** – strategies of greed and gathering as much as possible to oneself to increase what one has at the expense of someone else.
2 **'I must stay as I am'** – threats to identity to bolster and maintain self-definition or position as things seem in danger of slipping away from the players who hold some of the cards.
3 **'I want what you are!'** – hunger for control, strategies of domination over identity of others that will feed the sense of status amongst insecure managers.
4 **'I want to be who you are'** – power as imitation of highly prized and cool people.
5 **'You will pay for what you have done!'** – domination and violence as retribution and exchange.

It is factors such as these that will cause leaders at every level to pursue practices that result in the experience social participants have of being devalued. As we are exploring, this takes place as, on the ground, those on the receiving end of power-play are treated with indifference, invasive indignity or inequality (i.e. the experience of being diminished).

In a somewhat different context, James Madison, fourth president of the USA and political genius,[26] wrote in the Federalist Papers, that 'if angels were to govern men, neither external not internal controls on government would be necessary'. If men (and women) were angels, no government is needed; therefore a well-regulated state is a vital barrier against anarchy. Leaders of organisations do not put into practice factors that promote human flourishing because men are not angels.

Senior leaders especially can be motivated not by money as an extrinsic motivation but by power. This fits in well with the conceptual structure being proposed here since the drive towards being of high value is configured by many as a zero sum game. 'I win if you lose.'

Conclusion

The journey summarised here provokes reflection on the need to revisit the usual categories of the motivational drivers. We are motivated by the pursuit of value but experiences of life mean we are shaped by its opposite. To see how the dynamics of needing to pursue our value plays out in everyday life, it is helpful to focus on its contrast.

To follow up on this chapter, a proper account would need to be given of how the pursuit of a high value is situated within classic accounts of the drivers including Freudian and psycho-dynamic. A description would need to be drawn about this approach to motivation sits also within personality structure and developmental psychology.

The endemic struggle for our value in public and private worlds is an important dimension ignored in most psychological and sociological descriptions of the world. It therefore presents a challenge to theory. Why has this dimension not been an active dynamic in accounts of human action?

The suggestion I want to advocate is that amidst the multidimensional complexity of human behaviour, we are motivated at least in part by the pursuit of worth. The psychology of the unconscious should derive from mental forces which must include the impulse towards high value. The motivator to be of worth by all strategies open to us is overwhelming either in its presence or absence. It is rooted in 'value-in-oneself'. With it we flourish; without it we wither.

Value is a foundational principle of human action. Conveying worth is not merely an aspiration but a dimension of the human operating system: an ineradicable trait. Without a sense of value, we are cramped and constrained. Or we wither. With a rising sense of a valuable self, we function at our optimum and offer pathways of hope, combining significance with belonging and bringing out the best in people.

Notes

 1 *PM News Programme*, BBC Radio 4, 13 January 2008.
 2 'Millennials at Work: Reshaping the Workplace', PWC, May 2016, https://www.pwc.com/m1/en/services/consulting/documents/millennials-at-work.pdf, accessed May 2016.
 3 'Millennials at Work'.
 4 Kanigel, R. (1997), *The One Best Way: Frederick Winslow Taylor and the Enigma of Efficiency*. New York: Viking.
 5 Cambridge Institute for Management Technology, http://www.ifm.eng.cam.ac.uk/research/dstools/vrooms-expectancy-theory/, accessed February 2017.
 6 McGregor, D. (1960), *The Human Side of Enterprise*. New York: McGraw-Hill.
 7 McClelland, D.C. (2010), *The Achieving Society*. Eastford, CT: Martino Fine Books.
 8 Maslow, A. (1977), 'A Theory of Metamotivation: The Biological Rooting of the Value-Life', in *The Healthy Personality*, ed. H.-M. Chiang and A. Maslow. New York: D. Van Nostrand Co., p. 28.
 9 Peters, T.J. and Waterman, R.H. (1982), *In Search of Excellence: Lessons from America's Best Run Companies*. New York: Harper & Row.
10 Workplace Savings and Benefits – Communication and Engagement, 10 September 2013.
11 NHS Staff Survey 2015, https://www.england.nhs.uk/2016/02/staff-survey-results.
12 Adair, J. (1987), *Effective Motivation*. Guildford: Talbot Adair Press.
13 Kidder, T. (1998), *The Soul of a New Machine*. New York: Random House.
14 Author's client notes – used with permission and name withheld.
15 Wain, B. (2010), *Malaysian Maverick: Mahathir Mohamad in Turbulent Times*. Basingstoke: Palgrave Macmillan.
16 Letter, Freud to Breuer. Jones, E. (1964), *The Life and Work of Sigmund Freud*. Harmondsworth: Penguin Books, p. 181.
17 Maslow (1977), p. 28.
18 Freud, S. (1922), *Beyond the Pleasure Principle*. London: Hogarth Press.
19 Gay, P. (2006), *Freud: A Life for Our Time*. London: Max.
20 Freud, S. (1927), *The Ego and the Id*. London: Hogarth Press.
21 Author's client notes – used with permission and name withheld.
22 Author's client notes – used with permission and name withheld.
23 Ellis, A. (1979), *Reason and Emotion in Psychotherapy*. Sacramento, CA: The Citadel Press.
24 *The Today Programme*, BBC Radio 4, 12 December 2007.
25 *Best Companies Guide* (2007), Wrexham: Best Companies.
26 Cheney, L. (2014), *James Madison: A Life Re-considered*. New York: Penguin.

Index

 Taylor & Francis eBooks

Helping you to choose the right eBooks for your Library

Add Routledge titles to your library's digital collection today. Taylor and Francis ebooks contains over 50,000 titles in the Humanities, Social Sciences, Behavioural Sciences, Built Environment and Law.

Choose from a range of subject packages or create your own!

Benefits for you

» Free MARC records
» COUNTER-compliant usage statistics
» Flexible purchase and pricing options
» All titles DRM-free.

Benefits for your user

» Off-site, anytime access via Athens or referring URL
» Print or copy pages or chapters
» Full content search
» Bookmark, highlight and annotate text
» Access to thousands of pages of quality research at the click of a button.

REQUEST YOUR **FREE** INSTITUTIONAL TRIAL TODAY

Free Trials Available
We offer free trials to qualifying academic, corporate and government customers.

eCollections – Choose from over 30 subject eCollections, including:

Archaeology	Language Learning
Architecture	Law
Asian Studies	Literature
Business & Management	Media & Communication
Classical Studies	Middle East Studies
Construction	Music
Creative & Media Arts	Philosophy
Criminology & Criminal Justice	Planning
Economics	Politics
Education	Psychology & Mental Health
Energy	Religion
Engineering	Security
English Language & Linguistics	Social Work
Environment & Sustainability	Sociology
Geography	Sport
Health Studies	Theatre & Performance
History	Tourism, Hospitality & Events

For more information, pricing enquiries or to order a free trial, please contact your local sales team:
www.tandfebooks.com/page/sales